AWS Certified Cloud Practitioner (CLF-C02) Study Guide

In-Depth Exam Prep and Practice

Tom Taulli

O'REILLY®

AWS Certified Cloud Practitioner (CLF-C02) Study Guide

by Tom Taulli

Published by O'Reilly Media, Inc., 141 Stony Circle, Suite 195, Santa Rosa, CA 95401.

O'Reilly books may be purchased for educational, business, or sales promotional use. Online editions are also available for most titles (*https://oreilly.com*). For more information, contact our corporate/institutional sales department: 800-998-9938 or *corporate@oreilly.com*.

Acquisitions Editor: Megan Laddusaw
Development Editor: Jeff Bleiel
Production Editor: Ashley Stussy
Copyeditor: Liz Wheeler
Proofreader: Krsta Technology Solutions

Indexer: BIM Creatives, LLC
Cover Designer: Susan Brown
Cover Illustrator: José Marzan Jr.
Interior Designer: David Futato
Interior Illustrator: Kate Dullea

January 2026:   First Edition

Revision History for the First Edition

2026-01-07:   First Release

See *https://oreilly.com/catalog/errata.csp?isbn=9798341640221* for release details.

979-8-341-64022-1

[LSI]

Table of Contents

Preface

Cloud computing is at the core of how modern businesses operate. Every time you stream a movie, use an app, or check your bank account online, there's a good chance Amazon Web Services (AWS) is running behind the scenes. What started as a way to rent computing power has grown into a global ecosystem powering innovation in every industry imaginable.

This is why understanding AWS isn't just for developers or IT pros. It's for anyone who wants to stay relevant in today's tech-driven world. Whether you work in business, finance, marketing, operations, or tech, cloud literacy is becoming a must-have skill. And one of the best ways to prove your understanding is by earning the AWS Certified Cloud Practitioner certification.

This certification gives you a solid foundation in the cloud: how it works, why it matters, and how AWS delivers services that keep organizations running securely, efficiently, and at scale. It covers everything, including compute, storage, networking, AI, analytics, and cost optimization. You'll also learn the principles of security, billing, and global infrastructure.

The best part? You don't need a technical background to get started. This certification is designed for beginners—that is, people who want to understand the big picture and gain the confidence to speak the language of the cloud.

This book is your step-by-step guide. Inside, you'll find clear explanations and practical examples of every topic on the exam. Whether your goal is to launch a new career, level up in your current role, or build a foundation for more advanced AWS certifications, you're at the right place.

What's Covered

Here's a brief look at each chapter:

Chapter 1, "Introduction to the AWS Certified Cloud Practitioner (CLF-C02) Exam", provides an overview of the exam, including its purpose, audience, and career benefits. It outlines key exam topics, structure, and logistics such as cost, format, and scoring. The chapter also highlights related AWS certifications and resources for continued learning.

Chapter 2, "Getting Started with AWS", guides readers through setting up an AWS account, exploring the Free Tier, and navigating the AWS Management Console. It introduces key services such as EC2, S3, RDS, Lambda, and IAM, along with essential cost management tools like Budgets and Cost Explorer.

Chapter 3, "Cloud Computing Foundations", introduces the core principles of cloud computing, tracing its evolution and explaining how it enables scalable, on-demand access to IT resources. It outlines deployment models (public, private, and hybrid) and service models (IaaS, PaaS, and SaaS). The chapter also highlights the key benefits of cloud adoption, including cost efficiency, flexibility, and global reach.

Chapter 4, "Fundamentals of AWS", compares traditional on-premises infrastructure with AWS's flexible, pay-as-you-go model and introduces key financial concepts like TCO, CapEx versus OpEx, and licensing options. It covers optimization strategies such as rightsizing and automation, along with the AWS Well-Architected and Cloud Adoption Frameworks for building secure and efficient systems.

Chapter 5, "AWS Compliance and Governance", explains how compliance, governance, and security work together to maintain a secure and well-managed cloud environment. It reviews major compliance frameworks like HIPAA, PCI DSS, FedRAMP, and GDPR, and introduces AWS tools such as Config, Audit Manager, Organizations, and Artifact that support compliance and governance efforts. The chapter concludes by emphasizing AWS's shared responsibility model.

Chapter 6, "AWS Identity and Access Management (IAM)", explains how IAM controls access to AWS resources through users, groups, roles, and policies. It covers key concepts like authentication versus authorization, password policies, MFA, and permission boundaries to enforce least-privilege security.

Chapter 7, "Security", explains how AWS and customers share responsibility for protecting cloud environments and data. It introduces the defense-in-depth approach, layering tools and practices like IAM, encryption, and monitoring to guard against threats such as ransomware and phishing. The chapter highlights essential AWS security services—GuardDuty, KMS, CloudTrail, WAF, and Security Hub—and shows how they work together to detect, prevent, and respond to attacks.

Chapter 8, "AWS Global Infrastructure", explains how AWS's worldwide network of regions, availability zones, and edge locations supports low-latency, highly available applications. It explores key components like CloudFront, Route 53, Shield, and Global Accelerator, along with newer offerings such as Outposts, Local Zones, and Wavelength Zones for edge computing.

Chapter 9, "AWS Compute, Containers, and Serverless", explores the core ways AWS delivers processing power through EC2 instances, containers, and serverless technologies. It explains how to configure and secure EC2, manage scalable containerized workloads with ECS and EKS, and build event-driven applications using AWS Lambda. The chapter concludes with Auto Scaling and Elastic Load Balancing, which maintain performance and cost efficiency by automatically adapting to workload demands.

Chapter 10, "AWS Storage Services", covers the major AWS options for storing and protecting data, including S3 for object storage, EBS for block storage, EFS and FSx for file storage, Storage Gateway for hybrid environments, and AWS Backup for centralized protection.

Chapter 11, "AWS Database Services", compares self-managed EC2 databases with fully managed AWS options like RDS, Aurora, DynamoDB, and ElastiCache. It explains how relational, NoSQL, in-memory, and analytical databases differ in structure, scalability, and use cases.

Chapter 12, "AWS Networking Services", explains how AWS builds secure, scalable network architectures. It covers VPCs for isolating and controlling cloud resources, Route 53 for global DNS routing and resiliency, and connectivity options like Site-to-Site VPN and Direct Connect for linking on-premises systems to AWS.

Chapter 13, "Artificial Intelligence and Data Analytics Tools", introduces AI concepts, including machine learning, deep learning, and generative AI, showing how they enable intelligent systems and content creation. It explores key AWS AI services like SageMaker for model development, Lex for conversational bots, and Kendra for enterprise search.

Chapter 14, "AWS Developer Tools and Other Essential Services", explores AWS solutions that streamline application development, integration, and management. It covers tools like EventBridge, SNS, and SQS for connecting systems; CodeBuild, CodePipeline, and X-Ray for automating DevOps workflows; and services like Amazon Connect and SES for customer engagement.

Chapter 15, "Billing, Budgeting, and Cost Management in AWS", explains AWS pricing models—on-demand, Reserved Instances, Savings Plans, Spot, and others—and how to choose based on workload needs. It introduces key cost management tools like Cost Explorer, Budgets, and the Pricing Calculator, along with tagging and AWS Organizations for expense tracking.

Chapter 16, "Strategies and Techniques for Successfully Taking the AWS Certified Cloud Practitioner Exam", offers study guidance and exam-day strategies to help you prepare effectively. It covers time management, test-taking techniques, and the key exam domains.

Most chapters in this book include a quiz to reinforce key concepts, and a comprehensive final practice quiz is provided in Appendix A, "Practice Exam" to help solidify your understanding.

Conventions Used in This Book

The following typographical conventions are used in this book:

Italic
> Indicates new terms, URLs, email addresses, filenames, and file extensions.

`Constant width`
> Used for program listings, as well as within paragraphs to refer to program elements such as variable or function names, databases, data types, environment variables, statements, and keywords.

`Constant width bold`
> Shows commands or other text that should be typed literally by the user.

O'Reilly Online Learning

O'REILLY® For more than 40 years, *O'Reilly Media* has provided technology and business training, knowledge, and insight to help companies succeed.

Our unique network of experts and innovators share their knowledge and expertise through books, articles, and our online learning platform. O'Reilly's online learning platform gives you on-demand access to live training courses, in-depth learning paths, interactive coding environments, and a vast collection of text and video from O'Reilly and 200+ other publishers. For more information, visit *https://oreilly.com*.

How to Contact Us

Please address comments and questions concerning this book to the publisher:

O'Reilly Media, Inc.
141 Stony Circle, Suite 195
Santa Rosa, CA 95401
800-889-8969 (in the United States or Canada)
707-827-7019 (international or local)
707-829-0104 (fax)
support@oreilly.com
https://oreilly.com/about/contact.html

We have a web page for this book, where we list errata and any additional information. You can access this page at *https://oreil.ly/aws-cert-cloud-pract-1e*.

For news and information about our books and courses, visit *https://oreilly.com*.

Find us on LinkedIn: *https://linkedin.com/company/oreilly-media*

Watch us on YouTube: *https://youtube.com/oreillymedia*

Acknowledgments

I want to thank the awesome team at O'Reilly. They include Megan Laddusaw, Jeff Bleiel, Kristen Brown, and Ashley Stussy.

I also had the benefit of outstanding tech reviewers. They are Pramesh Anuragi, Arjun Bali, and Rachit Jain.

CHAPTER 1

Introduction to the AWS Certified Cloud Practitioner (CLF-C02) Exam

If you're interested in cloud computing but not sure where to begin, the AWS Certified Cloud Practitioner (CLF-C02) exam is a great place to start. In this book, you'll learn how to prepare for it, such as learning about core cloud concepts and systems, how AWS delivers its services, and why so many companies are shifting their infrastructure there. Expect to run into terms like *compute*, *storage*, and *networking*—but don't worry, it's all introduced in a way that makes sense if you're new to this space. The focus is on understanding, not memorizing buzzwords.

And this exam isn't just about technology. It also covers the business side of things—pricing models, billing basics, security responsibilities, and compliance. This broader scope makes it especially useful if you're in a nontechnical role. Whether you're in sales, marketing, project management, or working closely with IT teams, this certification helps you speak the language and see how the cloud fits into the bigger business picture.

In this chapter, we'll break down what the CLF-C02 exam looks like: what topics it covers, how it's scored, and the kinds of questions you'll see. That way, you can plan your preparation without flying blind.

Why Should You Take the Exam?

More companies are moving to the cloud every year. So having a basic understanding of how it all works can give your resume an edge—no matter what your job title is.

You don't have to be aiming for a cloud engineer role to benefit from this certification. It shows that you understand the fundamentals: what AWS offers, how cloud services support business, and how to talk about cloud strategy without getting lost in jargon. For people entering the technology field—or shifting into a cloud-adjacent role—it's a great way to get your foot in the door.

Let's look at other reasons to take the exam.

Recognition

Employers recognize the AWS Certified Cloud Practitioner as a respected credential. It signals that you're not just cloud-curious—you've taken the time to learn the ropes. And that kind of initiative stands out.

Whether you're looking to join a cloud-focused team or just want to contribute more confidently to cloud-related projects, this certification says you're ready to be part of the team.

The Cloud Megatrend

Across industries, organizations are doubling down on digital transformation, and the cloud sits at the center of it all. It offers what businesses want: scalability, flexibility, and lower costs compared to traditional, on-premises setups.

By 2025, analysts expect the global cloud market to hit around $912.77 billion (*https://oreil.ly/fFrjB*). And that's just the beginning. If current trends hold, the market could swell to $5.15 trillion by 2034. That's not a typo—it's a projected compound annual growth rate (CAGR) of 21.2% over the next ten years. A big part of what's fueling that surge is the shift to cloud-first strategies, where companies prioritize cloud-based tools and infrastructure from the start.

Public cloud services are driving much of the momentum. In fact, spending in this area alone is expected to hit $723.4 billion in 2025—a 21.5% jump over the previous year. The software as a service (SaaS) segment continues to dominate, with spending forecasted to climb toward $300 billion.

AWS Remains Dominant

AWS continues to lead the global cloud infrastructure market, holding onto a 30% share in the first quarter of 2025 (*https://oreil.ly/lMqZj*). This puts it ahead of Microsoft, which came in at 20%, and Google Cloud, which captured 12%.

During that same quarter, AWS pulled in $29.3 billion in revenue (*https://oreil.ly/oh3-7*)—a solid 17% jump compared to Q1 of last year. Operating income for the segment hit $11.5 billion, up from $9.4 billion in the first quarter of 2024.

Salary Boost

In the US, professionals holding the CLF-C02 certification earn around $85,866 a year on average (*https://oreil.ly/fimse*). Not bad for a starter credential.

Even better, it tends to come with a raise. A survey from Jefferson Frank (*https://oreil.ly/gSA43*) found that 73% of AWS-certified professionals saw a salary bump after passing their exam—with the average increase landing at 27%. This is a solid return on a relatively small time investment.

Prefer hourly work? Certified Cloud Practitioners typically pull in between $25 and $40 per hour, depending on your experience level, where you're based, and who's hiring.

The real value of the CLF-C02 certification is the doors it might open. Once you have it, you're on the radar for a wide range of cloud roles—especially if you keep building on your skills with additional certifications or hands-on experience.

Here are some common roles, along with average US salaries (*https://oreil.ly/fimse*):

- AWS cloud engineer—$108,230
- AWS DevOps engineer—$106,947
- AWS cloud architect—$126,154
- AWS developer—$99,189

Of course, these roles usually require more than the CLF-C02 certification. But if you're starting out, this certification gives you a strong foundation—and shows employers you're serious about the cloud.

Who Should Take the Exam?

A wide range of individuals can benefit from taking the CLF-C02 exam. Let's look at some categories that certified individuals have come from.

Business Professionals and Nontechnical Roles

If you work in sales, marketing, product development, or project management, getting certified by passing this exam can give you an edge. The knowledge you gain from preparing for this exam helps you understand how AWS services translate into business value, which makes conversations with technical teams smoother and more productive. With a better grasp of cloud concepts, you'll be equipped to contribute meaningfully to cloud-related projects and decisions—even if you've never written a line of code.

IT Staff and Technologists New to the Cloud

For system administrators, developers, or IT support staff who haven't worked deeply with cloud platforms, the CLF-C02 certification is a good option. If you're planning to pursue more advanced certifications—or step into roles focused on cloud architecture, DevOps, or security—it builds the groundwork.

Students and Career Changers

Trying to break into the technology industry? Or making a pivot into cloud computing? The CLF-C02 certification gives you a clear signal to employers that you're serious. It looks good on a resume and gives you the language and concepts you'll need to hold your own in interviews or internships.

Topics Covered in the Exam

AWS provides a simple guide (*https://oreil.ly/w__yf*) to the CLF-C02 exam. It outlines the topics covered, the types of questions to expect, and the scoring methodology.

Table 1-1 gives an overview of these key areas.

Table 1-1. Topics on the CLF-C02 exam

Domain	Percent of exam	What you'll be expected to know/do
Domain 1: Cloud Concepts	24%	• Define and explain the benefits of cloud computing (e.g., elasticity, scalability, agility) • Understand the AWS Cloud value proposition and economic benefits • Compare different cloud deployment models (public, private, hybrid) • Identify the basic global infrastructure of the AWS Cloud • Describe key concepts such as high availability and fault tolerance
Domain 2: Security and Compliance	30%	• Understand the AWS Shared Responsibility Model • Understand access management, such as Identity and Access Management (IAM) roles, users, and groups • Recognize AWS security services like AWS WAF (Web Application Firewall), Shield, Security Hub, Macie, and GuardDuty • Understand data protection mechanisms (encryption, key management) • Identify compliance programs and AWS artifact usage
Domain 3: Cloud Technology and Services	34%	• Describe the basic functions of core AWS services including Elastic Compute Cloud (EC2), Simple Storage Service (S3), Relational Database Service (RDS), and Lambda • Understand the AWS global infrastructure (Regions, Availability Zones, Edge Locations) • Differentiate between compute, storage, database, and networking services • Understand the concepts of containers and serverless computing • Identify AWS service categories and their use cases

Domain	Percent of exam	What you'll be expected to know/do
Domain 4: Billing, Pricing, and Support	12%	• Understand AWS pricing models (On-Demand, Reserved, and Spot Instances) • Identify key AWS billing and cost management tools (Cost Explorer, Budgets) • Explain the AWS Free Tier and how to track usage • Understand the features of AWS Support Plans • Recognize the AWS Marketplace and its role in procurement

Keep in mind that not every topic listed in these domains will appear on your exam. This is merely a list of possible topics from which questions will be drawn.

Exam Details

The AWS Certification exam features 65 questions total, but keep in mind that only 50 count toward your final score. The remaining 15 are experimental. AWS uses them to test new questions for future exams, so they won't impact your result. You're better off guessing when you're unsure, rather than not answering, because a question that isn't answered will be marked as incorrect.

The exam includes these types of questions:

Multiple choice
    One right answer among three distractors.

Multiple response
    Two or more correct choices selected from a list of five or more options.

Every question is designed to focus on one topic with fact-based answers. You won't find any trick questions or a mix of multiple subject areas in one question. For multiple-answer questions, you need to choose every correct option—there's no partial credit.

You'll receive a score between 100 and 1,000, and passing requires a score of at least 700. AWS uses a scaled scoring system, which standardizes the results across different versions of the exam. This is to ensure fairness. The exam duration is 90 minutes, and the cost is typically $100, though this may vary by location.

Exam Delivery Methods

You can choose between two exam delivery methods. Each has its own set of rules and environment requirements.

Online proctored exam (via Pearson VUE OnVUE)

If you're planning to take the CLF-C02 exam online through Pearson VUE's OnVUE platform, you'll need to prepare your testing environment carefully. Start by choosing a private, quiet, and well-lit room where you won't be interrupted. No one else is allowed to enter once the exam begins. Your desk must be completely clear of any unauthorized materials such as books, notes, or devices. You can only use one monitor and, before the test starts, you'll be asked to use your webcam to scan the entire room and workspace to confirm that you're following exam policies.

During the exam, your webcam and microphone must stay on the entire time for continuous monitoring. You can't leave your seat or take unscheduled breaks, even for a quick restroom trip. Certain behaviors—like speaking aloud, looking away from the screen, covering your mouth, or interacting with someone off-camera—can result in your exam being terminated. Make sure your system is ready by running a pre-exam check, and confirm that your internet connection is stable. Your webcam and mic must clearly capture your face and voice, especially during ID verification and the room scan. Speaking of ID, you'll need to show one valid, unexpired government-issued photo ID with your name and signature. The name must match exactly with the one in your AWS Certification Account.

In-person test center exam (via Pearson VUE)

If you're taking your AWS Certification exam at a Pearson VUE testing center, you'll be using the equipment provided on-site. When you arrive, you'll store personal items like phones, bags, and study materials in a designated area. These won't be accessible during the test. The environment is controlled and closely monitored to ensure a fair testing experience for everyone.

A live proctor will be present throughout your exam to enforce the rules and maintain security. You can take unscheduled breaks if needed, but the exam clock keeps ticking, and you'll have to complete a check-in process each time you return. Be sure to bring two forms of identification: a primary government-issued ID that includes your photo and signature, and a secondary ID that shows either your name and signature or your name and photo. Both IDs must be valid and unexpired.

Registration and Rescheduling

To take the CLF-C02 exam, you must be at least 13 years old. If you're between the ages of 13 and 17, AWS has certain requirements, including the consent of a parent or legal guardian. You can learn more about the requirements at the AWS Certification FAQs page (*https://oreil.ly/kFUyg*).

To register for the exam, go to *https://oreil.ly/mvIHl*. From there, select "Schedule an exam." You will then provide profile information about yourself: name, address, phone, etc. You will get the exam dashboard. You will go to the left menu bar and select Exam Registration and then choose "Schedule an exam."

You can cancel or reschedule up to 24 hours before your scheduled exam without penalty. If you need to change your appointment less than 24 hours in advance, you might forfeit your fee. Should you miss the exam entirely, you won't be refunded, and you must wait at least 24 hours before rescheduling. Remember, missing your appointment doesn't count as failing.

If a medical emergency occurs, contact Pearson VUE directly for support and, if appropriate, provide documentation to waive the fee or reschedule without additional costs.

Should you need to retake the exam after a failed attempt, a 14-day waiting period applies. Every exam attempt requires payment of the full fee.

There are accommodations for those with disabilities or who are nonnative English speakers (e.g., getting an extra 30 minutes for the exam). However, you need to request this before scheduling your exam by selecting "Request accommodations" on your account dashboard.

When you pass, AWS will award you a digital badge through Credly's Acclaim platform. It's a way to showcase your achievement on social media, email signatures, or your personal website. Your certification remains valid for three years. After this, you need to get recertified. But you will be eligible for a 50% discount on the fee for the exam.

Other AWS Certifications

AWS offers four main types of certifications, each geared toward a different level of experience and expertise. At the base level, there are the foundational certifications. These are designed for beginners, so you don't need any previous experience to study for them. The CLF-C02 exam falls into this category.

Moving up, you'll find the following types of certifications:

Associate
> These are role-specific—think developer, solutions architect, or data engineer. AWS suggests having some hands-on experience before diving in.

Professional
> Aimed at those looking to sharpen their skills in designing applications or automating systems. For this level, AWS recommends at least two years of experience.

Specialty
> These focus on deep knowledge in specific areas. The experience required depends on which specialty you're pursuing.

Once you've passed the CLF-C02 exam, there are various other exams you might consider taking, as you can see in Table 1-2.

Table 1-2. Other exams to consider after obtaining the CLF-C02 certification

Certification	What the exam covers
AWS Certified SysOps Administrator (*https://oreil.ly/VFssU*)	• Monitoring, logging, and remediation (20%) • Reliability and business continuity (16%) • Deployment, provisioning, and automation (18%) • Security and compliance (16%) • Networking and content delivery (18%) • Cost and performance optimization (12%)
AWS Certified Solutions Architect (*https://oreil.ly/QNhdK*)	• Design of secure architectures (30%) • Design of resilient architectures (26%) • Design of high-performing architectures (24%) • Design of cost-optimized architectures (20%)
AWS Certified Developer (*https://oreil.ly/4FiJo*)	• Development with Amazon Web Services (32%) • Security (26%) • Deployment (24%) • Troubleshooting and optimization (18%)
AWS Certified Data Engineer (*https://oreil.ly/FbiHT*)	• Data ingestion and transformation (34%) • Data store management (26%) • Data operations and support (22%) • Data security and governance (18%)

AWS Resources

AWS offers more than just a study guide (*https://oreil.ly/Epbs0*). You'll also find a handful of online courses for the CLF-C02 exam (*https://oreil.ly/rWIKl*). One is free, and the rest come with a price tag.

So, with all that already available, why pick up this book?

Those AWS resources are definitely worth checking out. They're helpful and well put together. But this book takes things further. It breaks down the concepts in more depth, walks you through real-world examples, and gives you plenty of practice questions to test your knowledge. You'll also find a glossary of key terms. This is especially handy since many exam questions hinge on understanding specific definitions.

And besides, some people just prefer learning from a book. If that's you, you're in the right place.

Updates

The CLF-C02 certification evolves as AWS rolls out new services and updates existing ones. To help you keep up with those changes, I've set up a website (*https://oreil.ly/NP5Nv*) where I'll post important updates and anything else you should know along the way.

Conclusion

In this chapter, we learned the details of the CLF-C02 exam, what topics it covers, and why it's a valuable credential—whether you're aiming to break into the technology field, shift into a cloud-related role, or build a stronger understanding of AWS. We also looked at the structure of the exam, how it's delivered, and what to expect on test day. From salary potential to real-world relevance, the CLF-C02 certification offers a solid return on investment.

In the next chapter, we will get an overview of AWS Cloud concepts, benefits, and foundational principles.

CHAPTER 2

Getting Started with AWS

In this chapter, we'll explore AWS, and you'll learn what you need to know for the exam. To get started, you'll need to set up an account. I'll show you how to do this and fill you in on the benefits of the AWS Free Tier.

Then we'll explore the AWS Management Console, and I'll walk you through the most valuable AWS services, such as EC2, S3, RDS, IAM, and Lambda. I'll also introduce AWS's essential cost management tools. Understanding all these pieces will make the rest of AWS much easier to grasp.

Free Tier

If you're just getting started with AWS, it's worth taking a close look at the AWS Free Tier. It's essentially Amazon's way of letting you kick the tires on their massive cloud ecosystem without racking up a bill right away. But like most good things, the details matter.

There are actually three flavors of the Free Tier: a six-month offer, an always-available tier, and a set of short-term trials. Each one works a little differently, so let's break them down.

Six-Month Free Tier

This one kicks in the moment you create a new AWS account. For the next six months, you get a monthly quota of popular services for free. This is essentially your cloud sandbox—with some guardrails.

You'll get 750 hours of EC2 usage per month (enough to run a small instance 24/7), 5 GB of S3 storage, and 750 hours of a managed database using RDS, among other things. It's plenty to host a low-traffic web app or tinker with a side project. Just keep an eye on the limits. If you go over them, you'll start seeing charges.

Always Free

Not everything shuts off when the six months are up. Some services are "always free," meaning the free usage tier sticks around as long as you have an AWS account. This includes one million Lambda invocations per month (for serverless apps), 25 GB of storage with DynamoDB, and some basic CloudWatch monitoring.

These offers aren't just for hobbyists. They're useful for lightweight production workloads or for handling sporadic traffic.

Short-Term Trials

A third category often gets overlooked: short-term trials. These are time-limited but start only when you first use the service. For example, Amazon Lightsail—an easy-to-use virtual private server (VPS) option—gives you 750 free hours a month for three months. Other services like SageMaker (for machine learning) and Redshift (for analytics) also offer time-based trials to help you explore more specialized tools.

However, when it comes to the Free Tier, here's what you need to keep in mind: if you're part of an AWS organization, only one account gets to use the Free Tier benefits. So if you're spinning up test environments in multiple linked accounts, you might end up surprised by charges.

Setting Up Your AWS Account

Getting started with AWS doesn't take long, but there are a few steps worth walking through carefully. AWS is powerful, but like anything in technology, it pays to slow down at the beginning so that you don't miss something important later.

Here's how to get your account up and running:

1. Go to *https://aws.amazon.com* and click "Create account." You'll find the button tucked in the top-right corner of the page.

2. Enter your basic login information. After that, AWS will send you an email to confirm your address.

3. Fill out your contact details. This includes your full name, phone number, and address. You'll also choose an account type—Personal or Business. If you're experimenting or learning, Personal is fine.

4. Add a payment method. Even if you plan to stick with the Free Tier, AWS still requires a valid credit or debit card. They won't charge you unless you go over the free limits, but it's how they verify real users.

5. Verify your phone number. You can choose either a text message or a voice call to receive a PIN. Enter the PIN to confirm you're reachable.

6. Pick your support plan. Unless you have specific needs, go with the Basic support plan—it's free and perfectly adequate when you're starting out.

Once everything checks out, you'll land in the AWS console, which you can see in Figure 2-1. This is your home base for everything you'll do in AWS.

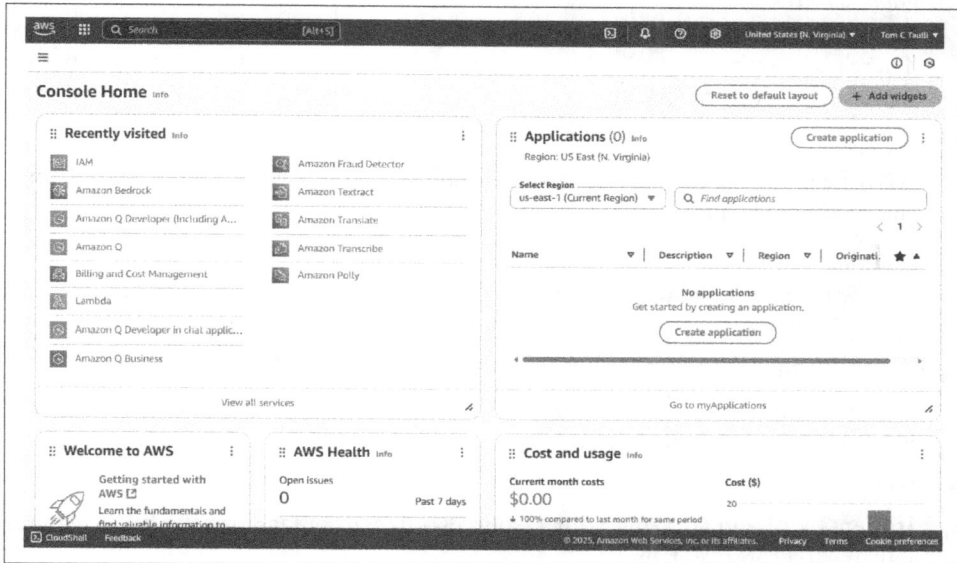

Figure 2-1. AWS console

You will start out as a root user. This is tied directly to the email address you used during sign-up. The root user has full access to everything in your AWS environment, including billing, security settings, and every service AWS offers. It's the account with the keys to the kingdom.

Because of that, the best practice is not to use the root user for your day-to-day work. Instead, AWS recommends that you immediately create an IAM (Identity and Access Management) user. AWS IAM lets you set up individual accounts with just the permissions needed for a specific task or role—nothing more. That way, if your credentials ever get compromised, the damage is limited.

When setting up an AWS account, it's a good idea to add multifactor authentication (MFA). This will add another layer of security.

Exploring the AWS Management Console

The Management Console can look a little overwhelming at first, but it's more approachable than it seems. AWS gives you a dashboard made up of widgets—little panels that show useful information or shortcuts.

Here's a quick tour of what you'll see:

Available services
> Click the square grid icon in the top-left to bring up a full list of AWS services. There's a search box too, which comes in handy once you start remembering names like "EC2" or "S3."

Recently visited
> AWS keeps track of services you've used recently, so you can jump back into them without hunting.

Applications
> This widget shows your deployed apps and the AWS regions they live in. You can also spin up a new application from here.

Welcome to AWS
> Think of this as your AWS orientation. You'll find links to documentation, tutorials, and general getting-started material.

AWS Health
> If there's an issue affecting your resources—like an outage or scheduled maintenance—it'll show up here.

Cost and usage
> This is your billing system. It shows your current month's spend and gives you a forecast based on your usage.

Security
> AWS flags anything that looks off, like missing patches, overly permissive settings, or anything that could put your account at risk.

And yes, you can rearrange the widgets. Drag them around until the console suits your preferences.

Keeping AWS Costs Under Control

Even if you're just experimenting or running small workloads, you may still rack up unexpected charges. One missed setting, one overprovisioned resource, and suddenly your "Free Tier" isn't so free anymore.

Fortunately, AWS gives you tools to stay ahead of surprises. You have to know where to look—and how to set things up right from the start. Here is a quick overview; we'll cover these services in more detail in future chapters.

Billing Dashboard

You'll find most of what you need in the Billing and Cost Management Dashboard. Type *billing* into the AWS console's search bar and click Billing and Cost Management. Figure 2-2 shows this dashboard.

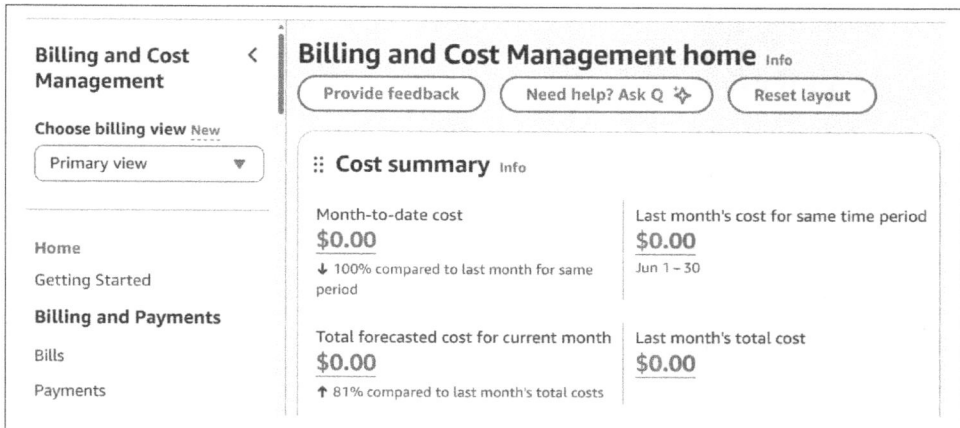

Figure 2-2. The dashboard for AWS Billing and Cost Management

Here, you can do the following:

- View your current charges
- Set preferences for invoice delivery and currency
- Track your Free Tier usage
- Opt in to billing alerts
- Dig into detailed reports on usage and cost

Budgets

Budgets let you draw a clear line in the sand: "I don't want to spend more than X." AWS will let you know when you're getting close or when you've crossed the line.

To create a budget, follow these steps:

1. In the AWS console, search for "budgets."
2. Choose "Create budget," then select "Cost budget."

3. Give your budget a name.

4. Set the amount (fixed or recurring).

5. Choose whether it's monthly, quarterly, or custom.

6. Configure your alerts—this is where you can choose thresholds, like "alert me at 80%."

You can set email notifications, SNS (Simple Notification Service) topics, or both. The first two budgets are free, which is usually enough for most individuals or small teams.

Free Tier Usage Alerts

If you're using AWS under the Free Tier, you should enable usage alerts. They'll warn you when you're approaching or exceeding Free Tier limits—before those overage charges kick in.

To enable alerts, follow these steps:

1. Go to Billing Preferences

2. Check the box to receive Free Tier usage alerts

3. Provide an email address

Managing AWS costs doesn't have to be stressful. A little upfront effort—like setting budgets and enabling alerts—goes a long way. Treat it like a smoke alarm: it might feel optional, right up until it saves your bacon.

Core AWS Services

AWS offers a massive catalog of services—well over 200 at last count—covering everything from computing and storage to AI, analytics, and Internet of Things (IoT). This range gives you much flexibility. But for the CLF-C02 exam, you don't need to know all of them. The exam focuses on the foundational pieces—the core services that power cloud infrastructure, keep it secure, and help manage costs. These are the pieces that will be most relevant to your preparation for the exam.

We'll cover the AWS services worth prioritizing (and we'll certainly cover these in more depth in the rest of the chapters). They show up often in real-world use cases, and more importantly, they reflect core AWS concepts like elasticity, the Shared Responsibility Model, and pay-as-you-go pricing. Here's a quick breakdown of the services:

Amazon EC2 (Elastic Compute Cloud)

EC2 is a virtual machine in the cloud. It lets you spin up servers quickly, choose your operating system (OS), pick from a range of instance types, and configure the networking to fit your needs. It's flexible and powerful, and it can be used for both test environments and full-blown production apps.

EC2 is a classic infrastructure as a service (IaaS) offering. You'll also see it come up a lot in cost optimization strategies like rightsizing, where you match instance size to actual usage.

Amazon S3 (Simple Storage Service)

Amazon S3 is an object storage service designed for storing and retrieving data at scale. It supports a wide range of use cases, such as storing media files, backup data, and application assets. The service provides high durability, availability, and accessibility over the internet. Think of it as an external hard drive with unlimited storage at low rates.

Amazon RDS (Relational Database Service)

Amazon RDS is a managed service for relational databases that supports multiple database engines, including MySQL, PostgreSQL, Oracle, and SQL Server. It automates administrative tasks such as software patching, backups, and database scaling, reducing the need for manual management.

Amazon Redshift

Redshift is AWS's managed data warehouse built for heavy analytics. If your job involves slicing and dicing large datasets or building out business intelligence dashboards, this is your tool.

AWS Lambda

Lambda lets you run code without provisioning servers. You just write your function, define what triggers it—like a file upload or an API request—and AWS handles the rest. It's especially useful for automation and microservices.

Amazon CloudWatch

CloudWatch is your eyes and ears in the AWS ecosystem. It collects metrics, logs, and events so that you can monitor performance, trigger alerts, and dig into issues when things go sideways.

AWS IAM (Identity and Access Management)

IAM handles permissions and access. You can create users, assign them to groups, and set up fine-grained access policies.

IAM is essential for every AWS environment. Whether you're locking down S3 buckets or controlling access to EC2 instances, this is your gatekeeper.

AWS CloudTrail

By default, CloudTrail logs all the API calls made in your account, such as who did what, when, and from where. This visibility is crucial for security, auditing, and compliance.

If something strange happens, CloudTrail helps you track down what went wrong (or who made the change). It's not flashy, but it's one of AWS's most important behind-the-scenes services.

AWS Cost Explorer

This tool gives you a visual breakdown of where your money is going. You can view spending over time, drill into usage by service, and spot trends that could lead to savings or surprises.

It's a must-use if you're serious about keeping costs under control, especially in multiaccount setups or fast-growing environments.

However, the AWS Cost Explorer does not provide real-time details. It can take up to 24 hours for the updates.

AWS Budgets

Budgets lets you set spending thresholds and get notified before things spiral. You can track both cost and usage, making it a smart tool for individuals, teams, or anyone watching the Free Tier limits.

AWS Bedrock

AWS Bedrock is a platform that allows for building generative AI applications. With it, you can select from a list of foundation models, such as those from Amazon, Anthropic, Mistral, and Meta. You can also configure the models and integrate them as APIs.

Besides these capabilities, AWS Bedrock allows for evaluating the performance of AI applications and scaling them for production.

Conclusion

In this chapter, we explored the core AWS services that every cloud practitioner should know—services like EC2, S3, RDS, Lambda, IAM, and CloudWatch that form the foundation of most cloud architectures. These tools are building blocks of real-world solutions used by startups, enterprises, and governments alike.

You also got a tour of the AWS Free Tier, learned how to set up your account the right way, and discovered essential cost management tools like Budgets and Cost Explorer. Taken together, these basics will help you start strong, avoid common mistakes, and make informed decisions as you continue your AWS journey.

In the next chapter, we'll shift our focus to understanding cloud architecture principles.

Chapter Quiz

To check your answers, please refer to the "Chapter 2 Answer Key" on page 205.

1. What is a key purpose of the AWS Free Tier?

    A. To provide permanent access to all AWS services

    B. To test only serverless services

    C. To let users explore AWS services at no cost within specific limits

    D. To avoid the need for a credit card during signup

2. Why should you avoid using the AWS root user for daily tasks?

    A. It cannot access billing features.

    B. It expires after 30 days.

    C. It has full access and poses a security risk if compromised.

    D. It requires reauthentication every hour.

3. What is a key function of AWS Identity and Access Management (IAM)?

    A. Managing user access and permissions

    B. Running serverless applications

    C. Tracking spending and usage

    D. Storing objects in the cloud

4. What is Amazon Elastic Compute Cloud (EC2) primarily used for?

    A. Running virtual servers in the cloud

    B. Hosting object storage

    C. Managing relational databases

    D. Creating IAM policies

5. Which AWS service logs all API calls and helps with security auditing?

    A. Amazon Redshift

    B. AWS IAM

    C. AWS CloudTrail

    D. Amazon CloudWatch

CHAPTER 3

Cloud Computing Foundations

This chapter takes you through the fundamentals behind cloud computing: what it is, where it came from, how it works, and why it matters.

Along the way, we highlight why businesses of all sizes are leaning into the cloud. Some of the benefits include lower costs, faster innovation, global reach, and the ability to scale up or down as needed. These aren't just buzzwords. They're real advantages that help teams move quicker and respond to change without getting bogged down in infrastructure headaches.

Regarding the exam, you'll be asked to distinguish between deployment models like public, private, and hybrid cloud, and to understand the differences between service models such as IaaS, PaaS, and SaaS. You'll also see questions that assess your grasp of the core benefits of cloud computing—like high availability, pay-as-you-go pricing, and global scalability. By understanding both the "what" and the "why" of cloud computing, you'll be better equipped to answer scenario-based questions that test real-world applications of these ideas.

Cloud Computing

The phrase "cloud computing" has been hyped, marketed, rebranded, and stretched to fit all kinds of products and services. Depending on who you ask, it might mean anything from streaming movies on Netflix to running entire companies' infrastructure. This kind of broad usage can make the definition slippery. So, to ground the idea, let's start with how AWS defines it (*https://oreil.ly/40eqG*):

"Cloud computing is the on-demand delivery of IT resources over the Internet with pay-as-you-go pricing. Instead of buying, owning, and maintaining physical data centers and servers, you can access technology services, such as computing power, storage, and databases, on an as-needed basis from a cloud provider like Amazon Web Services (AWS)."

This is a solid foundation. In plain terms, cloud computing lets you rent computing resources instead of buying them. Think of it like electricity. You don't run your own power plant. Rather, you plug in and pay for what you use. The cloud works the same way. Need a server for an hour? Fire one up, run your job, and shut it down. Done. No hardware to rack. No maintenance team. No upfront capital expense.

This model changes the game, especially for businesses that want to stay nimble. Startups can launch products without sinking cash into infrastructure. Enterprises can scale up for traffic spikes—say for the holiday seasons—without overprovisioning. And everyone benefits from faster deployment, more flexibility, and the ability to focus on building rather than babysitting servers.

Of course, there's more to it, but at its core, cloud computing is about turning IT into a utility. You use what you need, when you need it, and leave the rest to someone else.

A Brief History of Cloud Computing

Cloud computing emerged in the 1990s, bolstered by the arrival of the World Wide Web. It became possible for users to interact with software and services through a browser. Companies like Amazon and eBay built entire businesses around this model.

In 1999, Salesforce took the next step by launching a fully online customer relationship management (CRM) system. Instead of selling software that businesses had to install and manage, Salesforce delivered it entirely over the web. This SaaS model made it clear that cloud-based apps could be easier to use, cheaper to maintain, and faster to scale.

The real inflection point came in the early 2000s whenAmazon launched AWS. At first, it was a quiet rollout. It involved a few services, such as for storage and hosting web applications. But those offerings gave developers something they'd never had before: the ability to rent storage and computing power by the hour, without buying any hardware. This model would soon reshape how businesses of every size think about infrastructure.

At its heart, cloud computing builds on the familiar client-server model. A client (usually a browser or app) makes a request, and a server processes it and sends back the response, as you can see in Figure 3-1.

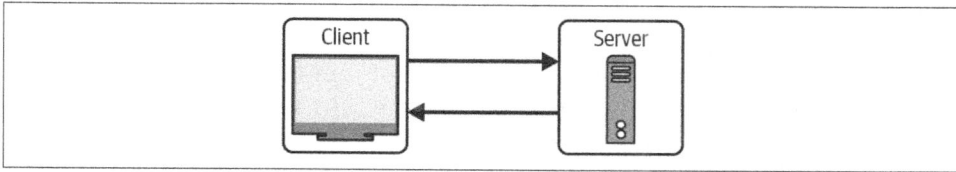

Figure 3-1. The client-server model

This architecture is what powers nearly everything we do online, from loading a website to spinning up virtual machines (VMs) in a data center thousands of miles away.

So while cloud computing feels like a recent development, it's really the product of decades of evolution.

Cloud Deployment Models

When it comes to defining a cloud strategy, organizations need to weigh several factors, including which parts of their application stack they're moving, how they prefer to manage resources, and what kind of IT infrastructure they already have in place.

There are three primary cloud deployment models to work with: cloud-based, on-premises, and hybrid. Each comes with its own trade-offs and strengths.

Cloud-Based (Public Cloud)

In a cloud-based setup, everything lives in the cloud—compute, storage, networking, databases, the whole stack. This model works well for new applications built specifically for the cloud, but many teams also migrate legacy apps into this environment. You can choose between low-level infrastructure like VMs (more control, more effort) or higher-level services like managed databases and serverless functions that abstract away the nitty-gritty.

Example: A tech startup might spin up web servers on AWS EC2, store files in Amazon S3, and use RDS for its backend database—all without needing a physical data center.

On-Premises (Private Cloud)

If your organization hosts everything in its own data center, you're in on-prem territory. This is also called a private cloud when it uses virtualization and cloud-style management tools. This model gives you maximum control over hardware, security, and compliance, which can be crucial in industries like finance or healthcare.

Example: A hospital might run its patient management system on local servers using VMware to virtualize the infrastructure, keeping sensitive data within its firewall for privacy and compliance.

Hybrid Cloud

Hybrid cloud blends the two. It lets you keep part of your infrastructure on-premises while extending other parts into the cloud. This model is especially useful when you have legacy systems that can't move easily, or when regulations require certain data to stay in-house. Hybrid setups offer flexibility and scalability while maintaining control where you need it.

Example: A retail company might run its customer-facing website and analytics in the cloud but keep its inventory and point-of-sale systems on-prem for performance and data privacy reasons.

How to Choose?

Choosing the right model depends on a mix of technical and business needs:

Security and compliance
How sensitive is your data? Are there legal or industry rules you must follow?

Scalability
Do your workloads spike seasonally or need rapid scaling?

Cost
What's your budget, and how much flexibility do you need with spending?

Existing infrastructure
What do you already have, and can it integrate with cloud services?

Many companies end up with a hybrid model, as it gives them the best of both worlds. You can scale quickly when needed, keep critical data close, and gradually modernize your systems without ripping everything out at once. The key is to match your deployment model to your specific goals.

Cloud Models

Depending on what you need—whether it's raw computing power, a ready-to-go development environment, or an application that works out of the box—you'll interact with the cloud in different ways. Broadly speaking, those ways fall into three buckets: IaaS, PaaS, and SaaS. Let's break them down.

IaaS

If you're looking for the cloud equivalent of renting a data center, infrastructure as a service (IaaS) is your model. It gives you access to the nuts and bolts of computing—VMs, storage, and networking—without asking you to manage physical servers.

You pay for what you use, and you get full control over the environment. This means you can choose your OS, install the software you need, and configure the systems how you like. It's a good fit for developers, systems administrators, or anyone who wants maximum flexibility without the hassle of maintaining hardware.

Typical use cases:

- Running older, on-premises applications in the cloud
- Hosting VMs
- Spinning up development and test environments on demand

Why teams like IaaS:

- Full control over systems and software
- Easy to scale up or down services, such as EC2 and S3

PaaS

With the platform as a service model, you don't think about infrastructure at all. The platform gives you everything you need to build and deploy software—runtime, databases, frameworks, and continuous integration and continuous delivery or deployment (CI/CD) tools—without touching the underlying servers.

This model is a sweet spot for developers who want to move fast. You focus on writing code, and the platform handles the rest, like provisioning, scaling, and patching.

Typical use cases:

- Building web or mobile applications
- Working with microservices
- Creating and managing APIs

Why developers like PaaS:

- No server management required
- Speeds up the release cycle
- Built-in tools for scaling and automation

SaaS

This is the model you've probably used the most, even if you didn't know the name. Software as a service applications are fully built, fully managed, and ready to use in your browser. Some examples include Gmail, Dropbox, or Microsoft 365. You sign in, and you're good to go.

With SaaS, the provider handles software, updates, and security. You just use the app. It's a good choice for businesses and individuals who want tools that work without the overhead.

Typical use cases:

- Email
- CRM platforms
- Project and task management tools

Why SaaS is so popular:

- No setup or maintenance required
- Users always have access to the latest version

Each of these models serves a different purpose, and the best choice depends on what you're trying to build or run as well as security considerations. If you just need software, go with SaaS. If you want to build software without worrying about infrastructure, PaaS is a good choice. And if you want total control, IaaS puts you in the driver's seat.

Figure 3-2 shows the key aspects of these three cloud models.

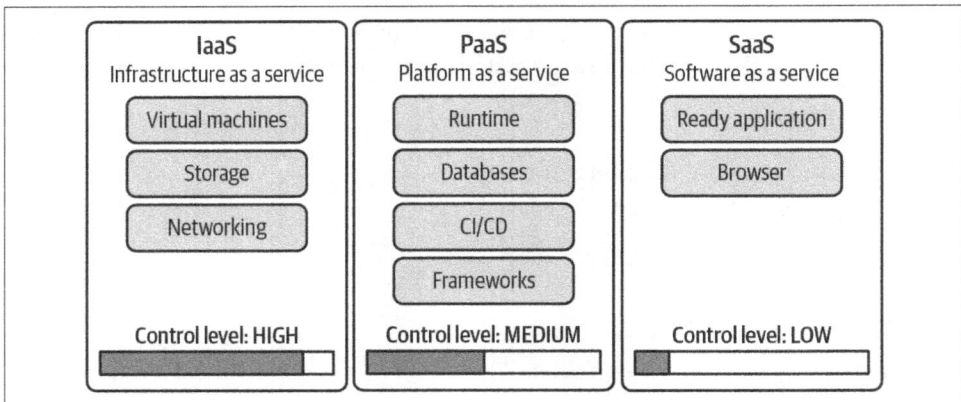

Figure 3-2. Comparisons among the three cloud models

Cloud Benefits

Since the 1990s, individuals and businesses have been transitioning from using independent, isolated computer systems to a cloud model, where infrastructure, platforms, and software are shared. This transition is still ongoing; many businesses are still making the change. There are several obvious advantages that the cloud offers:

Replace large upfront costs with pay-as-you-go pricing

Buying servers and building out data centers used to be the norm. It was expensive, slow, and locked up a lot of cash. Cloud services like Amazon EC2 flipped that script. Now, you only pay for what you use, when you use it. It's like trading a giant upfront bill for a flexible monthly tab, and the services scale with you.

Eliminate the burden of managing physical infrastructure

Keeping physical infrastructure up and running takes lots of time, money, and expertise. Power, cooling, repairs—it all adds up. Cloud providers take care of all this grunt work. So instead of patching servers, your team can spend their time building better apps and delivering real value to customers.

High availability

High availability means your systems stay up and running, even when something goes wrong. In the cloud, providers build in safeguards like backup systems, failover setups, and tools that automatically recover from failures. These layers of protection help prevent downtime. If you rely on applications that just can't go offline—like online stores, healthcare platforms, or financial systems—high availability is what keeps everything moving smoothly without interruptions.

Avoid over- or underprovisioning resources

Planning for peak traffic is tough. Overprovision, and you waste money. Underprovision, and performance takes a hit. The cloud solves this with elasticity, which is the ability to automatically scale resources up or down based on demand. AWS services like Auto Scaling and AWS Lambda support this.

Leverage massive economies of scale

Big cloud providers buy in serious volume, which adds up to thousands and thousands of servers and massive bandwidth. This buying power means lower costs per unit, and those savings get passed down to you. It's hard to match that kind of efficiency when you're operating your own infrastructure.

Accelerate innovation with greater speed and agility

Setting up new servers used to take days or even weeks. In the cloud, it's minutes, if not seconds. Need to run code without thinking about infrastructure at all? Services like AWS Lambda let you do just that. You can test, tweak, and ship features faster, which means more room for experimentation and innovation.

Deploy globally in minutes

Want to serve customers in Tokyo, London, and São Paulo—all at once? With the cloud, you can spin up resources across the world in just a few clicks. Providers like AWS have data centers in many regions across the globe, so you can keep latency low and performance high, no matter where your users are.

Conclusion

In this chapter, we looked at the building blocks of cloud computing, starting with how it evolved into today's powerful platforms like AWS. We also unpacked the different deployment models—public, private, and hybrid—as well as the core service models like IaaS, PaaS, and SaaS.

We then looked into why businesses are so drawn to the cloud, such as the lower costs, easier scaling, global reach, and the kind of agility that helps teams move fast without getting stuck in infrastructure overhead. Put together, these ideas give you a solid foundation for understanding how cloud computing helps organizations stay nimble, innovate quickly, and handle whatever the digital world throws their way.

Chapter Quiz

To check your answers, please refer to the "Chapter 3 Answer Key" on page 205.

1. Which cloud deployment model involves an organization hosting everything in its own data center, often using virtualization and cloud-style management tools?

   A. Public cloud

   B. Private cloud

   C. Hybrid cloud

   D. Blended cloud

2. When choosing a cloud deployment model, what factor is critical if an organization's workloads spike seasonally or need rapid scaling?

   A. Existing infrastructure that cannot integrate with cloud services

   B. Strict data sovereignty laws requiring all data to remain on-premises

   C. Scalability

   D. A fixed budget with no flexibility for variable spending

3. What is a key advantage of the software as a service (SaaS) model for businesses and individuals?

   A. It offers complete control over the underlying hardware and operating system.

   B. No setup or maintenance is required by the user, and they always have the latest version.

   C. It requires users to perform their own software updates and security patches.

   D. It is primarily designed for developers to build custom applications.

4. Which cloud deployment model is described as offering flexibility and scalability while maintaining control where needed, often useful for legacy systems or specific regulatory requirements?

   A. Public cloud

   B. Private cloud

   C. SaaS cloud

   D. Hybrid cloud

5. What does "high availability" mean in the context of cloud computing?

   A. Ensuring that applications can only run in a single Availability Zone

   B. Reducing costs by eliminating redundancy in infrastructure

   C. Designing systems to remain operational with minimal downtime

   D. Using larger instance types to handle failures

CHAPTER 4

Fundamentals of AWS

Cloud computing has fundamentally transformed the way organizations manage IT resources. Instead of investing heavily in physical infrastructure, businesses are now turning to cloud platforms like AWS to gain flexibility, reduce costs, and accelerate innovation.

This chapter provides a comprehensive overview of the fundamentals of AWS, starting with a comparison between traditional on-premises setups and cloud-based environments. We'll then go on to look at the key financial concepts like the total cost of ownership (TCO), examine licensing strategies, and dive into cloud native benefits like rightsizing, automation, and scalability. The chapter also introduces important frameworks like the AWS Well-Architected Framework and the AWS Cloud Adoption Framework. They provide practical guidance for designing secure, resilient, and cost-effective cloud solutions.

Cloud Economics

One of the cloud's most powerful advantages isn't technical at all—it's economic. Cloud economics has reshaped how organizations think about IT spending, shifting the conversation from servers and data centers to flexibility, speed, and financial agility. Understanding how cloud costs work, and how they differ from traditional infrastructure investments, is key to making smart decisions in the cloud.

In the next few sections, we'll unpack some of the main benefits and features that drive cloud economics.

On-Premises Versus Cloud Computing Environments

When you're weighing IT infrastructure options, the cost differences between running operations on-premises and moving to the cloud can be eye-opening. One of the key metrics that helps make sense of this is the TCO. This isn't just about the price tag on a server. Instead, it wraps in everything, such as purchase costs, operating expenses, ongoing maintenance, and the people who keep it all running.

Going the on-premises route often means you're footing a sizable bill. Here's a breakdown of where the money goes:

Hardware
Entry-level servers might cost you around $1,000 to $2,500, but once you step into enterprise-grade gear, you're easily looking at $10,000 or more per server.

Storage
High-capacity, high-performance enterprise storage solutions can set you back upwards of $50,000.

Networking gear
Routers, switches, firewalls—especially the kind that scale well and don't compromise on security—can push your networking spend past $50,000.

Software licenses
Operating systems, virtualization platforms, and middleware licenses can easily add up. Annual costs can exceed $5,000, depending on what you're running.

Data center space
Whether you build or lease, data center costs don't come cheap. Factor in power, cooling, and physical security, and you're looking at over $1,000 per square foot.

Staff and maintenance
Skilled IT personnel are essential, and salaries often hit six figures. This is before you even factor in patching, updates, or support contracts.

These costs are a big reason why so many companies are migrating to the cloud. With lower upfront expenses, predictable monthly fees, and the ability to scale up (or down) as needed, cloud services offer a level of financial flexibility that traditional infrastructure often can't match.

Capital Versus Operating Expenses

Capital expenditure (CapEx) generally refers to on-premises investments—spending up front to acquire physical assets like buildings, data centers, servers, and perpetual software licenses. These are long-term purchases you expect to keep and use over multiple years. While the initial cost can be large, the benefit is greater control. But you must forecast your needs years in advance, which is challenging if usage drops or surges unexpectedly.

Operating expenditure (OpEx), by contrast, includes operational costs that arise from day-to-day usage of services like compute, storage, SaaS subscriptions, and managed offerings. With cloud services, you pay as you go—typically monthly, quarterly, or annually—with little or no upfront cost. This pay-as-you-use model offers flexibility and lets your spending scale with demand.

Dividing expenses into CapEx and OpEx is common in the IT industry. It's a way to get a sense of the financial impact. These two terms also often show up on exam questions.

Bring-Your-Own-License (BYOL) Versus Included License Models

When you're deploying software on AWS, one of the first things to figure out is how you'll handle licensing. You've got two main paths: you can use the Bring Your Own License (BYOL) experience or use AWS's included licenses. Each has its pros, cons, and gotchas. Choosing the right model can save you money, reduce headaches, or both.

Bring Your Own License (BYOL)

If your organization already holds software licenses—such as Windows Server, SQL Server, or Oracle—BYOL on AWS offers a way to reduce costs and maintain compliance. For workloads that tie licensing to physical hardware (like older Windows or SQL Server core/socket-based licenses), deploying on Amazon EC2 Dedicated Hosts preserves the physical core and socket visibility required by licensing terms. This alignment can yield up to 50% savings.

Alternatively, if your Microsoft licenses are covered by active Software Assurance (SA), you can use License Mobility to shift eligible products—like SQL Server, Exchange, or SharePoint—to shared tenancy EC2 instances. This approach avoids the need for Dedicated Hosts, streamlines deployment, and still lets you use existing licenses, provided you complete the required Microsoft verification.

To use this service, you must submit Microsoft's License Mobility Verification Form (*https://oreil.ly/vfJ9X*) and receive approval before deploying workloads.

In both scenarios, the responsibility for license tracking and compliance remains with you, even though AWS offers tools like AWS License Manager to help. Ultimately, BYOL gives you the flexibility to reuse existing investments while reducing AWS spend, as long as you align infrastructure and licensing correctly.

AWS License Included model

The AWS License Included model uses the pay-as-you-go system to wrap the software licensing costs into the hourly price of the instance. You spin it up, use the software, and AWS takes care of the licensing details.

Using AWS-included licenses instead of your own is especially useful if you want flexibility. Need to scale up fast or experiment without wrestling with licensing paperwork? This model does particularly well here. For example, Amazon RDS for Oracle lets you skip the Oracle license purchase entirely. AWS supplies it as part of the package.

The trade-off, though, is cost. If you're running a workload for the long haul, it might end up being more expensive to use bundled licenses than to reuse licenses you already own. So while it's simpler, that simplicity can come with a price tag.

Making the right call

Determining which approach to use comes down to your situation.

If your company already owns licenses and your workloads are stable or predictable, BYOL might make more financial sense. You get to stretch your existing investments further. But if you're prioritizing agility, want to avoid compliance overhead, or need to move fast, the AWS License Included model could be the better fit, even if it costs a little more over time.

Whichever path you choose, tools like AWS License Manager can help you stay organized. It tracks what you're using and where, helping you stay compliant and avoid unexpected costs down the line.

Rightsizing

In AWS, *rightsizing* means fine-tuning your cloud resources—especially EC2 and RDS instances—so that they match what your workloads need. It's about having enough capacity to keep things running smoothly, but not having so many resources that you're paying for unused horsepower.

To achieve the right balance, you'll need to dig into usage data. Look for instances that are overprovisioned (too much CPU allocation or memory sitting idle) or under-provisioned (just barely handling the load). Once you spot the outliers, you can adjust instance types or sizes to better fit the actual demand.

This isn't a one-and-done task. Workloads evolve, and what fits today might be over-sized next quarter. This is why it works best to adopt rightsizing as an ongoing routine. Tools like AWS Compute Optimizer and Cost Explorer make this easier by offering data-driven recommendations based on how your infrastructure has behaved over time.

When done right, rightsizing can unlock major savings. By reviewing usage trends—typically over a 14- to 93-day window—you can spot opportunities to scale down, consolidate, or shift workloads without hurting performance. It also pairs nicely with long-term pricing strategies like Reserved Instances or Savings Plans, helping you reserve only what you truly need.

Automation

Automation takes the grunt work out of repetitive tasks like provisioning servers, managing configurations, and applying patches. For example, AWS Systems Manager Automation lets you build runbooks—basically, reusable workflows—that handle routine maintenance or deployment jobs across services like EC2 and RDS. This frees up your team to focus on higher-level strategy instead of constantly putting out fires.

Importantly, AWS makes this easy because its services are automation tools themselves. AWS Systems Manager is an automation engine, Auto Scaling automates resource scaling based on demand, and Compute Optimizer automates cost saving insights. Having the platform itself centered around automation reduces manual toil and ensures consistency.

When your application needs to handle unpredictable traffic, automation has your back there too. Services like Elastic Beanstalk and AWS Lambda automatically scale your application based on demand, so you don't have to scramble to spin up more servers during a spike.

Security and compliance also get a boost. Automated tools like AWS Config and CloudTrail keep an eye on your environment by tracking resource changes and logging user activity. This kind of visibility makes it easier to stay compliant and respond quickly if something goes sideways.

With the right automation in place, you can move faster, spend less, and build cloud systems that practically run themselves.

Scale

By pooling the demands of hundreds of thousands of customers, AWS can buy hardware and software in massive quantities. This scale drives down costs, and AWS passes those savings along to its users.

AWS also squeezes maximum efficiency out of its global infrastructure. It spreads costs across a huge customer base, which lowers the per-user price of services like storage and compute.

Its worldwide network of data centers and availability zones adds another layer of value. AWS can route workloads intelligently, balance performance, and maintain high availability—all while keeping operations cost-effective.

AWS's ongoing investments in innovation and infrastructure help drive costs even lower over time. As the platform evolves, customers continue to benefit from better performance, richer features, agility, and reduced pricing.

AWS Well-Architected Framework

The AWS Well-Architected Framework serves as a guide, offering a structured approach of design principles, best practices, and tools. However, it doesn't automatically configure or optimize your workloads. Instead, it helps your team critically assess your architecture, uncover risks, and determine what needs to be done in areas like performance, security, cost, and resilience. Armed with this guidance, you're responsible for executing the necessary steps—such as tagging resources, conducting load tests, enabling auto scaling, applying cost optimization strategies, and implementing security controls—in order to steadily improve your systems over time.

The framework is built around six key pillars:

Operational excellence
> Operational excellence is about keeping systems healthy and adapting quickly when things change—which they always seem to do. In AWS, this means treating operations like code. You automate what you can, track what matters, and build feedback loops into your workflow.
>
> To avoid surprises, you can run controlled failure drills, often called game days. You'll learn how your team and systems respond under pressure. This will help you identify where you need to focus to make your organization more resilient. The goal of these exercises isn't to overhaul the whole system, but to identify areas for improvement and make small, reversible changes. This is an ongoing process; you'll keep learning as you go.

Security
> Security should be a continuous practice. For this, AWS follows a Shared Responsibility Model. AWS secures the cloud infrastructure, but you're in charge of securing your data and workloads. This includes managing who can access what and when, encrypting everything important, and setting up systems to alert you when something goes sideways. Tools like AWS Config and CloudTrail can help, but regular risk reviews and staying on top of compliance are just as important. The more you automate your defenses, the faster you can respond.

Reliability
> Reliability means your system holds up, even when something breaks. AWS gives you tools to build for failure: spread workloads across availability zones, automate recovery, and make sure your monitoring practices provide useful information, rather than just noise. You should also test your backups and failover processes often. Use infrastructure as code to keep deployments consistent, and design for horizontal scaling so that you're ready when demand spikes.
>
> Resilient systems aren't an accident—they're planned that way.

Performance efficiency

Performance efficiency means meeting or exceeding your performance goals using the most appropriate cloud resources and evolving alongside those goals over time. It starts by making smart architecture choices—selecting the right compute (serverless, containers, or instances), storage, database, and networking solutions—matched to your workload's behavior. You should embrace design principles like using serverless architectures to remove infrastructure management and experimenting often to tune performance. After implementation, monitor key performance metrics, set up alarms, and run load tests under pressure to validate and optimize. When patterns shift, employ auto-scaling to adjust capacity and rightsize resources based on real-world data.

In essence, performance efficiency is an ongoing cycle: choose wisely, observe closely, and adjust continuously.

Cost optimization

Cost optimization helps you get the most value from AWS without overspending. Tag your resources, track usage patterns, and take advantage of pricing models like Spot Instances or reserved capacity. Budgeting tools can catch runaway costs early, and managed services can offload some of the operational burden.

Sustainability

A focus on sustainability pushes teams to go beyond performance and cost—centering on the environmental impact of their cloud workloads. The AWS Well-Architected Framework supports this by offering guidance to help reduce idle resources, optimize energy use, choose efficient regions, and minimize unnecessary data transfer.

Table 4-1 shows a summary of the AWS Well-Architected Framework.

Table 4-1. The AWS Well-Architected Framework

Pillar	What this pillar provides
Operational excellence	• Treat operations like code and automate where possible • Run game days to test how systems respond under stress • Make small, reversible changes and build in feedback loops
Security	• Follow the shared responsibility model: AWS secures the infrastructure, you secure your data • Encrypt critical information and control access • Use tools like AWS Config and CloudTrail, and automate security alerts
Reliability	• Distribute workloads across availability zones and automate recovery • Regularly test backups and failover processes • Use infrastructure as code and design for horizontal scaling
Performance efficiency	• Choose the right compute resources, including serverless and containers • Use managed services to reduce operational overhead • Monitor metrics and test workloads under pressure

Pillar	What this pillar provides
Cost optimization	• Tag resources and monitor usage patterns • Leverage pricing models like Spot Instances and reserved capacity • Use budgeting tools and managed services to avoid unnecessary spending
Sustainability	• Reduce idle resources and unnecessary data transfers • Optimize energy use and select efficient regions • Align architecture decisions with sustainability goals

AWS Cloud Adoption Framework

The AWS Cloud Adoption Framework (CAF) is Amazon's comprehensive guide for organizations that have committed to AWS and are ready to move beyond on-premises infrastructure. While the Well-Architected Framework focuses on the technical design and optimization of specific workloads, the CAF takes a broader view. It helps you assess and build the strategic, organizational, and operational capabilities needed for a successful cloud transformation.

The CAF is typically used before or alongside the Well-Architected Framework. It helps you answer questions like: "Are we ready—organizationally, technically, and culturally—to adopt AWS at scale?" Once those foundations are in place, the CAF comes into play to assess, refine, and optimize the design of your actual workloads.

The CAF is organized around six key perspectives: business, people, governance, platform, security, and operations. These help you align cloud adoption with business goals, develop governance and training plans, set up foundational cloud environments, and prepare your organization for long-term operations.

Business perspective
> The business perspective helps ensure your cloud investments support your broader business goals. This is focused on evaluating your cloud strategy, prioritizing investments, and defining key business outcomes. Decision makers—like the CEO, CFO, CIO, or CTO—will find this perspective especially valuable, as it aligns cloud initiatives with financial objectives, strategy, and innovation efforts.
>
> Rather than focusing on infrastructure, this perspective centers on what the cloud can enable: accelerating digital transformation, justifying investment through measurable benefits, assessing the right things to move, and shaping new value propositions. This helps guide leadership in defining the "why" before diving into "how."

People perspective
> This perspective focuses on how teams are organized, how leadership works, and how you support your workforce as roles and responsibilities evolve.
>
> You'll look at things like upskilling, leadership development, and change management. If you're in HR, talent development, or managing cross-functional

teams, this one's in your lane. The goal is to foster a culture that's ready to learn and adapt.

Governance perspective

The governance perspective guides organizations in aligning cloud strategy with business objectives while managing risk and compliance. It helps you define the skills, processes, and control mechanisms needed to run cloud programs responsibly. Stakeholders like the CIO, enterprise architects, program/product managers, analysts, and portfolio owners use this perspective to learn how to shape governance structures, update organizational processes, and enable oversight.

In practice, companies give relevant team members access to the governance perspective to understand and assess existing gaps. They then use this insight to design governance functions, such as program management, benefits and risk management, financial oversight, application portfolio reviews, and data governance. Once the "what and why" are understood, the company assigns specific roles to carry out these governance actions.

Platform perspective

This is where the technology takes center stage. The platform perspective provides guidance on how to design, build, and run your cloud systems. This includes modernizing old workloads, creating cloud native apps, and setting up continuous integration and delivery pipelines.

If you're a solutions architect, engineer, or IT manager, this is familiar territory. It's about building something that lasts and scales with your needs.

Security perspective

The security perspective is where organizations learn how to embed protection across their cloud environments. The focus is on confidentiality, integrity, and availability of data and workloads. It outlines nine foundational security capabilities—such as IAM, threat detection, and incident response—that security professionals must address.

For someone studying the framework, the key takeaway is this: these capabilities are intended for practitioners responsible for cloud security, especially CISOs, security architects, compliance officers, and internal audit teams.

Operations perspective

Operations is where strategy becomes reality. This perspective is about how you monitor, manage, and maintain your cloud services day to day. It includes your operating model, incident response strategy, and disaster recovery planning.

The key stakeholders here are IT operations leads, DevOps teams, and support managers. It's not the flashiest area, but it's the one that keeps everything humming behind the scenes.

Figure 4-1 shows a summary of the perspectives.

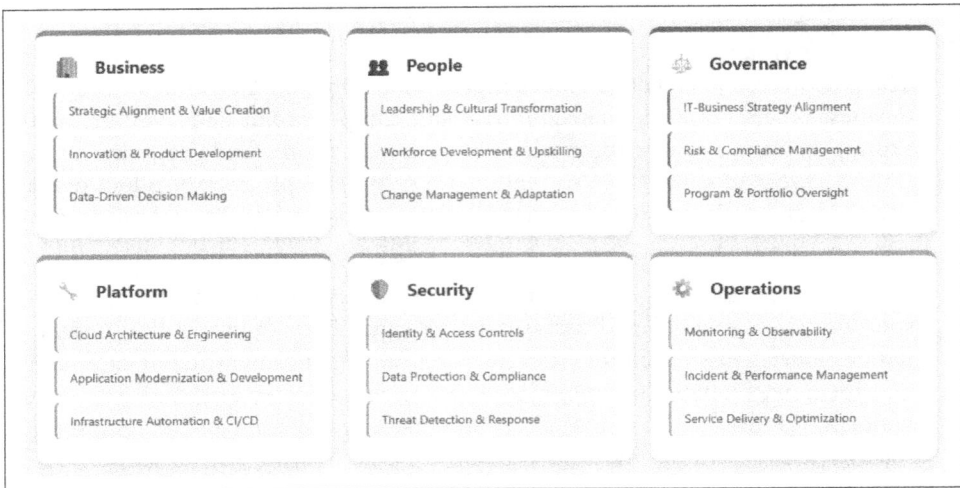

Business

Strategic Alignment & Value Creation

Innovation & Product Development

Data-Driven Decision Making

People

Leadership & Cultural Transformation

Workforce Development & Upskilling

Change Management & Adaptation

Governance

IT-Business Strategy Alignment

Risk & Compliance Management

Program & Portfolio Oversight

Platform

Cloud Architecture & Engineering

Application Modernization & Development

Infrastructure Automation & CI/CD

Security

Identity & Access Controls

Data Protection & Compliance

Threat Detection & Response

Operations

Monitoring & Observability

Incident & Performance Management

Service Delivery & Optimization

Figure 4-1. AWS Cloud Adoption Framework

Migration

Moving to the cloud is a strategic shift that can unlock better scalability, flexibility, and long-term cost savings. But getting there takes a lot of planning. AWS provides a practical toolkit known as the six migration strategies, commonly referred to as the 6 Rs.

Each of the six strategies offers a different path to the cloud. There's no one-size-fits-all solution, and that's the point. By understanding what each option offers, you can build a smart migration plan.

Let's break them down:

Rehost
Rehosting is the "lift and shift" move. You take your application as-is and drop it into the cloud, no code changes required. It's fast and relatively simple. It is for when you need to get out of a data center quickly or migrate a large batch of systems. The trade-off, though, is you won't get the full benefit of cloud native tools, and you may bring along some of your old inefficiencies. Still, for many, it's a solid first step.

Replatform
Replatforming means you tweak your application just enough to make it work better in the cloud, but without overhauling the whole system. Maybe you swap out a self-hosted database for a managed service like Amazon RDS. It's more work than rehosting but gives you a smoother, more cloud-friendly experience

without a full rewrite. It is modernization without some of the challenges of a full rebuild.

Refactor or re-architect

Refactoring or re-architecting goes deep. You redesign and rebuild the app to take full advantage of cloud native capabilities, such as microservices, serverless functions, or scalable, distributed databases. This approach takes time and resources. But if your current architecture is holding you back—or if you're trying to innovate faster—it's often worth the investment.

Repurchase

Repurchasing means swapping your old application for a new, cloud native one—usually a SaaS product. For example, instead of hosting your own CRM, you move to something like Salesforce. You don't migrate the application—you replace it. But this usually requires reworking internal processes or retraining teams.

Retain

Sometimes the best move is… no move. At least for now. Maybe the application just got an upgrade, has regulatory constraints, or depends on systems that aren't cloud-ready. In these cases, you hit pause. You keep the application on-premises while you work on migrating everything else. Retaining lets you focus on what's ready now without derailing the bigger plan.

Retire

Every organization has applications that no one really uses anymore. Maybe they served a purpose once, but now they're dead weight. Retiring those systems frees up time, budget, and mental space. It's often a great place to start your migration journey because it helps you clean house before moving forward.

Choosing the right strategy for each app means asking the right questions: How complex is it? How critical is it to the business? What kind of resources do you have to work with? The answers will point you toward the most effective approach.

AWS Snow Family

The AWS Snow Family is a set of physical, rugged devices designed to help customers move large amounts of data to and from AWS when internet connections are slow, expensive, or unreliable. These devices are commonly used in remote locations, in disconnected environments, during large migrations, or where data volumes are so large that transferring over the network would take too long or cost too much.

There are three main Snow device categories you need to know for the exam: Snowcone, Snowball, and Snowmobile. Snowcone is the smallest and most portable option —used for small edge use cases, IoT deployments, and limited-power/limited-space situations (like vehicles, ships, job sites, field sensors). Snowball is used for large-scale data transfer (tens of terabytes to petabytes) and can also support edge compute workloads depending on the model. Snowmobile is literally a tractor-trailer that can transfer exabyte-scale data for massive migrations.

However, AWS is de-emphasizing Snowball going forward. New orders will only be available to existing customers after November 2025. However, Snow Family knowledge is still testable because the exam objective is concept reasoning: if bandwidth is limited, or you need petabyte-scale offline transfer—choose Snow.

Conclusion

In this chapter, we learned how AWS transforms traditional IT practices by offering a flexible, scalable, and cost-effective alternative to on-premises infrastructure. We looked at the economic advantages of cloud computing, including the shift from capital expenditures to operating expenditures, and examined critical financial strategies like rightsizing and licensing models such as BYOL and the AWS License Included model.

We also introduced foundational frameworks such as the AWS Well-Architected Framework and the AWS Cloud Adoption Framework, which help organizations build reliable, secure, and efficient cloud environments while navigating cultural, operational, and technical shifts.

In the next chapter, we'll look at cloud governance and compliance with the AWS platform.

Chapter Quiz

To check your answers, please refer to the "Chapter 4 Answer Key" on page 206.

1. What is one major financial advantage of moving from on-premises infrastructure to the cloud?

    A. Increased hardware investments

    B. Higher initial capital costs

    C. Longer depreciation timelines

    D. Lower total cost of ownership (TCO)

2. Which of the following is not one of the 6 Rs of cloud migration?

   A. Rehost

   B. Repackage

   C. Replatform

   D. Refactor

3. What is the purpose of the sustainability pillar in the Well-Architected Framework?

   A. Enforce legal compliance

   B. Reduce environmental impact

   C. Increase profit margins

   D. Boost staff productivity

4. Which Cloud Adoption Framework (CAF) perspective focuses on aligning IT with business goals and financial accountability?

   A. Platform

   B. Governance

   C. Security

   D. People

5. What's a key benefit of using the repurchase migration strategy?

   A. Retains all legacy customizations

   B. Eliminates compliance needs

   C. Keeps infrastructure on-premises

   D. Replaces legacy apps with software as a service (SaaS)

CHAPTER 5

AWS Compliance and Governance

When you're running workloads in AWS, it's easy to blur the lines between compliance, governance, and security. They're tightly linked, but each plays a distinct role in keeping your cloud environment secure, well-managed, and in line with regulations. Understanding how they differ—and how they work together—goes a long way toward building systems that are both efficient and trustworthy.

In this chapter, we'll take a look at compliance, along with governance. We'll begin coverage of the topic of security in the next chapter by looking at the AWS IAM service. Keep in mind that compliance is more emphasized in the exam. So, our coverage of governance will be fairly brief. For this topic, you will need to understand a couple of tools like AWS Organizations and AWS Config.

Understanding the Differences

Let's first look at the differences between compliance, governance, and security.

Compliance

Compliance is about playing by the rules. Whether those rules come from laws, industry standards, or your own internal policies, compliance means making sure your systems and data handling practices follow them.

In the AWS ecosystem, compliance typically centers on protecting customer data, managing risk, and providing accountability. AWS helps with this by providing infrastructure that's built to meet recognized security standards. Their Compliance program covers a wide range of frameworks.

By aligning with these standards, AWS makes it easier for organizations to meet their own compliance requirements, no matter the industry or geography.

It's also important to keep in mind that theAWS Shared Responsibility Model applies to compliance duties. AWS ensures that the cloud infrastructure meets industry standards, while customers are responsible for configuring services like encryption and IAM policies to comply with regulations like the US's Health Insurance Portability and Accountability Act (HIPAA) and the EU's General Data Protection Regulation (GDPR).

Governance

If compliance is about following rules, governance is about creating and enforcing them. It's the broader framework that keeps your cloud operations aligned with business goals and risk tolerance.

In practice, governance involves setting policies, defining roles, and putting the right processes in place to make sure your AWS resources are used responsibly. This includes managing access, enforcing security standards, and ensuring that teams follow best practices across the board.

Good governance is also a powerful way to keep cloud costs in check. With tools like AWS Budgets and service control policies (SCPs), you can set spending limits, flag usage overages, and restrict unnecessary resource usage. This can help make sure your cloud investments stay aligned with your organization's goals.

AWS offers several tools to support this effort. Services like AWS Organizations, AWS Control Tower, and AWS Config help you manage multiple accounts, apply consistent policies, and monitor changes over time. With the right setup, governance becomes less about policing behavior and more about enabling teams to work safely at scale.

Security

Security is about protection. It's the set of technical and procedural safeguards that defend your data, systems, and workloads from threats—both external and internal.

AWS offers tools like IAM (Identity and Access Management), KMS (Key Management Service), and AWS Shield (a managed distributed denial of service protection service). These services help you control who can access what, encrypt sensitive data, and protect against attacks. Security is covered in detail in Chapter 7.

When used together—and used well—compliance, governance, and security don't just keep you out of trouble. They create a strong foundation for operating confidently in the cloud.

Compliance Frameworks Overview

When it comes to compliance, AWS helps organizations meet a wide range of industry, national, and international requirements. These requirements may come in the form of standards (like PCI DSS), programs (like FedRAMP), regulations (like HIPAA), or audit reports (like SOC 1 and 2). In this section, we'll walk through them—and clarify how AWS helps you align with each.

Note that AWS doesn't create these programs. Instead, it offers services and documentation that help you meet their requirements—whether by providing audit reports, offering compliant infrastructure, or listing authorized services.

PCI DSS

The Payment Card Industry Data Security Standard (PCI DSS) sets strict guidelines for processing, storing, and transmitting credit card data. AWS offers a PCI-compliant environment for services that handle payment information. If your application touches cardholder data, you'll need to make sure both your architecture and operational practices meet PCI requirements.

ISO

The International Organization for Standardization (ISO) sets globally recognized standards for information security, risk management, and quality assurance. AWS maintains compliance with key ISO certifications, some originally published jointly with the International Electrotechnical Commission (IEC). These include ISO/IEC 27001 (information security management), ISO/IEC 27017 (cloud-specific security controls), and ISO/IEC 27018 (protection of personal data in the cloud). These certifications demonstrate that AWS's security and privacy practices meet rigorous international benchmarks.

NIST

The US National Institute of Standards and Technology (NIST) provides widely adopted standards for cybersecurity, including NIST 800-53, an information security standard, and the NIST Cybersecurity Framework (CSF), as well as requirements like NIST Special Publication (SP) 800-171 for protecting Controlled Unclassified Information (CUI) for nonfederal systems. (CUI is a category of information determined by the US federal government.) AWS aligns many of its services and controls with NIST guidelines, making it easier for US federal agencies and other organizations to meet their security objectives.

FedRAMP

The Federal Risk and Authorization Management Program (FedRAMP) is a US government program that standardizes security assessment and authorization for cloud services used by federal agencies. AWS offers a catalog of services that have received FedRAMP authorization, meaning they've been reviewed and approved under the program's strict security standards.

However, not all AWS services are FedRAMP-authorized, and authorizations can differ based on the Region or deployment model. AWS GovCloud (US) divides the US into an eastern and a western region and offers compliance guidance. Standard regions, like the Northeast, the Southwest, etc., may also be used as a deployment model, and different authorizations might apply. That's why, if you're working with government data, it's essential to confirm that the specific AWS services you plan to use are on the list of FedRAMP-authorized offerings. You can do this through AWS Artifact or the official FedRAMP Marketplace (*https://oreil.ly/PfYTy*).

FINMA

FINMA, the Swiss Financial Market Supervisory Authority, governs financial institutions operating in Switzerland. AWS supports compliance with FINMA requirements through specific documentation, risk transparency, and audit support tailored to financial firms. If you're operating in Swiss finance, you'll need to map AWS services to FINMA's outsourcing and risk control guidelines to stay compliant.

HIPAA

The US's Health Insurance Portability and Accountability Act (HIPAA) mandates strict protections for handling protected health information (PHI). AWS enables HIPAA compliance through services covered under a Business Associate Addendum (BAA). Once you sign a BAA with AWS, you're cleared to build HIPAA-compliant applications using supported services. But it's still up to you to configure those services correctly and implement proper access controls and encryption.

GDPR

The EU's General Data Protection Regulation (GDPR) governs data protection and privacy for individuals in the European Union. It requires strict safeguards for how organizations collect, store, and process personal data. AWS supports GDPR compliance through its Data Processing Addendum (DPA), which is available via AWS Artifact, and provides a wide range of services with built-in privacy and security features such as encryption, access controls, and logging. Still, customers remain responsible for implementing appropriate safeguards in their own applications and ensuring that data subject rights—such as access and erasure—are upheld.

SOC 1 and SOC 2

SOC (System and Organization Controls) reports are designed to assess how well a service provider manages and protects data. These reports were developed by the American Institute of Certified Public Accountants (AICPA). They are intended to verify that an organization working with data has appropriate internal controls in place. The reports are categorized into types: SOC 1 focuses on financial reporting controls, while SOC 2 evaluates broader operational criteria like security, availability, and confidentiality. These reports are especially important for organizations that need to demonstrate trustworthiness to customers and partners. AWS provides SOC reports so that you can understand the security controls in place.

In Table 5-1, you'll see a comparison of these frameworks.

Table 5-1. Compliance frameworks

Framework	Primary focus
PCI DSS	Secure handling of credit card data (processing, storing, transmitting)
ISO	International security and risk management standards (e.g., ISO/IEC 27001, 27017, 27018)
NIST	US cybersecurity standards (e.g., NIST 800-53, CSF)
FedRAMP	US federal government security standards for cloud services
FINMA	Swiss financial regulatory compliance
HIPAA	Safeguards for protected health information
GDPR	Data protection and privacy for EU residents
SOC 1	Controls over financial reporting
SOC 2	Controls for security, availability, confidentiality

Note that not all AWS Regions support every compliance framework. Always check the AWS Services in Scope by Compliance Program before architecting a workload with regulatory requirements.

Working with Compliance Frameworks

When you're building in the cloud, it's easy to assume that meeting one compliance framework means you're covered across the board. Unfortunately, that's not the case. Being compliant with SOC 2 requirements, for example, doesn't mean you're automatically compliant with HIPAA, PCI DSS, or any other regulatory standard. Each framework has its own rules, requirements, and expectations.

Another common misconception: just because a service is available in an AWS Region doesn't mean it meets every compliance requirement there. AWS makes a wide range of services globally available, but it's up to you to verify which ones are approved for the specific frameworks your organization needs to follow.

Moreover, don't treat compliance like a checklist. Each framework demands its own set of controls, configurations, and documentation. AWS gives you a powerful toolkit and a foundation for compliance, but staying on top of it is an active, ongoing effort.

Compliance Tools

We'll shift our focus to the AWS-native tools that help you put compliance practices into action. They help you monitor, enforce, and report on how well your AWS environment is meeting the rules, whether they're driven by external regulations or your organization's internal policies.

Some of these tools help with risk detection and remediation (like Amazon Inspector), others assist with tracking configuration drift or enforcing organizational policies (like AWS Config or Control Tower), and some streamline audit preparation (like AWS Audit Manager).

In Chapter 2, tools like Amazon CloudWatch and AWS CloudTrail are covered. Now let's explore several additional services that are especially useful for managing compliance.

Amazon Inspector
> Amazon Inspector is a security scanner for your EC2 instances and workloads. It automatically checks for vulnerabilities, such as outdated software, open ports, or misconfigured networks. It flags issues that could create risk or break compliance rules so you can fix them fast.

AWS Config
> AWS Config keeps track of your cloud environment's configuration over time. It records changes, evaluates them against rules you set, and helps ensure that resources stay compliant. If something drifts out of line, you'll know right away and you can automate responses if needed.

AWS Trusted Advisor
> Trusted Advisor acts like a virtual consultant. It reviews your AWS environment and offers recommendations to improve security, reduce costs, and boost performance. While it doesn't enforce changes, it gives valuable insights you can use to stay on track with best practices, including compliance.

AWS Audit Manager
> AWS Audit Manager helps you simplify the process of preparing for audits by automating evidence collection. It maps AWS resource activity to control requirements from frameworks like PCI DSS, HIPAA, and SOC 2. Audit Manager also integrates with services like AWS Config and CloudTrail to collect evidence automatically, which shows how it streamlines compliance workflows.

AWS Organizations
> AWS Organizations helps you manage multiple AWS accounts from a central location. This makes it easier to organize your environment, apply governance policies, and streamline operations. You can group accounts into organizational units (OUs), set up new ones quickly, and use SCP to enforce permissions and

establish guardrails across accounts. This not only simplifies security and compliance but also consolidates billing. Plus, it integrates with other AWS services. This lets you manage configurations, share resources, and push security policies organization-wide without jumping through hoops.

For example, you can use SCPs to block developers in a sandbox account from accidentally spinning up expensive GPU instances. Similarly, tagging policies can enforce consistent cost allocation across departments—such as requiring a `Cost Center` or `Project` tag on every resource—so that finance teams can accurately track and charge back cloud spend.

AWS Control Tower

AWS Control Tower automates the setup of a secure, well-governed multiaccount AWS environment by creating a landing zone built on AWS best practices. It applies specific guardrails to enforce governance and compliance, including preventive guardrails (for example, restricting root user actions) and detective guardrails (such as monitoring for noncompliant resources). Control Tower integrates with tools like AWS Organizations, IAM Identity Center, and AWS Service Catalog to handle provisioning, access, and resource management at scale.

AWS License Manager

AWS License Manager helps you keep software licensing under control, whether you're running workloads in AWS, on-premises, or both. It supports major vendors like Microsoft, SAP, and Oracle, letting you define rules, track usage, and enforce policies to avoid overuse or violations. The service gives you visibility into license consumption across accounts, automates compliance checks, and reduces the chances of audit surprises or unplanned costs.

AWS Security Hub

AWS Security Hub provides a single dashboard that aggregates security findings from multiple AWS services like Inspector, GuardDuty, and Config, as well as supported third-party tools. It continuously checks your environment against compliance frameworks such as the Center for Internet Security (CIS) Benchmarks, PCI DSS, and NIST CSF. (AWS provides a set of security configuration practices to align with the CIS Benchmarks program, called the CIS AWS Foundations Benchmarks.) This helps you maintain a real-time compliance posture without having to manually stitch together data from different sources.

AWS Budgets

AWS Budgets lets you set custom cost and usage limits for your AWS environment and get alerts when you approach or exceed them. While it's primarily a financial governance tool, it also supports compliance objectives by enforcing accountability for spending policies, reducing the risk of "shadow IT" (IT systems deployed with the aim of bypassing limitations or restrictions) or uncontrolled resource growth. For example, you can tie budget alerts to automated actions—like restricting new resource launches in noncompliant accounts—helping ensure that financial policies and operational guardrails go hand in hand.

In Table 5-2, you'll find a comparison of the AWS tools for compliance.

Table 5-2. Compliance tools

Tool	Primary function
Amazon Inspector	Scans EC2 instances and workloads for vulnerabilities
AWS Config	Tracks and records configuration changes across AWS resources
AWS Trusted Advisor	Provides best practice recommendations for security, cost, and performance
AWS Audit Manager	Automates evidence collection for audits
AWS Organizations	Helps you manage multiple AWS accounts from a central location
AWS Control Tower	Automates the setup of a secure, well-governed multiaccount AWS environment
AWS License Manager	Helps manage software licenses
AWS Security Hub	Centralizes and aggregates security findings across AWS services and third-party tools; continuously checks compliance against standards like PCI DSS, and NIST CSF
AWS Budgets	Enables cost and usage monitoring with custom limits and alerts; supports financial governance and helps enforce spending compliance

Compliance Documentation

When audits or legal reviews roll around, you'll need documentation. AWS provides a set of tools and resources that make it easy to access the compliance materials you need without waiting on support tickets or chasing down PDFs.

AWS Artifact

AWS Artifact is a repository of compliance reports and agreements. It offers instant access to third-party audit reports—like SOC, PCI DSS, and ISO certifications—as well as legal documents like HIPAA Business Associate Agreements. Everything's organized in one place and tied to your AWS account, so you can pull what you need, when you need it.

Here's how to use AWS Artifact:

1. Log in to AWS.
2. Go to the search box on the top left and enter "ASW Artifact."
3. Select it.
4. You have two options: View reports and View agreements.
5. Select the second one.

6. Figure 5-1 shows a list of the agreements.

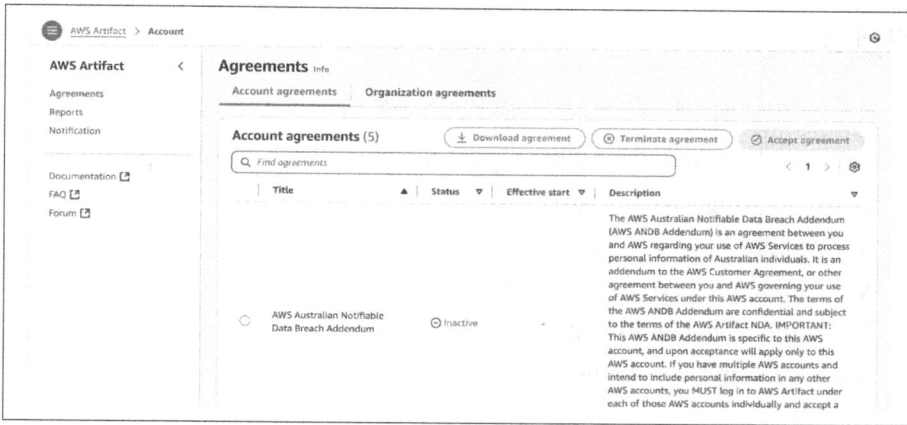

Figure 5-1. List of agreements in AWS Artifact

7. At the top of the screen, you can select the agreements for your AWS account or organization.

8. Select the first agreement.

9. You can then download it as well as accept the agreement. You will also likely need to agree to a nondisclosure agreement.

Once you accept an agreement, it's logged as part of your account's compliance records and stays available for reference whenever you need it. This comes in handy during audits or when working in regulated industries. Just note that some agreements are required based on the services you're using.

AWS Customer Compliance Center

If you're looking for guidance on navigating compliance in the cloud, the AWS Compliance Center is worth bookmarking. It includes whitepapers, FAQs, auditing checklists, and customer case studies from regulated industries. You'll also find resources tailored for legal teams, auditors, and compliance pros who need to understand how AWS fits into their regulatory picture.

Conclusion

Compliance keeps your workloads in line with regulatory and internal standards, while governance provides the structure—policies, roles, and oversight—that guides how cloud resources are used. We covered key frameworks like HIPAA, PCI DSS, and FedRAMP, and walked through AWS tools that support compliance, including Config, Audit Manager, License Manager, and Artifact.

Up next, we'll look at identity management in AWS.

Chapter Quiz

To check your answers, please refer to the "Chapter 5 Answer Key" on page 206.

1. What is the primary purpose of governance in AWS?

    A. Encrypting data in transit

    B. Monitoring security events

    C. Preventing distributed denial-of-service (DDoS) attacks

    D. Defining and enforcing policies to guide cloud operations

2. Which compliance framework is focused on the US federal government cloud service standards?

    A. Health Insurance Portability and Accountability Act (HIPAA)

    B. Federal Risk and Authorization Management Program (FedRAMP)

    C. Payment Card Industry Data Security Standard (PCI DSS)

    D. Swiss Financial Market Supervisory Authority (FINMA)

3. What tool continuously tracks and evaluates AWS resource configurations?

    A. AWS Artifact

    B. AWS Config

    C. Amazon GuardDuty

    D. AWS Shield

4. Which service helps scan Elastic Compute Cloud (EC2) instances for misconfigurations or vulnerabilities?

    A. AWS Shield

    B. AWS CloudTrail

    C. Amazon Inspector

    D. AWS Config

5. What is the purpose of service control policies (SCPs) in AWS Organizations?

    A. To restrict access to AWS services across accounts

    B. To scan for DDoS attacks

    C. To store audit logs

    D. To generate compliance documentation

CHAPTER 6

AWS Identity and Access Management (IAM)

When you're working in the cloud, one of the first things you need to figure out is who has access to what. Controlling that access—both who gets in and what they're allowed to do once they're there—is exactly what AWS Identity and Access Management is built for. IAM lets you define users, groups, roles, and policies to control access across your AWS environment. Whether you're setting up multifactor authentication, allowing users to log in, or following the principle of least privilege, IAM is a core part of keeping your cloud setup secure.

For the AWS Certified Cloud Practitioner exam, expect IAM to show up. The exam covers basic AWS security concepts, and IAM is a big part of that. You'll need to understand what IAM does, how policies work, and when to use roles or groups depending on the situation.

Identity

Identity plays a central role in how we keep things organized. Just like you need a driver's license or passport to prove who you are in the real world, systems need a way to recognize users, applications, and devices. And not just recognize them, but verify they're allowed to do what they're trying to do.

When we talk about identity in computing, we're casting a wide net. It's not just people logging into email or cloud dashboards. It includes applications talking to each other, devices joining networks, and services requesting access behind the scenes. In every case, identity forms the backbone of security. If you can't verify who or what is trying to access something, how can you trust them?

The most familiar form of identity management is the classic username and password combination. Usually, your username is your email address or some version of your name.

But the password is where it gets tricky. Most systems now demand a mix of uppercase and lowercase letters, numbers, and special characters. The goal is to make your password tough to guess, especially for attackers using automated tools.

Now, what about apps and devices? These don't log in with usernames and passwords like people do. Instead, they often use digital certificates, which rely on public key cryptography (a method that uses a pair of mathematically related keys) and digital signatures to prove identity. Applications might also include version numbers or serial numbers as identifiers, especially when connecting to networks or APIs.

Here's a quick breakdown of what happens during a typical login flow for an application:

User input
    The login form collects a username and password.

Client-side checks
    Before anything gets sent, the browser or application may check the input, like making sure the password is long enough or the phone number looks valid.

Secure transmission
    The credentials get sent to the server over HTTPS to keep them encrypted in transit.

Authentication
    The server looks up the username and compares the submitted password against a hashed version stored in the database. AWS IAM never stores passwords in plain text.

Session creation
    Once authenticated, the server creates a session token to track the user's activity while they're logged in.

None of this is simple. And building an identity system from scratch isn't something most organizations want to tackle. This is why many turn to identity providers (IdPs), which are specialized services like Okta, Microsoft Entra ID, or Google Workspace that handle tasks such as user registration, login, authentication, and session management. These platforms take the heavy lifting out of identity so that teams can focus on their core product.

While AWS IAM is central to identity and access management, it is not itself an identity provider. Instead, IAM controls who can access AWS resources and what actions they can perform. It often integrates with external IdPs, trusting their authentication.

An example is when users are allowed to sign in through an external IdP and then assume roles in AWS. For workforce users (those who use your AWS account), AWS also offers IAM Identity Center, which can act as AWS's native IdP. In practice, IAM and IdPs serve different purposes but are tightly connected when building secure, scalable systems.

Authentication Versus Authorization

Authentication and authorization often get lumped together, but they play very different roles. If you're working in AWS—or any cloud platform—knowing the difference is essential for keeping your environment locked down.

Let's start with authentication. This is how AWS verifies who you are. Typically, that means logging in with a username and password. But if that's all you're using, you're not going far enough, because passwords can be guessed or leaked. Adding MFA, which is covered in the section "Multifactor Authentication (MFA)" on page 64, significantly raises the bar for security. You can also connect AWS to external IdPs using the AWS IAM Identity Center. This is especially useful in larger organizations where central identity management is already in place.

But knowing who someone is doesn't mean you should trust them with everything. That's where authorization comes in.

Once AWS knows who's trying to do something, it needs a determination of what they're allowed to do, which is something the account holder decides. AWS handles this through IAM, using policies, roles, and permission boundaries to draw the lines. Think of it as the difference between unlocking the front door (authentication) and deciding which rooms someone can enter once they're inside (authorization).

The golden rule here is the principle of *least privilege*: only grant the permissions someone needs to do their job—nothing more. It's tempting to give broad access "just in case," especially when you're in a rush, but that habit leads to trouble fast. If an account with excessive permissions gets compromised, the attacker has the keys to your kingdom.

When you put all of this together—strong authentication, tight authorization, and layered controls—you build a secure access model that can scale with your AWS usage. And in the world of cloud security, that's half the battle.

Basics of IAM

As your AWS setup grows, managing permissions for each user one at a time turns into a logistical mess. This is where IAM proves its worth. It lets you define who can access what—centrally—using a combination of users, groups, and policies.

Consider an IAM user as a single person or application that needs to work with your AWS resources. Instead of assigning permissions to every user individually, you can create groups based on job roles or responsibilities, and then attach permissions to those groups. However, it's important to note that IAM user groups cannot be nested. This is a common point of confusion.

Another critical concept is the AWS root user. This account has full access to all AWS services and billing. It should only be used for tasks requiring elevated privileges, such as enabling MFA or changing account settings, and it must always be protected with MFA.

By combining IAM users, groups, and policies—while keeping the root user tightly controlled—you can build a permission model that's both secure and scalable.

Take a look at the example in Figure 6-1.

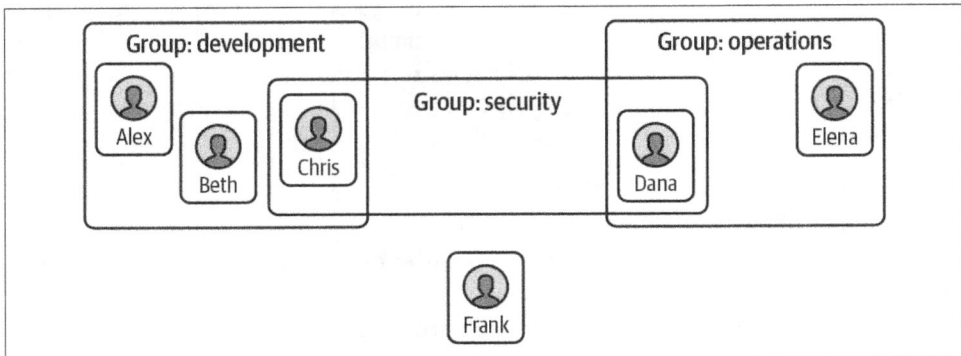

Figure 6-1. IAM groups

Here, Alex and Beth are part of the Development group, while Elena belongs to Operations. Chris and Dana also have roles in the Security group because they need to access resources across both development and operations systems for security oversight and compliance checks. IAM doesn't mind overlapping memberships. Users can belong to multiple groups without any issues.

Chris bridges Development and Security, giving him access to both code repositories and security monitoring tools. Dana spans Security and Operations, allowing her to audit operational systems while maintaining security protocols across infrastructure.

Technically, you can have someone like Frank floating around without a group, and you could assign him permissions as an individual, but that's asking for trouble. It's safer and much easier to keep things tidy by managing permissions through groups instead of one-off user settings.

It's also important to remember the AWS Shared Responsibility Model. AWS secures the infrastructure that runs its services (security of the cloud), while customers are responsible for managing access to their resources using IAM (security in the cloud). Group management, role assignments, and least-privilege policies fall squarely on the customer's side of that responsibility.

Creating an IAM User

In this section, we'll go over how to create a new user in IAM.

1. Log in to AWS.
2. At the top right, enter this in the search box: "IAM."
3. Select IAM. Figure 6-2 shows the dashboard.

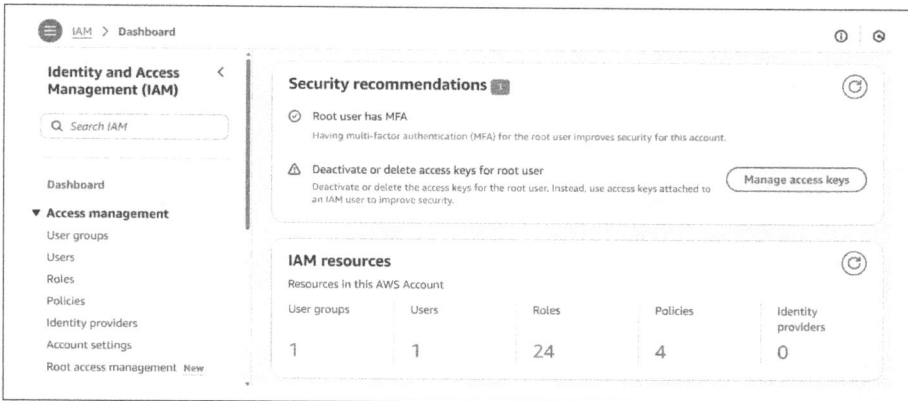

Figure 6-2. The IAM dashboard

4. At the top, you will see security recommendations. And below, there is a tally of the number of user groups, users, roles, policies, and identity providers. On the sidebar, you can drill down into these categories.
5. On the left sidebar, select Users. Here, you will see a list of your IAM users.
6. On the top right, select "Create user."
7. Enter a username, which can be up to 64 characters and have letters and numbers and some special characters like # and -.
8. Select "Provide user access to the AWS Management Console" for human users needing console access, or choose programmatic access (via access keys) for applications or scripts, following the principle of least privilege.
9. Select "I want to create an IAM user." You can then use either a custom or auto-generated password.
10. Choose Next.

11. This is where you create the permissions. But, as discussed in the section "Basics of IAM" on page 57, you should do this for a group. So select Create group.

12. You will create a name for the group.

13. There are over 1,000 prebuilt policies you can select, some of which you can see in Figure 6-3.

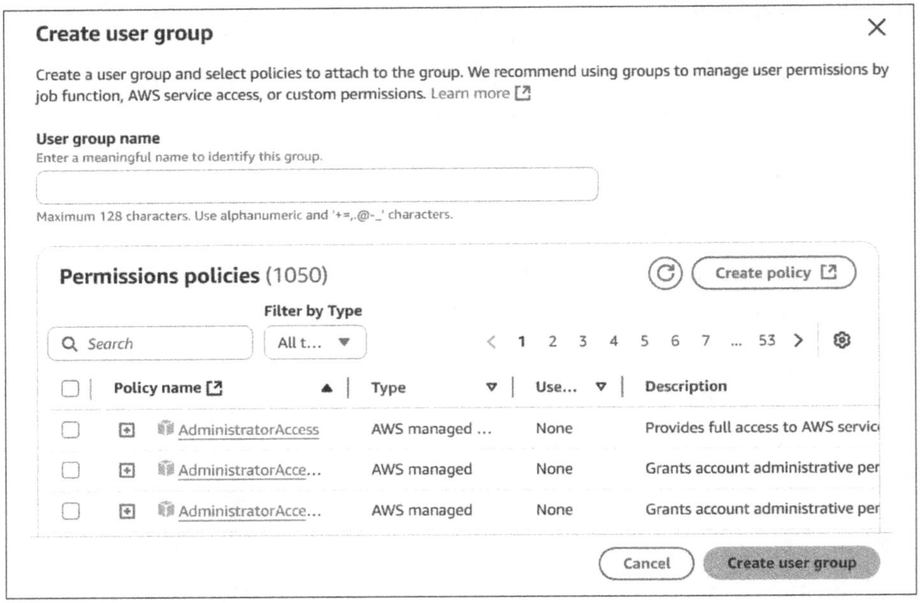

Figure 6-3. The form to create a user group

14. The policies specify what actions are allowed or denied, on which resources, and under what conditions—such as based on IP address, time of day, or whether the request is made using Secure Sockets Layer (SSL). This allows for fine-grained access control across AWS services. You can also create your own policy.

15. You add the user to the group.

16. Select Next.

17. You will see a review of the details for the user.

18. Select "Create user."

Keep in mind that IAM is a global service. This means you will not select a region for it, since it is available across all of the AWS platform.

Policies

Policies are JavaScript Object Notation (JSON) documents that define permissions—what actions are allowed or denied, on which AWS resources, and under what conditions.

Policies can be attached to any of the following:

- Users directly
- Groups (collections of users)
- Roles (temporary identities used by AWS services or for cross-account access)

Each IAM policy generally follows the structure in Table 6-1.

Table 6-1. Policy structure

Key field	Description
Versions	Specifies the policy language version. "2012-10-17" is most commonly used.
Statement	One or more rules that define permissions.
Effect	"Allow" or "Deny"—controls whether the action is permitted.
Action	The specific API operations permitted (e.g., ec2:RunInstances).
Resource	The AWS resource(s) the actions apply to—can be * or specific Amazon Resource Names (ARNs).
Condition (optional)	Additional constraints (e.g., IP address, time).

Suppose you have a group called "Developer". You attach the following policy to this group:

```
{
  "Version": "2012-10-17",
  "Statement": [
    {
      "Effect": "Allow",
      "Action": [
        "ec2:RunInstances",
        "ec2:StopInstances",
        "ec2:TerminateInstances",
        "ec2:DescribeInstances"
      ],
      "Resource": "*"
    },
    {
      "Effect": "Allow",
      "Action": [
        "s3:PutObject",
        "s3:GetObject",
        "s3:ListBucket"
      ],
```

```
      "Resource": "*"
    },
    {
      "Effect": "Allow",
      "Action": [
        "cloudwatch:GetMetricData",
        "logs:DescribeLogGroups",
        "logs:GetLogEvents"
      ],
      "Resource": "*"
    }
  ]
}
```

Here's what is happening:

- EC2 permissions allow users to launch, stop, terminate, and describe instances.

- S3 permissions grant the ability to upload, download, and list objects.

- CloudWatch Logs lets users view metrics and logs for performance monitoring.

This is a balanced policy. Developers get the tools they need to do their jobs—such as to build, test, or debug—without compromising security. They cannot change IAM configurations or network security settings.

When you attach a policy to a group, all users within that group automatically inherit those permissions. If a user is a member of multiple groups, their total permissions combine all group policies plus any directly assigned individual policies.

Let's use an example where an IAM policy is applied to two different groups, as seen in Figure 6-4.

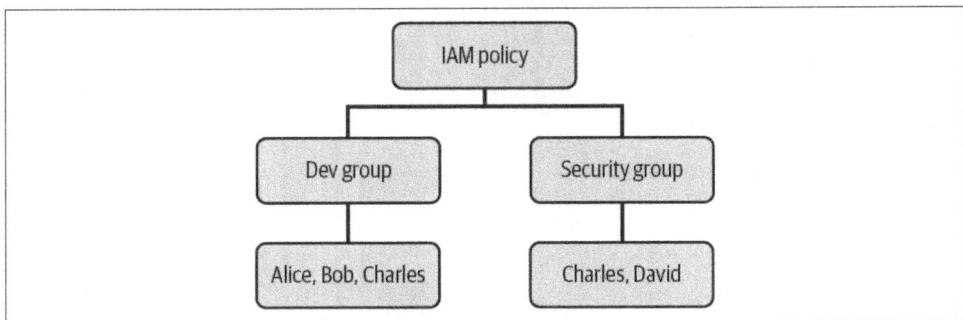

Figure 6-4. Inheritance of an IAM policy

Users inherit permissions based on their group memberships, with overlapping users receiving combined permissions from all their groups.

This is the breakdown:

- Alice and Bob receive permissions exclusively from the Developer group.
- Charles belongs to both the Developer and Security groups, so he receives the combined permissions from both groups.
- David receives permissions from the Security group and may additionally have individual policies applied directly to his account.

When you delete a user from a group, they immediately lose all permissions that were inherited from that group. This happens instantly with no delay or grace period. However, the user retains any permissions from other groups they still belong to, individual policies directly attached to their account, and any roles they can assume.

This immediate permission revocation is actually a security feature designed to ensure that access control changes take effect without leaving security gaps.

Most IAM systems don't automatically notify the user that their permissions have changed, so they'll discover it when they try to access something and get denied. When removing users from groups, especially in production environments, it's good practice to communicate the change beforehand and verify they have alternative access paths if needed for their work.

In addition to identity- and group-based policies, IAM also supports permission boundaries. A permission boundary sets the maximum permissions an IAM user or role can have. Even if a policy grants broader access, the permission boundary acts as a ceiling. This helps to ensure the principle of least privilege is enforced.

This is especially useful in delegated administration scenarios. For example, if you allow a team lead to create IAM users for their project, you can apply a permission boundary so that any new users they create cannot exceed the defined limits.

Setting a Password Policy

When you're managing access to IAM, you can create a password policy. It's a basic step, but it goes a long way in protecting your account. By creating clear, consistent rules around passwords, you make it harder for bad actors to slip in through weak or reused credentials.

AWS lets you customize this policy with a few key settings:

Minimum password length
> You decide how long passwords need to be. Having 8 or 12 characters is common.

Character requirements
> You can require a mix of uppercase and lowercase letters, numbers, and special characters.

Expiration rules
> Want users to reset passwords every 90 days? You can set that up easily. It helps reduce the chance of long-term exposure if a password gets compromised.

Password reuse prevention
> AWS can remember up to 24 past passwords and block users from recycling them.

User control
> You can choose whether users are allowed to change their own passwords. In most cases, especially with expiration policies in place, you'll probably want to let them.

This policy applies across the entire AWS account. So every IAM user is subject to it unless you explicitly say otherwise. However, the password policies do not apply to the root user. For this, you will need to secure the account with MFA.

On its own, a good password policy makesbrute force attacks and basic credential stuffing much harder. (Brute force attacks involve guessing a huge number of possible passwords, andcredential stuffing uses known usernames or email addresses and their corresponding passwords to gain further access.) But if you're dealing with sensitive accounts—like admin roles or the root user—adding MFA is important. It adds another layer of defense that passwords alone just can't match.

This is how you can create a password policy:

1. Go back to the IAM dashboard.
2. On the left sidebar, select "Account settings."
3. Click Edit. Here, you can select either the IAM default or custom.

Multifactor Authentication (MFA)

Using MFA is critical with IAM. It's one of the simplest, most effective ways to stop unauthorized access—especially if a password ever gets exposed. This is why AWS treats MFA as a best practice, and in many cases, it's mandatory for high-risk actions like changing IAM policies or managing billing.

MFA adds an extra layer of security by requiring users to prove their identity with two or more different types of authentication factors. But a username doesn't count. It's considered public and often easy to guess.

Real factors fall into three categories:

Something you know
> Usually a password or passphrase. Sometimes it's an answer to a security question.

Something you have

A device you physically possess, like a phone that receives a one-time password or passcode (OTP) via an authenticator app (Google Authenticator, Authy, and so on). AWS also supports hardware tokens that generate time-based codes.

Something you are

Biometrics like fingerprints or facial recognition. AWS doesn't directly collect biometric data, but it can work with identity providers (like AWS IAM Identity Center or other IdPs) that support biometric logins.

By requiring at least two of these factors, AWS dramatically increases account security. MFA makes life harder for attackers using tactics like phishing (when an attacker tries to trick a user into revealing sensitive information), brute-force guessing, or hijacking sessions. One Microsoft study (*https://oreil.ly/T493f*) reported that MFA blocks over 99% of account takeover attempts. And a separate study (*https://oreil.ly/zi81c*) from Google, NYU, and UC San Diego found that MFA stopped every automated bot attack and thwarted 96% of phishing efforts.

Setting up MFA in AWS is straightforward. You've got a few options, depending on your needs:

- Attach IAM policies that enforce MFA for sensitive operations.
- Use virtual MFA apps on smartphones or go with hardware MFA devices.
- If you're using the AWS IAM Identity Center, you can also plug in Universal 2nd Factor (U2F) security keys (like YubiKeys) that follow the FIDO (Fast Identity Online Alliance) standard.

Passwordless

Using MFA can certainly be a hassle, as it means going through several steps. Then again, the added complexity plays a big role in making MFA more secure. Still, strong security doesn't have to come at the cost of user convenience. This is where passwordless authentication makes a difference. Instead of relying on passwords or one-time codes, it uses biometrics like facial recognition or fingerprint scans to verify identity.

One of the key advantages of passwordless authentication is how it handles sensitive data. Biometric information never leaves the user's device. It stays local, which protects privacy and limits the damage in the event of a server breach. Behind the scenes, this process uses public-key cryptography. When you first set it up, your device generates two keys: the public key, which is sent to the authentication service, and the private key, which stays safely stored on your device. That way, even if someone breaks into the system, they can't do anything without the private key you control.

AWS has leaned into passwordless authentication. Amazon Cognito, for example, now supports modern, password-free sign-in methods. Users can authenticate using passkeys based on WebAuthn (Web Authentication, a standard published by the World Wide Web Consortium) and FIDO2 standards (jointly established by FIDO and the World Wide Web Consortium), which let them log in using built-in tools like Apple's Face ID, Apple's Touch ID, or Windows Hello. There's also support for OTPs sent by email or Short Message Service (SMS). These features are part of the Cognito Essentials tier and are available in all standard AWS Regions, except for the Gov-Cloud regions in the US.

IAM also supports passkeys as a method for MFA. Both root and IAM users can register passkeys based on FIDO standards, whether through built-in biometrics or physical security keys.

Finally, AWS Amplify makes it easy to bring passwordless authentication into your web or mobile apps. By integrating directly with Cognito, Amplify lets developers implement options like email or SMS OTPs, as well as WebAuthn passkeys. This means you can offer a secure, password-free login experience without adding a lot of complexity to your codebase.

Accessing AWS

So far in this book, we've looked at how to access AWS using the Management Console. But there are two other approaches, which include the AWS Command Line Interface (CLI) and the AWS software development kits (SDKs).

AWS Command Line Interface (CLI)

The AWS CLI allows you to run commands in your terminal. It's fast and allows for scripts and automation.

The CLI is available for the following:

Windows
    Runs on a 64-bit version of Windows 10 or newer

macOS
    Supported from macOS 10.14 (Mojave) onward

Linux
    Operates on many distros like Amazon Linux, Ubuntu, CentOS, Fedora, RHEL (Red Hat Enterprise Linux), and Debian

Arm-based systems
    Runs on 64-bit Arm machines like Raspberry Pi

Once you've installed the CLI, you'll need to configure it with your AWS credentials. This can be done using the `aws configure` command, which prompts you to enter your access key ID, secret access key, default region, and output format. In the section "Credentials," I'll show how to create these keys.

When you use the CLI, you will always start with the `aws` command. Here's an example:

```
aws s3 cp file.txt s3://my-bucket/
```

This command takes a plain-text file and copies it into your specified S3 bucket.

Besides the CLI, there is also AWS CloudShell. It's a browser-based terminal built into the AWS Management Console. To access it, you'll click the shell icon in the top-right corner of the screen.

These are some of the features:

Multiple shells
You can choose from Bash, PowerShell, or Z shell.

Persistent storage
Each AWS Region gives you 1 GB of persistent storage, so you can save scripts, config files, and anything else you want to keep between sessions.

Built-in credentials
CloudShell automatically uses the permissions of the user signed in to the console.

Customizable interface
You can tweak the font size and choose between light and dark themes.

Multiple tabs
Open several terminal tabs and switch between them easily.

Session resilience
If your browser crashes or your connection drops, CloudShell uses `tmux` to restore your session.

AWS Software Development Kits (SDKs)

If you're building an application and want it to integrate to AWS directly, you can use the AWS SDKs. These are language-specific libraries. Here are just a few that are available:

- JavaScript
- Python
- Java

- .NET
- Go
- C++
- Swift

The SDKs take care of tasks like signing requests, handling retries, and catching errors. Moreover, they give you a consistent experience no matter what language you're using. This means if you switch from, say, Python to Go, you won't have to relearn everything from scratch.

Credentials

To use the CLI or SDKs, you need credentials. These prove that you're allowed to do what you're trying to do. AWS supports two main types. First, there are long-term credentials, which are access keys tied to a specific IAM user. Each one includes the following:

- An access key ID that functions like a username and is publicly identifiable.
- A secret access key that acts like a password.

They're persistent, meaning they last until you rotate or delete them.

You can generate long-term access keys through the AWS Management Console:

1. Go to the IAM dashboard.
2. Select Users on the left sidebar menu.
3. Select a user.
4. Click "Create access key."
5. Select the CLI use case option. Then you will confirm this.
6. Choose Next.
7. Select "Create access key."

For both your access key ID and secret access key, you should not share them and make sure they are stored securely.

Next, there are temporary security credentials. These are short-lived keys issued by the AWS Security Token Service (STS). They're usually linked to IAM roles and expire automatically after a set time. They're safer for day-to-day use, especially in production environments.

A best practice is to use temporary credentials whenever possible. They reduce the risk of leaks, which means less manual overhead and better security.

IAM Roles

A role in IAM is an identity with specific permissions that can be assumed by trusted entities, such as AWS services, users, or applications. Unlike IAM users, IAM roles do not have long-term credentials. Instead, they provide temporary security credentials for the duration of the role session.

Here are reasons to use IAM roles:

Delegating access
> Roles let you safely hand out permissions to applications or users that wouldn't normally have access to your AWS resources.

Cross-account access
> You can grant access to people or services in another AWS account without sharing permanent secrets.

Federated access
> If your users log in through a company directory or an external identity provider, roles can give them access without the need to create separate IAM users for each one.

You'll find IAM roles are especially useful in a few key scenarios:

AWS services acting on your behalf
> Suppose you've got an EC2 instance that needs to pull files from an S3 bucket. Instead of hardcoding credentials (which you should never do), you assign a role to the instance.

Cross-account collaboration
> Roles make it easy to share resources between multiple accounts without having to manage static keys.

External user access
> Whether someone logs in through Okta, Google, or your corporate single sign-on (SSO), you can use a role to give them temporary access. There is no IAM user required.

Let's now look at how to create a role in IAM:

1. Go to the IAM dashboard.
2. In the left sidebar menu, select Roles and then click "Create role."
3. Use the default selection for AWS.
4. For the use case, select EC2.
5. You can select one or more existing policies or a custom one.

6. Choose Next.

7. Enter the name for your role and write a description for it.

8. Select "Create role."

Security for IAM

AWS provides some tools to help secure IAM. We'll look at two of them, IAM credential reports and the IAM Access Advisor.

IAM Credential Reports

An IAM credential report gives you a snapshot of every IAM user in your AWS account. It shows whether each user has a password, active access keys, MFA enabled, or any old signing certificates enabled.

This report is especially helpful for identifying potential security issues. For example, you might find access keys that haven't been used in months or users without MFA enabled. Once you know about the situation, it's easy to clean things up—deactivate unused credentials, rotate keys, or enforce stronger authentication policies.

To generate the report, you will go to the IAM dashboard and select "Credential Report." You will then click "Download Credential Report." The file will be in a comma-delimited format (comma-separated values, or CSV), which you can use in tools like spreadsheets or databases.

IAM Access Advisor

The IAM Access Advisor provides insights into the permissions granted to IAM users and roles. This highlights the AWS services they can access and the last time those services were used. This tool is helpful for identifying unused permissions.

This capability is effective when following the principle of least privilege. For example, if someone has permissions to thirty services but has only used five in the last six months, that's a clear sign it's time to be more restrictive.

To use the IAM Access Advisor, you will go to the IAM dashboard and select either Users or Roles. Then you will choose a specific user or role, and click on the Last Access tab to view service access details.

Conclusion

To wrap things up, AWS IAM plays a central role in keeping your cloud environment secure. It lets you control who can access specific resources and what they're allowed to do—whether that's reading from an S3 bucket, launching EC2 instances, or accessing sensitive data. With the right mix of users, groups, roles, and policies, IAM gives you the tools to enforce clear, consistent access rules across your environment.

In the next chapter, we'll look at the various security tools in AWS.

Chapter Quiz

To check your answers, please refer to the "Chapter 6 Answer Key" on page 206.

1. What is the purpose of Identity and Access Management (IAM) in AWS?

   A. To control who can access AWS resources and what actions they can perform

   B. To monitor billing usage across accounts

   C. To automate infrastructure deployment

   D. To analyze logs for unusual behavior

2. Which IAM feature allows permission control based on job functions?

   A. Tags

   B. Password policies

   C. Groups

   D. Regions

3. Which type of credential is recommended for short-term programmatic access?

   A. IAM user access keys

   B. Console passwords

   C. Session tokens stored in Simple Storage Service (S3)

   D. Temporary credentials via IAM roles

4. What does the IAM Access Advisor help you do?

   A. View root user actions

   B. Identify unused permissions

   C. Change passwords

   D. Enable multifactor authentication (MFA)

5. Which field in an IAM policy allows you to restrict access by IP address?

   A. Resource

   B. Action

   C. Condition

   D. Statement

CHAPTER 7

Security

Security in the cloud isn't a nice-to-have anymore. It's the bedrock everything else rests on. As cyber threats keep evolving, both in number and complexity, staying safe requires more than just hoping your provider has things covered. Cloud providers and customers each play a part in keeping systems and data secure.

Threats come in all shapes and sizes: phishing attempts, ransomware, denial-of-service attacks, zero-day vulnerabilities you won't see coming. Knowing what's out there is important, but awareness alone won't be enough. Strong security relies on multiple layers—encryption, access controls, constant monitoring—all working together to create a solid defense.

In this chapter, we'll focus on what you need to know for the AWS Certified Cloud Practitioner exam when it comes to security. We'll cover the AWS shared responsibility model and walk through the core principles of defense-in-depth. You'll get a clear look at best practices for managing access and protecting data, and we'll look at key AWS tools like GuardDuty, CloudTrail, and the KMS—the ones that tend to pop up on the exam.

Why Security Matters

Cybersecurity didn't start as a formal discipline. It grew out of necessity—a need that emerged the moment computers became networked in the 1960s. Once systems could communicate, the idea of sending software from one machine to another became possible. This is when a door that attackers could use was created.

Since those early days, the cybersecurity world has grown—massively. By 2024, Grand View Research valued the global cybersecurity market at over $245 billion (*https://oreil.ly/JgXfZt*). This number is expected to more than double to $500 billion by 2030.

Why such explosive growth? The threat landscape keeps expanding. According to Microsoft, its customers face more than 600 million cyberattacks every single day. In the words (*https://oreil.ly/HlcXD*) of Corporate Vice President, Customer Security and Trust Tom Burt: "These cyberattacks are continuing at a breathtaking scale, and as they increasingly put human health at risk, the stakes for stopping them couldn't be higher."

Common Security Threats

Most attacks involve malware, a catch-all term for "malicious software." These programs infiltrate systems to steal, destroy, or lock away valuable data—or sometimes just to cause chaos.

Here are the big categories of threats that you should know for the exam:

Ransomware
> This kind of malware locks up your files or systems. You'll get a message: pay the ransom, or lose access. In 2024, the average ransom demand hit $5.2 million (*https://oreil.ly/4YPiO*), according to the US Treasury's Office of Foreign Assets Control (OFAC). Ransomware often sneaks in through other malware like worms or Trojan horses. Worms are programs that replicate themselves to spread to other computers; the latter masquerades as legitimate software to trick users into installing it.

Phishing
> You've probably seen this in your inbox—that is, an email urging you to "verify your account" or "click here for urgent action." Phishing uses fake messages to trick people into revealing sensitive information, like credit card numbers or passwords. A variation, called Domain Name System (DNS) spoofing, directs users to fake websites that look legitimate—like a login form for a bank or shopping site—but are controlled by attackers.

Distributed denial-of-service (DDoS) attacks
> These flood a website or application with traffic, overwhelming the system so that real users can't get through. It's like a digital traffic jam.

Man-in-the-middle (MitM) attacks
> Here, the attacker secretly intercepts communication between two systems. On unsecured WiFi networks, this can be surprisingly easy, especially if no encryption is in place.

Zero-day exploits
> These take advantage of software vulnerabilities that haven't been patched yet. The term "zero-day" refers to the fact that developers have zero days to respond before attackers can exploit the flaw. One notorious example is Log4Shell, which

surfaced in 2021 and affected roughly 10% of the world's digital infrastructure (*https://oreil.ly/L5xqm*).

Brute force attacks

These rely on automated tools to guess login credentials or on social engineering, where an attacker tricks someone into handing over their password. It's surprisingly effective.

Injection attacks

This technique involves inserting malicious code into web forms or apps to gain control over backend systems. It's a favorite for attackers targeting databases.

Some cyberattacks aren't just criminal—they're geopolitical. Nation-state actors have the resources and technical firepower to carry out highly advanced operations, sometimes over months or years.

AWS Shared Responsibility Model

The AWS Shared Responsibility Model defines how compliance, governance, and security duties are divided between AWS and the customer—with the primary focus on security. At a high level, AWS secures the cloud itself: the physical infrastructure, networking, and foundational services. Customers are responsible for securing what they put into the cloud: their applications, configurations, and data.

However, the balance of responsibilities depends on the type of AWS service being used. With IaaS offerings like Amazon EC2, customers manage more, including the operating system, network controls, and applications. With PaaS models, such as Amazon RDS, AWS takes on more of the heavy lifting, handling the OS and underlying platform, while customers focus mainly on data and access. With software as a service or fully managed services like AWS Lambda, AWS covers nearly everything below the application code itself, leaving customers primarily responsible for their code, business logic, and data governance.

Why is this model necessary? In a traditional on-premises setup, your team owns the entire stack—from physical access controls to firewall rules and everything in between. But in the cloud, you're renting part of a much larger system. Without clearly defined lines of responsibility, it's easy to assume AWS is handling something when it's actually in your hands. The Shared Responsibility Model helps eliminate this confusion, ensuring both AWS and customers know exactly where their security and compliance duties begin and end.

Figure 7-1 shows an illustration of the AWS Shared Responsibility Model. It highlights the main distinctions between AWS's responsibilities and those of the customer.

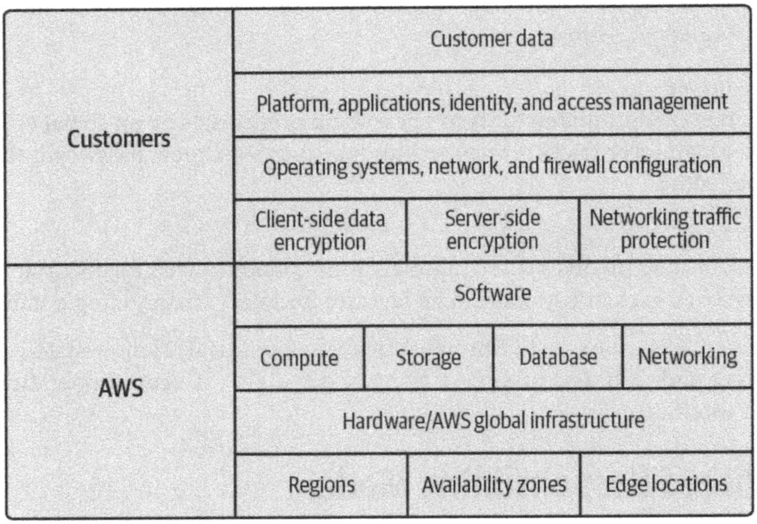
Customers
Customer data
Platform, applications, identity, and access management
Operating systems, network, and firewall configuration
Client-side data encryption
Server-side encryption
Networking traffic protection
AWS
Software
Compute
Storage
Database
Networking
Hardware/AWS global infrastructure
Regions
Availability zones
Edge locations

Figure 7-1. AWS Shared Responsibility Model

Let's look at the different levels of responsibility.

What AWS Secures: Security of the Cloud

AWS handles the heavy lifting at the infrastructure level. This includes the following:

- Locking down physical data centers (access control, power, and climate)
- Maintaining the global backbone, such as regions, availability zones, and edge locations
- Managing hardware and virtualization layers like servers and hypervisors
- Taking care of the core managed services stack like Amazon S3, RDS, and DynamoDB

Basically, AWS attempts to make sure the physical platform is secure so that you can build with confidence.

What You Secure: Security in the Cloud

Once AWS delivers a service, securing it becomes your job. How much you need to manage depends on the service, but here's what typically falls on your plate:

- Data management, which is about encryption, classification, and making sure you're following the right regulations.

- Application security, such as for writing secure code, patching your applications, and managing permissions.

- Access control, where you set up IAM roles and policies and enforce MFA.

- OS-level maintenance for EC2 and similar services. You're patching and hardening the OS.

- Network configuration, which is about the designing of virtual private clouds (VPCs), routing tables, and handling firewall rules.

The general rule: the more control AWS gives you, the more responsibility you take on.

However, there are scenarios where responsibilities are not solely with either AWS or the customer:

Patching
AWS patches managed services like RDS, but you handle patching for EC2 or your container images.

Configuration
AWS gives you secure defaults, but you still need to configure them for your use cases.

Training
AWS trains its staff. But you need to train yours to use the platform securely.

These shared areas are where misunderstandings often creep in, so pay close attention to them.

Shared Responsibility Example: Amazon RDS

Let's take an example of the shared responsibility model using Amazon RDS. This will give you a practical sense of what AWS handles and what you're still responsible for.

When you use RDS, AWS manages a lot of the heavy lifting behind the scenes. It takes care of the EC2 instances that run your databases, including patching the operating system and database engine. AWS also disables direct Secure Shell (SSH) access to the underlying machines, which means you don't have to worry about managing these servers directly. There is also automation of backups, failovers, and storage, so as to ensure the database is durable and highly available.

But once the RDS instance is up and running, it's your job to configure it properly. This starts with network security: setting up the correct inbound rules in your security groups and locking down access with IP whitelisting or VPC settings. You also need to decide whether your database should be publicly accessible.

User management inside the database is on you too. You're responsible for creating and assigning permissions to database users, making sure they have only enough access to do their jobs. If you want to enforce encryption in transit, you'll need to configure this through parameter groups. And if you want the data at rest to be encrypted, you have to enable it when you create the database.

Here's the key idea: AWS secures the infrastructure and handles the managed service layer, but you're still on the hook for how that service is used. If you misconfigure your RDS instance and someone gains access they shouldn't have, that's your responsibility—not AWS's.

The Model Keeps Evolving

As AWS rolls out new services, the shared responsibility model keeps expanding. And with artificial intelligence (AI) and machine learning (ML) workloads, there's a whole new category of responsibility—that is, securing training data, preventing model abuse, and ensuring ethical use of ML systems.

Defense-in-Depth

Defense-in-depth is a security philosophy and best practice that applies broadly to an IT environment, not just to AWS. It means building multiple layers of protection rather than relying on a single security control to keep your systems safe. In AWS, you build defense-in-depth by combining measures such as IAM, network segmentation, encryption, and monitoring. While AWS provides the tools and services to implement these layers, it's ultimately up to you to design and configure them to create a comprehensive security posture that protects your most critical assets from different angles of attack.

The idea comes from military strategy, and it makes a simple but important point: no single control is bulletproof. Firewalls can fail. Software can be misconfigured. People make mistakes. Defense-in-depth accepts that reality and plans for it by surrounding systems and data with a series of safeguards—technical, administrative, and physical. If one layer gets breached, others are still standing.

You're building a security posture that can take a hit and keep going. Even if a vulnerability slips through one layer, it shouldn't result in a full-blown breach. It's like the "Swiss cheese model" used in safety engineering. Each slice has holes, but stack enough of them together and those gaps rarely line up. That's the essence of this approach.

These are the layers of a defense-in-depth system. Each layer tackles a specific slice of the threat landscape:

Layer 1—Edge protection
> This is your first line of defense—the front door, so to speak. It deals with anything coming in from the outside world. The focus is to screen and absorb threats before they ever reach your core systems.

Layer 2—Inbound traffic filtering
> Once traffic clears the edge, this layer allows for a closer look. The goal is to enforce more detailed rules—checking protocols, ports, traffic patterns—and either block, reroute, or throttle anything suspicious.

Layer 3—Compute protection
> This layer involves hardening systems like servers, VMs, containers, and functions.

Layer 4—Data and identity safeguards
> Here, you focus on the sensitive data and the identities that access it.

Layer 5—Monitoring and detection
> This layer cuts across all the others. It's your visibility layer, allowing things like collecting logs, spotting anomalies, generating alerts, and triggering incident response workflows. Without it, you're flying blind. With it, you can catch breaches early, trace their origins, and act fast to contain them.

In the next section, we'll walk through each of these five layers by looking at the tools, services, and configurations available in AWS' ecosystem.

Layer 1: Edge Protection

The edge is where your infrastructure first meets the outside world. It's your perimeter—the digital frontier where you filter incoming traffic, block bad actors, and improve performance along the way. This is where you want threats handled early, far from your core systems.

Next, I'll cover how AWS helps you fortify that perimeter.

Amazon Route 53 and DNS Firewall

At first glance, Route 53 looks like just a DNS service. But under the hood, it's doing a lot more than name resolution. It acts as a global traffic director, routing users to the most responsive backend using latency-based routing, health checks, and automatic failover. When a system goes down, Route 53 reroutes traffic elsewhere. Users don't notice a thing, and neither do attackers trying to exploit a temporary gap.

Next, DNS Firewall adds a layer of threat defense by blocking DNS lookups for known malicious domains. This means attackers relying on malware callbacks or phishing domains get stopped at the lookup stage.

Amazon CloudFront

CloudFront is AWS's content delivery network (CDN), and it does more than just speed up your site. It takes pressure off your servers by caching static and dynamic content closer to users across a massive network of edge locations worldwide. When traffic surges—whether from a sudden wave of users or an attempted attack—Cloud-Front absorbs the load and keeps your origin servers steady.

CloudFront also layers in security: Transport Layer Security (TLS) encryption for safe delivery, signed URLs and cookies to lock down access, and geographic filtering to block regions you don't serve. You can even deploy custom logic at the edge using CloudFront Functions or Lambda@Edge, allowing lightweight filtering or header inspection before traffic goes any further.

AWS Shield

AWS Shield is the cloud provider's built-in DDoS protection service. It runs continuously in the background and deals with high-volume attacks that aim to overwhelm your applications or network.

Shield Standard is automatically included at no cost for every AWS customer. It provides baseline protection against common, most frequently observed network and transport layer attacks. This does not require any setup.

For organizations that need deeper safeguards, Shield Advanced builds on that foundation. It offers enhanced detection and mitigation capabilities, detailed attack diagnostics, and near-real-time visibility into events. Customers also gain access to AWS's 24/7 DDoS Response Team (DRT) and benefit from financial protections, such as coverage for unexpected scaling costs caused by attacks.

By operating at the infrastructure level, Shield uses anomaly detection and layered mitigation strategies that engage before most customers are even aware of a threat. This helps to keep applications resilient and available.

AWS WAF (Web Application Firewall)

AWS WAF (Web Application Firewall) focuses on application-layer traffic. Specifically, this is for HTTP and HTTPS requests. Think of it as a bouncer at the door that inspects every request before it reaches your app. You can define custom rules to fit your environment, such as blocking based on IP address, request size, headers, patterns like SQL injection, or geographic origin.

It's flexible. That is, you can set rules that are broad or highly specific. Features like rate limiting, bot control, geo-restrictions, and size constraints work together to protect against automated attacks, common exploits, and targeted threats.

WAF also integrates natively with AWS services such as CloudFront, API Gateway, and Application Load Balancers, allowing you to filter traffic at the edge—stopping malicious requests before they ever hit your application.

AWS Firewall Manager

Managing security across multiple AWS accounts and regions can get messy fast. AWS Firewall Manager helps you keep it all under control by centralizing rule enforcement. You create policies once, and they automatically apply across your organization—Route 53, WAF, Shield Advanced, and more.

It also keeps an eye on compliance, making sure any new resources follow the same protections without manual setup.

AWS Security Hub

The Security Hub aggregates and prioritizes security findings from across multiple AWS services—such as GuardDuty, Inspector, and Config—and presents them in a single, unified dashboard. This makes it easier to monitor your AWS environment for threats, misconfigurations, and compliance gaps.

The Security Hub also maps findings against common compliance standards like PCI DSS, NIST CSF, and CIS Benchmarks. This helps organizations continuously assess and improve their overall security posture. By centralizing insights, it reduces the need to manually check individual services and gives security teams a streamlined way to prioritize and remediate issues.

AWS Config

AWS Config is a service that continuously monitors and records the configuration of AWS resources. This allows you to track changes and evaluate them against compliance requirements. By maintaining a detailed history of resource states, Config helps organizations identify misconfigurations, enforce internal policies, and meet external audit requirements. For example, it can automatically check whether S3 buckets are publicly accessible, confirm that IAM policies follow least privilege, or verify that encryption settings are enabled. This continuous visibility not only strengthens security but also makes it easier to troubleshoot operational issues and prove compliance with regulatory standards.

Table 7-1 summarizes these edge protection AWS services.

Table 7-1. AWS security services for the edge

Service	Purpose	Key features
Amazon Route 53	A DNS system that also routes traffic efficiently	• Uses latency-based routing, health checks, and automatic failover to optimize performance • Instantly reroutes traffic during outages to maintain seamless user experience and security
Amazon CloudFront	Content delivery network to accelerate delivery and reduce server load	• Caches content at global edge locations • Absorbs traffic surges • TLS encryption • Signed URLs and cookies • Geo-filtering • Edge compute with CloudFront Functions or Lambda@Edge
AWS Shield	DDoS protection service for network and application availability	• Always-on protection • Shield Standard is free • Shield Advanced offers diagnostics, near-real-time visibility, response team access, and cost protection
AWS WAF	Web Application Firewall for filtering HTTP/HTTPS traffic	• Rule-based filtering (IP, size, headers, patterns) • Protection against SQL injection and bots • Geo-restrictions and rate limiting
AWS Firewall Manager	Centralized security policy management across multiple AWS accounts and services	• Organization-wide policy enforcement • Manages WAF, Shield, Route 53, and more • Ensures compliance for both new and existing resources
AWS Security Hub	Centralized security and compliance management across AWS services	• Aggregates findings from GuardDuty, Inspector, Config, and more • Provides a unified dashboard to prioritize and monitor security posture • Maps results to compliance frameworks like PCI DSS, NIST, and CIS Benchmarks
AWS Config	Continuous monitoring and compliance for AWS resources	• Records and evaluates configuration changes across AWS resources • Ensures compliance with security policies (e.g., S3 buckets not public) • Supports audits and remediation by tracking configuration history

Layer 2: Inbound Traffic Filtering

Once traffic makes it past the edge, it arrives at your Virtual Private Cloud (VPC) environment. This is a logically isolated part of AWS where your compute resources live. Inbound filtering at this stage gives you precise control over who can talk to your systems and how. It works at both the network and transport layers, inspecting traffic and making routing decisions to ensure only clean, approved data makes it through.

There are several AWS services that help you build this next layer of protection.

Elastic Load Balancing (ELB)

Elastic Load Balancing (ELB) acts as the front door for all incoming traffic to your application. Instead of letting requests hit your resources directly, ELB sits in front, routing each request to one of several healthy targets—like EC2 instances, containers, or specific IP addresses. It keeps a constant eye on these targets.

This setup hides the actual compute resources behind a single access point, making it much harder for attackers to zero in on individual hosts. This layer of abstraction helps protect your backend from direct hits.

At the same time, you're gaining resilience. If a resource fails or traffic spikes unexpectedly, the load balancer spreads requests across available capacity. Your users get a smoother experience, and your application stays up and responsive.

AWS Network Firewall

Sitting at the edge of your VPC—near internet gateways, VPNs, or Direct Connect links—AWS Network Firewall adds a much deeper layer of inspection. It combines stateful and stateless filtering. Stateful means it understands the context of a connection, like a conversation that started with a handshake and continues with replies. Once it allows this session, return traffic flows automatically. Stateless rules work faster but more simply, blocking or allowing individual packets without tracking the full session.

AWS Network Firewall can dive deep: decrypting TLS traffic, scanning protocols, and acting as an intrusion prevention system (IPS).

Security Groups and Network ACLs

Inside a VPC, Security Groups and network access control lists (NACLs) give you two more powerful tools to shape how traffic moves.

Security Groups are stateful and operate at the resource level. You assign them to instances or network interfaces. If a Security Group allows inbound traffic on a port, return traffic is automatically permitted. You can attach multiple groups to a single resource and define very specific rules around allowed IPs, ports, and protocols.

NACLs, by contrast, are stateless and work at the subnet level. This means they evaluate every packet both ways. So, you need to write rules for inbound and outbound traffic. NACLs also evaluate rules in numbered order and provide for both "allow" and "deny" actions. They're effective for enforcing broad rules early, before traffic even reaches your instances.

Table 7-2 summarizes these services and systems.

Table 7-2. AWS services for inbound traffic filtering

AWS Service	Function	Key Characteristics
Elastic Load Balancing (ELB)	Routes incoming traffic to healthy compute resources (EC2, containers, IPs) and removes unhealthy ones from rotation	• Acts as a single entry point (front door) • Hides backend infrastructure from direct exposure • Automatically distributes traffic across healthy targets • Enhances availability and fault tolerance
AWS Network Firewall	Protection at the edge of your VPC	• Supports both stateful and stateless rules • Can decrypt TLS, scan protocols, and act as an IPS • Positioned near internet gateways (IGWs), virtual private networks (VPNs), or Direct Connect links • Helps secure east–west and north–south traffic
Security Groups	Controls traffic at the resource level within a VPC	• Stateful: Return traffic is automatically allowed • Attached to elastic network interfaces (ENIs) or instances • Rules specify IPs, ports, and protocols • Multiple groups can be assigned to one resource
Network ACLs (NACLs)	Controls traffic at the subnet level, offering a broad layer of protection across multiple instances	• Stateless: Each direction must be explicitly allowed • Applies to all resources in a subnet • Evaluates rules in number order • Supports both allow and deny rules for inbound and outbound traffic

Layer 3: Compute Protection

At this stage, we are where your workloads live. Whether you're running VMs, containerized services, or serverless functions, Layer 3 is about protecting the systems that execute your code. This means keeping them resilient, patched, secure, and ready to scale.

Let's look at the key AWS tools that make this layer stronger.

Auto Scaling

When demand shifts, Auto Scaling responds. It automatically adjusts the number of running compute resources—whether EC2 instances, container tasks, or database replicas—based on real-time conditions. So, during a traffic spike, it spins up more capacity to handle the load. When things quiet down, it scales back to save costs.

Auto Scaling also contributes to security and stability by continuously evaluating instance health. If something isn't responding or shows signs of failure, it's replaced. This means only healthy, functional resources stay in rotation—without you having to intervene manually.

Amazon Inspector

Security starts with visibility, and that's where Amazon Inspector comes in. It's a vulnerability management service that scans your compute resources—like EC2, container images in the Amazon Elastic Container Registry (ECR), or Lambda functions—for known software flaws and unintended exposure.

For EC2, it runs vulnerability scans using either agent-based or agentless methods. It checks for issues like outdated OS packages, misconfigurations, and open network paths that shouldn't exist. With containers and Lambda, it scans during deployment, flagging any known common vulnerabilities and exposures (CVEs in your dependencies before they go live).

Inspector works behind the scenes continuously, kicking off assessments automatically when something changes—like a new version of an application or a new image pushed to the ECR. You can also connect it to Security Hub or EventBridge for automated workflows, alerts, or remediation pipelines.

AWS Systems Manager

Systems Manager is your control tower for operational hygiene across compute environments. It brings several key tools together under one roof:

- Patch Manager automates patching across EC2 instances, on-prem servers, or other managed nodes. You set baselines and schedules, and it handles the rollouts.

- Inventory gathers metadata on your systems—like installed software, configurations, and patches—so that you can detect drift, confirm what's running where, and track down unapproved changes fast.

- Compliance aggregates patch statuses and configuration data, giving you a clear view of where things stand. It also integrates with other AWS services for alerting and automated actions.

Together, these tools help you stay on top of your infrastructure without drowning in manual tasks. You get centralized visibility, automated patching, and better control over what's happening across your environment.

Table 7-3 is a summary of the compute protection services.

Table 7-3. Compute protection services

Service	Primary function	Key capabilities
Auto Scaling	Dynamically adjusts compute resources based on demand	• Automatically scales EC2s, Elastic Container Services (ECSs), or RDS instances • Reacts to real-time traffic and usage • Reduces resources when not needed to save costs
Amazon Inspector	Automated vulnerability scanning and exposure detection	• Scans EC2s (agent-based/agentless) • Analyzes container images in Amazon ECR • Checks Lambda functions at deploy time • Flags known CVEs and misconfigurations
AWS Systems Manager	Centralized management for operations, patching, and compliance across environments	• Patch Manager: Automates OS and software patching • Inventory: Tracks software, configurations, and changes • Compliance: Shows patch/config status across infrastructure

Layer 4: Data and Identity Safeguards

This layer is about protecting your most critical assets: the sensitive data your systems handle and the identities that access it. If Layers 1–3 are about keeping attackers out, Layer 4 assumes they might get in—and builds strong protections around the information they're after.

At the heart of this layer are two core principles: encrypt everything, and control who gets access. Even if someone breaks through a previous layer, the data should be useless without the right credentials and keys.

We've already covered IAM (Identity and Access Management) in detail in Chapter 6, so now let's shift focus to the piece that locks your data down—encryption.

Encryption takes readable data—called plain text—and scrambles it using mathematical algorithms and keys, turning it into ciphertext. Without the matching decryption key, the data stays unreadable.

There are two main types you'll use in AWS:

- Encryption at rest protects data stored on disk—like in S3 buckets, RDS databases, or Elastic Block Store (EBS) volumes. It keeps data safe even if someone accesses the storage directly.

- Encryption in transit secures data moving across the network—like traffic between microservices or from a user to an application. TLS is the most common protocol used here.

When you apply both consistently, you create a strong default. Data stays protected whether it's sitting still or flying across the wire.

Let's look at the various AWS services for encryption.

AWS Key Management Service (KMS)

First, there is the AWS KMS, which is for managing encryption keys. It handles the complexities behind the scenes, such as key generation, rotation, and secure storage.

Here's how it works: when you encrypt data, AWS services use a one-time "data key" for the actual encryption. The data key gets encrypted by a customer master key (CMK) stored in a hardware security module (HSM) managed by KMS. You never see the keys directly, but you always stay in control of their usage.

KMS supports both symmetric keys (the same key is used to encrypt and decrypt) and asymmetric keys (separate public and private keys), giving you flexibility depending on your use case—whether it's encrypting data or verifying signatures. Every time a key is used, KMS records the event in CloudTrail, so you get a complete, timestamped audit trail that shows exactly who accessed what, and when.

CloudHSM

If you need even tighter control over your cryptographic operations—say, for regulatory compliance or internal security requirements—custom key stores backed by CloudHSM let you take control. With CloudHSM, you manage your own HSMs inside your VPC. You get full ownership of the keys, including the ability to generate, store, and use them entirely within a device you control. AWS takes care of the physical security and maintenance, but you handle the keys directly. This is useful for scenarios where trust boundaries or legal frameworks require customer-controlled encryption infrastructure.

AWS Certificate Manager (ACM)

Encryption in transit needs TLS certificates, and AWS Certificate Manager (ACM) takes the complexity out of managing them. It can automatically issue, renew, and deploy certificates to services like ELB or CloudFront, so your applications always use HTTPS without any manual steps.

ACM works for both public-facing endpoints and private internal services. Either way, it removes the operational overhead and reduces the risk of expired or misconfigured certificates.

For sensitive data like API keys, database passwords, or tokens, AWS Secrets Manager complements ACM by securely storing and managing secrets. ACM also supports automatic rotation of credentials using AWS Lambda functions, which makes it especially useful when integrating with non-AWS systems that require custom rotation logic.

AWS Secrets Manager

Credentials are sensitive data like database passwords, API keys, or third-party tokens. Secrets Manager keeps them secure. It encrypts every secret with KMS, supports fine-grained access control, and offers automatic rotation for supported services.

It also integrates directly with other AWS tools—like RDS—so apps can pull credentials on the fly without hardcoding anything or exposing secrets in config files.

Table 7-4 summarizes the services for encryption.

Table 7-4. AWS services for encryption

Service	Purpose	Key features
AWS Key Management Service (KMS)	Manage encryption keys across AWS services	• Handles key generation, rotation, secure storage • Supports symmetric and asymmetric keys • Integrates with CloudTrail for audit logging
AWS CloudHSM	Dedicated hardware-based key management	• Customer-managed HSMs inside a VPC • Full ownership and control of keys • AWS manages physical security
AWS Certificate Manager (ACM)	Provision, manage, and deploy SSL/TLS certificates for secure connections	• TLS certificate management for encryption in transit • Supports ELB, CloudFront, etc. • For public and private services
AWS Secrets Manager	Secure storage and rotation of sensitive information like credentials	• Encrypts secrets with KMS • Fine-grained access control • Auto-rotation for supported services • Integrates with RDS and other AWS tools

Layer 5: Monitoring and Detection

This is the visibility layer. It's where you stop flying blind and start spotting trouble before it spreads. At this layer, logs get collected, unusual behavior gets flagged, alerts go out, and incident-response playbooks kick in automatically. The sooner you know something's off, the faster you can respond—and that can make all the difference.

Let's now look at the AWS tools for monitoring and detection.

Amazon GuardDuty

GuardDuty is AWS's built-in threat detection service. It's fully managed, constantly running, and uses ML to sift through massive streams of data. This includes Cloud-Trail events, VPC flow logs, DNS queries, and (if you opt in) things like Elastic Kubernetes Service (EKS) audit logs, RDS login attempts, S3 data access, Lambda activity, and more.

The service looks for signs of trouble, such as unauthorized API calls, malware in your workloads, data exfiltration, cryptomining, and runtime threats inside containers or EC2 instances. All of it gets analyzed using behavioral modeling, anomaly detection, and threat intelligence from AWS and partners.

Turning it on takes a single click. Once it's up, GuardDuty sends findings to Amazon EventBridge, which lets you wire up alerts, notifications, or automatic responses via Lambda, SNS, or whatever tooling fits your workflow. It also supports deeper visibility into services like EKS, Lambda, and EBS, and it recognizes specialized threat types like compromised credentials and targeted cryptomining.

AWS CloudTrail and Amazon CloudWatch

CloudTrail gives you the full story of what's happening in your AWS environment. Every API call and console action—who did what, when, and from where—is logged. This audit trail becomes essential during investigations, compliance reviews, and detection efforts. All this information feeds directly into services like GuardDuty, CloudWatch, and Security Hub.

CloudWatch, on the other hand, focuses on real-time visibility. It collects metrics (like CPU, memory, and network usage), ingests logs, and tracks custom signals. You can define filters and alarms to catch issues like repeated failed login attempts, unauthorized access, or traffic spikes. You can then surface those insights in dashboards or trigger auto-remediation actions.

You can integrate CloudTrail logs into CloudWatch Logs for deeper inspection. This unlocks proactive alerting and lets you zero in on unusual behavior before it snowballs.

AWS Security Hub

AWS Security Hub brings all your AWS security findings into one place. It aggregates data from services like GuardDuty, Macie, Inspector, IAM Access Analyzer, and supported third-party tools.

Beyond aggregation, Security Hub runs automated checks against standards like NIST and PCI DSS. This leverages AWS Config under the hood. It provides real-time visibility into your compliance posture across multiple accounts and regions.

It's important to note that Security Hub does not automatically fix issues. Instead, it integrates with other services—such as AWS Lambda, Systems Manager, or partner tools—for remediation workflows. Findings are standardized using the AWS Security Finding Format (ASFF). This makes it easy to route them through EventBridge for automation or ticketing systems.

Security Hub also integrates with Amazon Detective. This allows analysts to pivot directly from a finding into a visual investigation to trace root causes.

Amazon Macie

Macie focuses on protecting sensitive data stored in Amazon S3. It's built to discover, classify, and monitor personal and financial information automatically, using ML and pattern matching.

Once enabled (again, just one click), Macie starts scanning your S3 buckets—checking both data contents and access configurations. It flags issues like publicly exposed data or misconfigured permissions and generates findings labeled as "SensitiveData" or "Policy." These are stored for 90 days and routed through EventBridge for action. You can also send alerts to Security Hub or your existing pipelines via SNS, Lambda, or a security information and event management (SIEM) system, which collects, aggregates, and analyzes security data from across your entire IT environment.

For audit and compliance workflows, Macie can export detailed discovery reports to an encrypted S3 bucket using KMS. This makes it easier to document findings, analyze trends, and prepare for audits.

AWS Trusted Advisor

AWS Trusted Advisor acts as a best-practice guide. It continuously scans your AWS environment and offers automated recommendations to improve security, performance, fault tolerance, and cost efficiency. On the security front, it flags critical issues such as whether MFA is enabled on the root account, whether unused security group ports remain open, or if IAM access keys are old and unused.

Table 7-5 summarizes the AWS tools for monitoring and detection.

Table 7-5. Summary of AWS tools for monitoring and detection

Service	What it does	Key features and integrations
Amazon GuardDuty	Detects threats using machine learning across AWS data sources like CloudTrail, VPC Flow Logs, DNS queries, EKS audit logs, and more.	• One-click activation and always on • Integrates with EventBridge for automation • Detects advanced threats including container and EC2 runtime risks
CloudTrail and CloudWatch	CloudTrail logs every API call and console action for auditing and investigation. CloudWatch monitors performance metrics and logs in real time for operational visibility and alerts.	• CloudTrail feeds into GuardDuty and Security Hub • CloudWatch enables real-time alerts and dashboards • Logs can trigger auto-remediation actions
AWS Security Hub	Aggregates and standardizes security findings from AWS services and third-party tools. Provides compliance checks and centralized visibility.	• Pulls data from GuardDuty, Macie, Inspector, and more • Uses AWS Security Finding Format (ASFF) • Integrates with EventBridge and Amazon Detective for investigations

Service	What it does	Key features and integrations
Amazon Macie	Scans S3 buckets to discover and classify sensitive data using ML. Identifies exposure risks and access misconfigurations.	• One-click setup for automated S3 scanning • Flags and routes sensitive data findings via EventBridge • Exports encrypted reports to S3 for audits
AWS Trusted Advisor	Automated best-practice checks for AWS accounts.	• Highlights critical issues such as MFA not being enabled on the root account or unused security group ports left open • Helps align environments with AWS best practices without requiring manual audits

Third-Party Security Services in the AWS Marketplace

The AWS Marketplace is a curated ecosystem packed with third-party security tools that plug into your AWS environment. These tools range from next-generation firewalls and cloud native posture management (CSPM) platforms to SIEM systems, identity and access management solutions, and data protection software. Each one comes from an independent vendor, gets reviewed by AWS, and is ready for quick deployment.

Getting started is straightforward. Whether the product shows up as an Amazon Machine Image (AMI) or a SaaS offering, you can deploy it directly into your cloud environment. You don't need to sign a separate contract with each vendor, and the charges roll into your existing AWS bill. If you're on an Enterprise Discount Program, these purchases count toward your volume discounts too.

Before a product hits the Marketplace, AWS runs it through a series of automated checks—scanning AMIs for vulnerabilities and reviewing configurations for security gaps. Vendors are also required to patch in a timely manner and handle secrets securely. On top of that, there's Vendor Insights, a feature that pulls together key compliance information—like SOC 2, ISO 27001, FedRAMP certifications—in AWS Artifact. You also get ongoing compliance monitoring through tools like AWS Config and Audit Manager.

Resources for AWS Cloud Security

AWS offers a wide mix of resources designed to help you build, understand, and strengthen your security practices—no matter where you are in your cloud journey. Here are three key places to focus your attention:

AWS Knowledge Center
>   This is full of FAQs, how-to articles, and video guides that tackle common security questions like setting up IAM policies, turning on MFA, or locking down access via the CLI.

AWS Trust Center
> This is the home for foundational resources—whitepapers, compliance artifacts, vulnerability reporting tools, and current AWS advisories.

AWS Security Blog
> This is where things get more dynamic. Written by AWS security engineers and field experts, the AWS Security Blog dives into real-world scenarios, service updates, and deep dives on best practices. You'll find posts on everything from tagging secrets in AWS Secrets Manager to protecting generative AI workloads, along with insights from major events like AWS re:Inforce.

Conclusion

In this chapter, you got a look at the fundamentals of cloud security and how AWS gives you the tools to build systems that are both secure and resilient. We walked through today's shifting threat landscape and broke down some of the most common attacks—ransomware, phishing, and zero-day exploits, among them.

You also saw how AWS handles security as a shared responsibility, and how this model shapes what you're responsible for versus what AWS covers. We dug into the concept of defense-in-depth—using multiple layers of protection—and explored key services like GuardDuty, KMS, and CloudTrail that help make those layers possible.

In the next chapter, we'll look at the AWS global infrastructure, such as AWS Regions, availability zones, and edge locations.

Chapter Quiz

To check your answers, please refer to the "Chapter 7 Answer Key" on page 206.

1. In AWS's Shared Responsibility Model, what is AWS responsible for?

   A. Setting up Identity and Access Management (IAM) policies for customer applications

   B. Encrypting data in customer databases

   C. Securing the physical data centers and network infrastructure

   D. Installing antivirus software on Elastic Compute Cloud (EC2) instances

2. What is the function of AWS Web Application Firewall (WAF)?

   A. To store secrets like API tokens

   B. To block malicious web traffic at the application layer

   C. To automatically patch operating systems

   D. To manage Virtual Private Cloud (VPC) subnet routing

3. What AWS service allows for centralized enforcement of firewall rules across accounts?

   A. Route 53

   B. IAM

   C. Amazon Inspector

   D. AWS Firewall Manager

4. Which AWS service helps manage encryption keys used across services?

   A. AWS Key Management Service (KMS)

   B. AWS Shield

   C. Amazon Route 53

   D. Elastic Load Balancer

5. What is the primary function of AWS Security Hub?

   A. Managing encryption keys

   B. Aggregating security findings across AWS services

   C. Filtering web traffic

   D. Logging API calls

CHAPTER 8

AWS Global Infrastructure

A global application is one that's deployed across multiple geographic locations. In AWS, this typically means leveraging multiple AWS Regions, Availability Zones, and Edge Locations. The main benefit of this setup is that users will experience less delay when interacting with your application. Because of the sheer size of the planet, a user in India accessing a server in the United States will experience noticeable lag. But if your application is deployed closer to where your users are—say, in both the US and Asia—then everyone benefits from faster, more responsive performance.

Another major reason to go global is disaster recovery. You may not want to rely solely on a single AWS Region. While AWS is highly reliable, disasters like earthquakes, power outages, or political instability can impact a Region. Deploying your application across multiple Regions enhances resilience by enabling failover if one Region goes down. To make this seamless, however, you need to configure replication (such as S3 Cross-Region Replication), implement solid backup strategies, and use services like Amazon Route 53 for DNS failover. This layered approach ensures redundancy, maximizes uptime, and keeps your applications highly available even during Regional disruptions.

Finally, distributing your application globally can also strengthen defenses against cyberattacks. Threats like DDoS attacks are unfortunately common, but spreading infrastructure across multiple Regions makes it much harder for attackers to disrupt your entire system. With services such as AWS Shield providing DDoS protection and AWS Global Accelerator enabling intelligent traffic rerouting, you gain additional resilience. Pairing this with other security measures—like AWS WAF for filtering malicious requests and IAM for access control—further ensures that your application remains secure, reliable, and available worldwide.

In this chapter, we'll look at the AWS global infrastructure. We'll look at how data centers, Regions, Availability Zones, and Edge Locations work. We'll also look at the various AWS services, such as CloudFront, as well as deployment options. All of these are common topics on the exam.

Data Centers

At the core of any cloud platform lies the data center. It's the physical foundation behind all the powerful services we associate with the cloud. This is where you'll find the hardware like servers, storage units, networking gear, and other critical equipment. This is all housed in a dedicated facility.

The data center industry is massive. In the United States alone, there are more than 5,300 data centers (*https://oreil.ly/OGRcX*), making it the global leader. Worldwide, that number climbs to nearly 12,000 (*https://oreil.ly/uaFEQ*).

Most data centers share a common set of features:

Racks and cabinets
These are the frameworks for organizing servers, networking hardware, and storage. A standard rack measures 19 inches wide, and they are arranged in rows, which are usually enclosed in cabinets. Smart layout design here matters. This improves cooling efficiency and makes maintenance easier.

Cabling
Power and data flow through a dense network of cables, typically routed through ceilings or under raised floors. Managing this web of connections is critical for keeping the system running smoothly.

Power systems
Data centers rely on backup generators and uninterruptible power supplies (UPSs). These are usually powered by diesel so as to keep operations going even during outages.

Environmental controls
All the hardware in a data center generates considerable heat. Systems to regulate temperature and humidity are important to prevent overheating and maintain optimal performance.

Fire protection
Fires can spread fast in a data center. This is why these facilities are equipped with smoke detectors, heat sensors, and suppression systems like sprinklers to catch problems early and minimize damage.

Physical security
To protect against unauthorized access, data centers use a mix of surveillance cameras, fencing, biometric scanners, and secure login systems.

With all these systems in place, the cost of building and maintaining a data center adds up quickly. For example, in the US, the price to build one typically ranges between $7 million and $12 million per megawatt (MW) of capacity (*https://oreil.ly/ 89RPh*). In Europe, the cost runs a bit higher—between $8 million and $14 million per MW. This is mainly due to stricter environmental regulations. In developing Regions, the price tends to range between $4 million and $7 million per MW.

Operating costs come next, and energy is by far the largest expense. It often eats up 30% to 60% of a facility's ongoing budget (*https://oreil.ly/kZUaW*). Location plays a big role in how high the energy bill gets. Factors like access to cheap power sources and climate conditions matter a lot. For this reason, cloud companies often build their data centers near low-cost energy sources. Apple, for example, located one of its facilities in Foulum, Denmark, to take advantage of nearby hydroelectric power from Norway.

Not all data centers are built on the same scale. Some are compact and serve niche purposes, while others are massive and built for enterprise-level workloads. A typical cloud provider's data center might span about 100,000 square meters.

Then there are the giants.

Take Meta's project in Richland Parish, Louisiana: a planned four-million-square-foot data center with an estimated construction cost of $10 billion (*https://oreil.ly/7_fzV*). Once it's up and running—targeted for 2030—it'll support about 500 employees. On top of that, Meta is investing $200 million to upgrade local roads and water infrastructure. For energy, the company has partnered with Entergy Louisiana, which will build new power generation systems to support the facility.

Other tech giants are racing to build their own mega-scale data centers as well—Microsoft, Apple, Oracle, and Amazon are all in the mix. This growth is pushing demand for electricity sharply upward.

In fact, the Electric Power Research Institute predicts that by 2030, data centers could consume up to 9% of the US's total electricity (*https://oreil.ly/x8UpH*)—more than double today's levels.

This rapid growth presents a major challenge. The current power grid wasn't designed for such high loads from modern data centers. Upgrading the grid to handle this demand will be both costly and time-consuming.

Renewable energy sources like wind and solar are promising but unreliable due to their intermittent nature. Plus, there's the regulatory maze that slows down approvals for new energy projects.

In response to growing energy demands and the limitations of traditional and renewable power sources, several major tech companies are turning to nuclear energy as a viable solution. Amazon, for instance, acquired a 960-MW data center in March 2024 (*https://oreil.ly/5jJ14*) that draws its power directly from the Susquehanna nuclear facility in Pennsylvania. Meanwhile, Google announced a partnership with Kairos Power in October 2024 to develop small modular reactors (SMRs), with a goal of generating up to 500 MW of carbon-free electricity by 2035.

Nuclear power offers clear benefits. It's carbon-free and capable of providing steady energy at scale. But it also comes with serious risks. Accidents can be catastrophic, and new plants are extremely expensive and slow to build.

Still, as demand for cloud services keeps rising, and as workloads like AI place even greater strain on infrastructure, the need for reliable, scalable energy solutions isn't going away.

Regions and Availability Zones

AWS builds its global infrastructure around the concept of Regions, which are geographically distinct areas that each contain multiple Availability Zones, or AZs. These AZs function as independent data centers but are designed to work together. Every Region includes at least two AZs, all linked by high-speed, low-latency networking. This setup allows for rapid, synchronous data replication and supports robust, fault-tolerant architectures that can keep running even in the face of service disruptions or disasters.

One of the biggest strengths of this approach is Regional isolation. Each Region runs independently, so if a natural disaster, technical glitch, or political event affects one Region, the others remain untouched. Within a single Region, AZs are physically spread out to reduce the chance of a single incident taking down multiple zones. This physical separation helps maintain service continuity even during localized failures.

Each AZ comes equipped with its own power backup systems, including UPSs and generators, and draws electricity from different substations and grids. This design eliminates shared points of failure in power delivery. On the networking side, AZs connect using fully redundant, high-bandwidth fiber, and each one hooks into multiple Tier 1 transit providers. AWS also rolls out updates one zone at a time, which lowers the risk of system-wide issues.

Currently, AWS operates 39 Regions worldwide, spanning 123 Availability Zones. Figure 8-1 shows those for North America.

And they're still growing. New Regions are already in the pipeline, including locations in New Zealand, Saudi Arabia, and Chile, and a Sovereign EU Region, along with 13 additional AZs.

North America is home to nine AWS Regions, spanning the United States, Canada, and—since early 2025—Mexico. Besides these, there are the AWS GovCloud (US) Regions. They are specialized, isolated environments built to host sensitive data and regulated workloads for US government agencies, defense contractors, and organizations in highly regulated industries. These Regions are physically and logically separate from standard AWS commercial Regions. This provides an added layer of security and compliance.

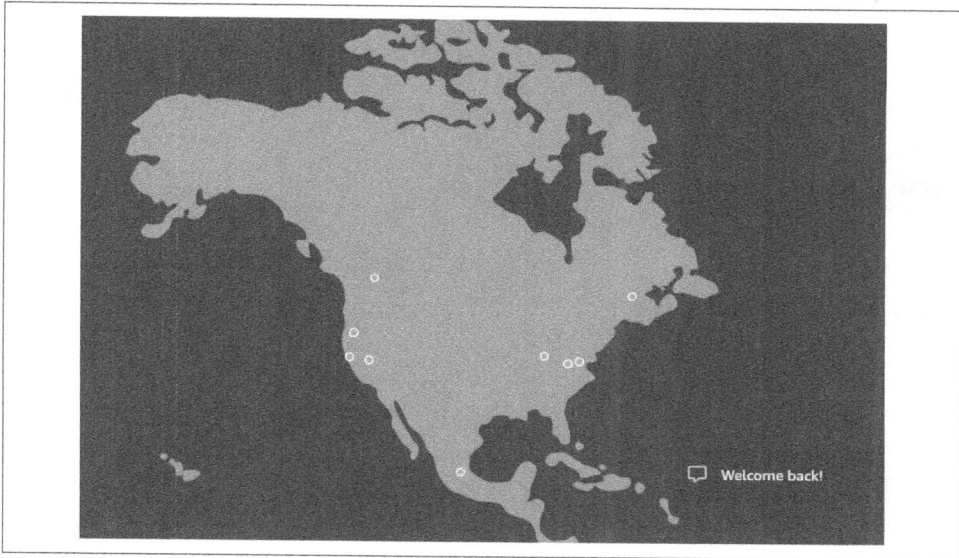

Figure 8-1. AWS Regions in North America

GovCloud supports strict regulatory requirements, including FedRAMP High, the most rigorous level of FedRAMP authorization, International Traffic in Arms Regulations (ITAR), and Department of Defense standards. This makes it suitable for handling Controlled Unclassified Information and other mission-critical workloads. Collectively, these Regions include 31 AZs. Table 8-1 shows the details.

Table 8-1. AWS Regions and Availability Zones in North America

Region name	Code	AZ	Launch year
US East (Northern Virginia)	us-east-1	6	2006
US East (Ohio)	us-east-2	3	2016
US West (Oregon)	us-west-2	4	2011
US West (Northern California)	us-west-1	3	2009
Canada (Central)	ca-central-1	3	2016
AWS GovCloud (US-West)	us-gov-west-1	3	2011
AWS GovCloud (US-East)	us-gov-east-1	3	2018
US West (Arizona)	us-west-3	3	2023
Mexico (Central)	mx-central-1	3	2025

Whenever you work with AWS—whether through the CLI, SDKs, or infrastructure-as-code tools like CloudFormation or Terraform—you'll need to specify Regions using their official codes (such as those listed in Table 8-1 for North America and Table 8-2 for some of the other global Regions). These codes follow a standardized naming convention, and they're essential for telling AWS where to create or manage your resources.

Table 8-2 shows some of the popular codes for foreign markets.

Table 8-2. AWS codes for Regions

Region	Code
Europe (Ireland)	eu-west-1
Europe (Frankfurt)	eu-central-1
Asia Pacific (Tokyo)	ap-northeast-1
Asia Pacific (Seoul)	ap-northeast-2
Asia Pacific (Mumbai)	ap-south-1
Asia Pacific (Singapore)	ap-southeast-1
Asia Pacific (Sydney)	ap-southeast-2
Africa (Cape Town)	af-south-1
Middle East (Bahrain)	me-south-1

Selecting Regions

Picking the right AWS Region is a strategic move that directly impacts how your applications perform, how much you'll pay, whether you meet regulatory requirements, and which AWS services you can actually use. To make the best choice, it helps to evaluate your needs across four key areas:

Compliance and data sovereignty
> Some industries and countries require certain data to remain within specific geographic boundaries. AWS supports these mandates through a broad selection of global Regions, dedicated Local Zones, and specialized offerings like the European Sovereign Cloud. To ensure compliance, review relevant laws such as GDPR or UK GDPR, along with your organization's internal policies. AWS tools like Control Tower and CloudHSM can further support compliance and control over data residency.

Proximity to users
> Latency can make or break the user experience. Again, deploying your infrastructure in Regions close to your users helps reduce round-trip time. For broader reach, services like CloudFront and Global Accelerator intelligently route traffic to the nearest available endpoint.

Service and feature availability

Not every AWS service is available in every Region. Major Regions usually receive new features first. Before choosing a Region, consult the AWS Services List to verify that the capabilities you need are available. If they're not, you may need to architect around it or delay implementation until AWS expands support.

Pricing and cost differences

AWS pricing varies significantly between Regions. For example, workloads in São Paulo can cost 50–70% more than the same setup in Northern Virginia. Use tools like the AWS Pricing Calculator or the Price List API to estimate expenses accurately. Also keep in mind that data transfer costs can vary. This is not just between Regions but also between Availability Zones. Inter-AZ transfers are not always free unless you're using certain services, such as S3 replication or workloads within the same placement group. To optimize costs further, consider Reserved Instances and Savings Plans, and carefully account for data transfer fees if your architecture spans multiple Regions or AZs.

Edge Locations

Beyond AWS Regions and Availability Zones, there's another key layer in the AWS global infrastructure that helps speed things up: Points of Presence (PoPs). These are physical sites that host Edge Locations and regional edge caches. They are strategically placed in major cities and densely populated areas to sit closer to end users. Unlike full AWS Regions, PoPs focus on specialized tasks such as caching content, handling DNS lookups, and defending against DDoS attacks.

AWS has built out a massive global network of PoPs—over 600 as of 2025—spanning more than 90 cities in 45+ countries. This network powers services like Amazon CloudFront, Route 53, AWS Shield, and AWS Global Accelerator, enabling low-latency content delivery, intelligent traffic routing, and stronger protection against threats. Together, these PoPs form the backbone of one of the most extensive content delivery and security systems in the world.

In Chapter 7, we saw how these services operate from a security perspective. Now, let's shift to how they fit into and benefit from AWS's broader global infrastructure.

Global Accelerator

The AWS Global Accelerator helps users around the world connect faster and more reliably, without you needing to do much extra work.

Here's how it works: Global Accelerator gives you two static IP addresses that don't change, no matter what. These IPs use a routing method called anycast, which means they're announced from dozens of AWS Edge Locations. When someone tries to access your application, their request hops onto AWS's private network from the nearest Edge Location. The private backbone usually beats the public internet in both speed and consistency.

If something goes wrong—like a failure in a Region—the Global Accelerator can shift traffic to a working endpoint in another Region almost instantly. The user won't notice anything and there will be no DNS changes.

Amazon Route 53

Amazon Route 53 manages DNS operations from the edge. It operates on a global anycast network and uses over 200 PoPs. When someone tries to resolve a domain like *myapp.mydomain.com*, the request is routed to the nearest PoP based on real-time network conditions. This minimizes latency and ensures users receive fast, reliable responses no matter where they are.

Route 53 is architected in two layers: a global control plane and a distributed data plane. The control plane lives in one AWS Region and handles tasks like creating or updating DNS records, setting up routing policies, and configuring health checks.

The data plane, on the other hand, is everywhere. It handles the DNS lookups and keeps an eye on endpoint health across PoPs, Regions, and Edge Locations. Even if the control plane goes offline temporarily, the data plane keeps running—resolving DNS queries and routing traffic as needed.

CloudFront

CloudFront runs on a layered system that includes Edge Locations, Regional Edge Caches (RECs), and AWS's private global backbone.

Here's how it works: when someone requests a file—maybe a video, image, or web page—CloudFront starts by checking the nearest Edge Location. If the file's already cached there, it's delivered instantly. If not, the request quietly moves up the chain to a REC, which has a much larger cache and holds onto content longer. If this is not enough, then CloudFront pulls the content from your origin server.

This tiered system cuts down on trips to the origin, reduces load on your backend, and speeds things up for users—all with no extra work on your part.

Behind the scenes, CloudFront doesn't rely on the public internet for these fetches. Its PoPs and RECs connect through AWS's own high-capacity fiber network—hundreds of terabits of fully redundant, low-latency connections that span AWS Regions and AZs.

AWS Shield

AWS Shield is built into the backbone of AWS. The service kicks in at the edge of the network, where it can stop threatening traffic before it gets anywhere near your application.

Every AWS account gets Shield Standard by default. It automatically filters out common DDoS attacks at the Edge Locations, which are the same PoPs used by services like CloudFront, Route 53, and Global Accelerator. When a surge of malicious traffic shows up, Shield Standard blocks it on the spot.

If an application has higher stakes—or you just want more control—Shield Advanced takes things further. It learns traffic patterns and uses custom rules, along with AWS WAF to catch more complex threats at the edge. It provides access to real-time dashboards, detailed flow logs, and support from AWS's dedicated DDoS Response Team.

AWS Outposts

AWS Outposts allow for running AWS services in a data center or co-location facility—a third-party data center where companies rent space for their own IT infrastructure. AWS takes care of everything: delivery, setup, and ongoing support.

There are two options for AWS Outposts:

- Full-size 42U racks are tall data center cabinets (about 80 inches high), preloaded with servers, storage, networking gear, and redundant power systems. They show up fully assembled and are ready to go.
- Compact servers are for tighter spaces like branch offices or factory floors.

Each Outposts rack comes with integrated switches and supports two key network connections:

- The service link is an encrypted connection that ties your Outpost to its parent AWS Region. It handles all the control traffic—like provisioning and updates—so AWS can provide centralized management.
- The local gateway provides a low-latency bridge between your Outpost and on-site systems, letting your apps talk to local resources without going out to the cloud and back.

Although the hardware sits in your building, it behaves like it's part of AWS. You use the same console, CLI, and APIs, but get the benefits of low latency, local data processing, and hardware management. If your AWS connection drops, your workloads keep running locally and sync back automatically once you're reconnected. In addition, AWS offers Direct Connect locations at over 100 global sites. This provides dedicated network connections to AWS Regions or Local Zones. It enables hybrid workloads to benefit from consistent low latency, higher bandwidth, and more reliable connectivity than the public internet alone.

Local Zones and Wavelength Zones

When applications require lower latency and more specialized hardware, AWS has capabilities that go beyond Regions and Edge Locations. This is where Local Zones and Wavelength Zones come in. They are AWS's way of moving compute and storage even closer to users.

Local Zones. When your users are far from the nearest AWS Region, delays start to creep in. Data takes longer to move, and applications can become sluggish. Local Zones fix this by dropping a smaller slice of AWS—compute, storage, and database power—into major cities. This helps enable ultra-low-latency applications like gaming or real-time analytics.

You start by opting in to a Local Zone and linking it to your existing VPC. From there, you carve out a subnet inside that zone—essentially reserving resources, just like you would in a standard AZ. Once that's set, you can launch your services—EC2 instances, EBS volumes, RDS databases—in the city. Your application stays connected to the main AWS Region through a fast, secure network, but now your core resources live closer to the action.

However, Local Zones aren't full-blown AWS Regions. They offer fewer service types and less hardware variety, and there's less built-in redundancy. So it's smart to have a backup plan—say, rerouting workloads to a regular AZ. And note that Local Zones often come with slightly higher hourly rates. Also, not all services are available, like RDS Aurora and EKS.

Wavelength Zones. Imagine AWS moving into a telecom provider's 5G data center—right alongside the equipment that powers your mobile connection. That's what a Wavelength Zone is. Instead of sending mobile data on a long trip to a distant AWS Region, it stays inside the carrier's network and gets processed right there, delivering near-instant responses and ultra-low latency.

Getting started with Wavelength is straightforward. You opt in, link it to your existing VPC, and spin up a subnet inside the Wavelength Zone. From there, you can launch familiar AWS services like EC2 for compute or EBS for storage. A key piece here is the carrier gateway—a specialized connector that ties your AWS instances directly to the telecom's 5G network. So when a user sends a request over 5G, your application gets it almost instantly, without that data ever leaving the carrier's network.

Even though these instances run at the network edge, they still stay connected to your primary AWS Region through a secure, high-speed private link. This means you can tap into Region-based services like RDS or DynamoDB, as if the edge resources were sitting in your cloud environment.

Wavelength Zones and Local Zones don't replace AWS Regions or AZs—they extend them. They're built for cases where location really matters, such as with real-time gaming, video streaming, or connected vehicles. You still rely on the core cloud for most services, but you gain the option to push latency-sensitive parts of your application closer to users. It's a flexible setup that helps you balance performance and scale, depending on what your application needs.

Table 8-3 shows a summary of theEdge Location services in AWS.

Table 8-3. Edge Location services in AWS

Services	Key features
Global Accelerator	• Provides static anycast IPs announced from Edge Locations • Routes traffic over AWS's private backbone for better speed and reliability • Automatically redirects traffic on failure without DNS changes
Amazon Route 53	• Resolves DNS at the edge using a global anycast network • Keeps latency low with 200+ Points of Presence • Data plane stays operational even if the control plane goes down
CloudFront	• Delivers cached content from Edge Locations and Regional caches • Uses AWS's private network for fast, secure content delivery • Reduces trips to the origin, improving speed and lowering backend load
AWS Shield	• Automatically blocks DDoS attacks at Edge Locations • Shield Advanced adds custom protections and real-time visibility • Integrated with services like CloudFront and Route 53
AWS Outposts	• Brings AWS infrastructure to your data center or branch • Supports the service link (to AWS Region) and local gateway (to on-prem systems) • Managed through AWS tools like the Console and the CLI
Local Zones	• Brings compute, storage, and database resources closer to users • Useful for latency-sensitive workloads in metro areas • Integrated with your VPC but offers fewer services than a full Region
Wavelength Zones	• Deploys AWS infrastructure inside telecom 5G data centers • Enables ultra-low latency for mobile and edge devices • Connected to an AWS Region via secure private link

Deploying AWS Services

In Chapter 6, we looked at the different ways to interact with AWS, like with the Management Console, the CLI, SDKs, and CloudShell. But these tools aren't just for poking around or adjusting settings. You can use them to provision and deploy AWS services.

Let's walk through the main options available:

AWS Management Console
> If you're getting started or need to do something quick, the AWS Management Console is a good option. It's for tasks like spinning up an EC2 instance, creating a new S3 bucket, or tweaking a security group. You can do it all from here without touching a line of code. The Management Console is useful when testing the waters or handling small, one-off tasks.

AWS CLI
> When you're ready to automate—or prefer working in a terminal—the AWS CLI gives you scriptable, repeatable control over AWS resources. For example, with a single command like `aws s3 cp file.txt s3://my-bucket`, you can move files around, launch services, or batch-process changes. The CLI is fast, efficient, and fits into your existing shell scripts or automation routines.

AWS SDKs
> If you're writing code and want AWS baked in, the SDKs are libraries that do the heavy lifting behind the scenes. They handle retries, authentication, and other low-level details, so you can focus on building your app.

AWS APIs
> Under the hood, everything—from the CLI to SDKs—talks to AWS through its APIs. These are direct HTTP endpoints that let you interact with AWS services at a low level. You probably won't use them directly unless you're building a custom tool or integrating AWS into something that doesn't support the CLI or SDKs. But if you need full control and don't mind handling authentication and formatting yourself, the APIs are there.

Infrastructure-as-code (IaC) tools
> If you're deploying the same infrastructure more than once—or managing multiple environments like dev, staging, and production—you'll want to look into IaC. Tools like CloudFormation, the AWS Cloud Development Kit (CDK), and Terraform let you define your infrastructure in code or config files. Once written, you can version, reuse, and roll back those definitions just like application code. It's a solid approach for consistency, collaboration, and staying sane as your environment grows.

Table 8-4 shows a summary of the different deployment options.

Table 8-4. Summary of AWS deployment options

AWS tool/method	Description and use cases
AWS Management Console	• For beginners and quick tasks • GUI-based; no coding required • Used for launching EC2, creating S3 buckets, etc. • Best for testing or one-off actions
AWS CLI	• Command Line Interface for automation • Scriptable and repeatable workflows • Fast and efficient for batch operations • Fits well in shell scripts and CI/CD
AWS SDKs	• Code libraries for multiple languages • Integrate AWS into applications directly • Handle retries, auth, and API calls • Ideal for developer workflows
AWS APIs	• Low-level HTTP interfaces to AWS services • Used under the hood by CLI/SDKs • Full control for custom integrations • Requires manual handling of auth/formatting
Infrastructure as code	• Defines infrastructure in code or config files • Tools: CloudFormation, CDK, Terraform • Supports versioning and reuse • Best for managing multi-env setups (dev/staging/prod)

Choosing Between One-Time Tasks and Repeatable Processes in AWS

When you're working in AWS, a common crossroads you'll hit is deciding whether to do something manually, or take the time to automate it for the future. This decision plays a big role in how efficient, scalable, and reliable your cloud setup turns out to be.

Manual, one-time tasks usually happen through the AWS console or a quick CLI command. They're fine for simple, occasional jobs—like spinning up a test server or tweaking a security group on the fly.

On the flip side, automation comes into play when you need to repeat a task regularly or keep things consistent across multiple environments. Tools like AWS CloudFormation, the CLI, SDKs, or Terraform make it easy to turn one-off efforts into codified, repeatable processes. It takes more time upfront, but the payoff is real: fewer errors, smoother scaling, and a setup you can trust to work the same way every time.

The key is knowing which path fits your situation. For production deployments or anything that involves multiple teams or Regions, automation is usually the smarter move. But if it's a quick fix or a throwaway test, manual might make more sense. Striking the right balance helps you stay flexible without sacrificing reliability.

Conclusion

This chapter covered how AWS builds a global, resilient infrastructure using Regions, AZs, and edge services like CloudFront, Route 53, and AWS Shield to deliver low-latency, high-availability applications. We also looked at how AWS extends its reach with Outposts, Local Zones, and Wavelength Zones for edge computing. Finally, we discussed deployment tools—Console, the CLI, SDKs, APIs, and IaC—and how to choose between manual tasks and automation based on your needs.

In the next chapter, we'll look at AWS compute services.

Chapter Quiz

To check your answers, please refer to the "Chapter 8 Answer Key" on page 207.

1. What is the main benefit of using multiple AWS Regions for global applications?

   A. To reduce costs for all storage services

   B. To increase Elastic Compute Cloud (EC2) instance speed

   C. To consolidate resource access logs

   D. To reduce latency and improve disaster recovery

2. Which AWS component is a physical location containing server racks, storage, and networking gear?

   A. Availability Zone

   B. Edge Location

   C. Region

   D. Data center

3. Which AWS service provides built-in distributed denial-of-service (DDoS) protection at Edge Locations?

   A. AWS Shield

   B. Amazon EC2

   C. AWS Config

   D. AWS Virtual Private Network (VPN)

4. Which AWS service uses a tiered caching structure, starting at Edge Locations and scaling up?

A. AWS Shield

B. Amazon Route 53

C. Amazon CloudFront

D. Amazon Elastic Block Store (EBS)

5. How do AWS Regions and Availability Zones (AZs) work together?

A. AZs host entire Regions.

B. Regions are made up of multiple isolated AZs.

C. AZs and Regions are the same.

D. Regions provide caching; AZs do not.

CHAPTER 9

AWS Compute, Containers, and Serverless

Compute is the engine behind running applications, crunching data, and delivering services. On AWS, compute takes several forms. You've got virtual servers through Amazon Elastic Compute Cloud (EC2), container-based setups with Elastic Container Service (ECS) and Elastic Kubernetes Service (EKS), and lightweight, event-driven code with AWS Lambda. Each option strikes a different balance between control, scalability, and how much management you want to handle yourself.

When preparing for the AWS Certified Cloud Practitioner exam, understanding compute is critical. So this chapter walks you through the essentials—how to launch and secure EC2 instances, what containers bring to the table, and how serverless can take infrastructure off your plate entirely. You'll also get familiar with features like Auto Scaling and Elastic Load Balancing (ELB), which help applications stay responsive and cost-effective, even under changing loads.

EC2

In Chapter 2, we saw how Amazon EC2 is one of the core building blocks in AWS's IaaS offerings. At its simplest, EC2 lets you spin up VMs in the cloud. You can launch them, shut them down, configure them to your needs, and manage them remotely. It's one of the most widely used services in AWS, and not surprisingly, it shows up frequently on the exam.

A big draw of EC2 is how quickly you can get started. Launching an instance usually takes just a few minutes once configured. But there are some important steps to consider before the launch. You'll need to select an AMI, choose an instance type (which defines the CPU, memory, and networking capacity), configure the VPC and subnet settings, assign security groups for inbound and outbound traffic, and provision storage for your workloads. These choices determine the performance, cost, and security posture of your instance.

Once launched, you get root access to the instance and can treat it like a regular server. Need to pause and pick things back up later? No problem. When you stop an instance, its data on the boot volume remains intact.

To help with rightsizing, AWS also provides the Compute Optimizer, which analyzes your instance usage and recommends better instance types. This helps avoid overprovisioning, keeps costs in check, and ensures you're getting the right balance of performance and efficiency for your workloads.

But EC2 is built to handle high availability and fault tolerance. For storage, you can attach persistent block storage volumes. To evenly distribute incoming traffic, there's a managed load-balancing service. And when demand fluctuates, an automatic scaling system can dynamically adjust the number of running compute instances.

EC2 Instance Types

EC2 also gives you flexibility in pricing. On-Demand Instances are pay-as-you-go, which is ideal when you don't want to commit long term. If you're looking for lower costs with some commitment, you can choose from Savings Plans. These include Compute Savings Plans (which apply broadly to EC2, Lambda, and Fargate), EC2-specific Savings Plans, and options tailored for Amazon SageMaker, which is used for ML and AI development.

For the deepest discounts, Spot Instances can offer up to 90% savings compared to On-Demand pricing. These are designed for interruptible workloads, such as batch processing, CI/CD pipelines, or other fault-tolerant tasks. However, pricing varies by instance type, region, and demand, and AWS may reclaim your instance at any time if capacity is needed.

Beyond pricing, it's also important to understand storage. EC2 instances can use Amazon EBS for persistent, detachable block storage that survives instance stops and terminations, or instance store volumes for high-performance but ephemeral storage that is lost when the instance stops or terminates. Choosing the right storage option is key to workload durability and performance.

Finally, AWS has been promoting Graviton-based instances (e.g., c7g, m7g), which use custom Arm-based processors. These instances often deliver better price/performance compared to x86-based instances and are increasingly featured on the exam. Many customers adopt Graviton to reduce costs while maintaining or improving workload efficiency.

So let's take a look at an EC2 instance—that is, c5.4xlarge. It's part of the compute-optimized family (that's the "C" in the name), fifth generation ("5"), and it's in the 4xlarge size tier. This provides you 16 vCPUs, 32 GB of RAM, and up to 10 Gbps of network bandwidth. This instance type is a good option if your application is CPU-hungry—think scientific modeling, high-performance web servers, or big batch jobs—and you want good performance without overspending.

AWS organizes EC2 instances into several broad families:

- General-purpose instances, like the M and T series, strike a balance between CPU usage, memory, and networking. They're good choices for things like web servers or development environments, which are workloads that don't spike in just one direction.

- Compute-optimized instances (C series) offer a high ratio of CPU performance to cost. If you're handling intense processing tasks like ad serving, ML inference, and game servers, this is a good choice.

- Memory-optimized instances (R, X, and Z series) come with large amounts of RAM, which is suitable for in-memory databases, caching layers, or data-heavy apps.

- Storage-optimized instances like the I, D, and H series focus on fast, local storage. This is a good fit for transactional databases (OLTP, or online transaction processing), NoSQL systems, data warehouses, or distributed storage platforms.

Security Groups

Security groups act like virtual firewalls that protect your EC2 instances by controlling the flow of traffic in and out. Rather than blocking traffic, they work by explicitly allowing only the types of traffic you specify. Each rule in a security group defines what kind of traffic is permitted, whether it's from a specific IP address, a range of IPs, or even another security group. That last option is especially useful for managing secure communication between instances without relying on fixed IP addresses.

For example, when you launch an EC2 instance, one of your first tasks is to connect to it securely to perform updates, fix issues, or configure settings. For Linux-based EC2 instances, the standard way to connect is through SSH, which is a reliable and encrypted command-line protocol.

How you connect depends on your computer. If you're using macOS or Linux, you're already set. You will open your terminal and use the built-in SSH client. Windows 10 and newer versions also come with built-in SSH support in the terminal, so the process is just as simple. If you're using an older version of Windows, you can still connect using a free tool like PuTTY, which provides a user-friendly interface with the same functionality.

Prefer to avoid setting up any software? AWS offers EC2 Instance Connect, a browser-based solution that works on any device and doesn't require SSH key management or installations. It's especially helpful when you're using a shared or unfamiliar computer and need quick access to your instance.

Regardless, AWS security groups are reusable. You can attach the same security group to multiple EC2 instances, and any single instance can have several groups assigned to it. This gives you flexibility to manage access in layers—without duplicating effort.

There's a catch, though: security groups are tied to a specific region and VPC. If you move to a different region or create a new VPC, you'll need to set them up again from scratch.

Security group rules act at the network level, which is at the edge. If traffic doesn't match the rules, it gets dropped before it ever touches your instance.

For a cleaner setup, it's a good idea to split different types of access into separate security groups. For instance, keep SSH access rules in one group and web traffic rules in another. By doing this, each group stays focused, easier to manage, and more secure. It also makes auditing and troubleshooting a lot simpler down the line.

When configuring security group rules, you'll work with specific port numbers that correspond to different services and protocols. Understanding these standard port assignments is essential for properly securing your instances while maintaining necessary functions:

Port 22: SSH/SFTP (SSH File Transfer Protocol)
   Allows secure login to Linux EC2 instances and secure file transfers.

Port 21: FTP (File Transfer Protocol)
   Used for basic file transfers and is not encrypted.

Port 80: HTTP (Hypertext Transfer Protocol)
   Handles standard, unencrypted web traffic.

Port 443: HTTPS (Hypertext Transfer Protocol Secure)
   Supports encrypted, secure web traffic—commonly used by most modern websites.

Port 3389: RDP (Remote Desktop Protocol)
   Enables remote desktop access to Windows-based EC2 instances.

Setting Up an EC2 Instance

Let's see how to create an EC2 instance.

1. Log in to AWS.
2. Search for EC2 and click on it.
3. Select Instances on the left sidebar menu.
4. Select "Launch an instance." Figure 9-1 shows the screen for this.

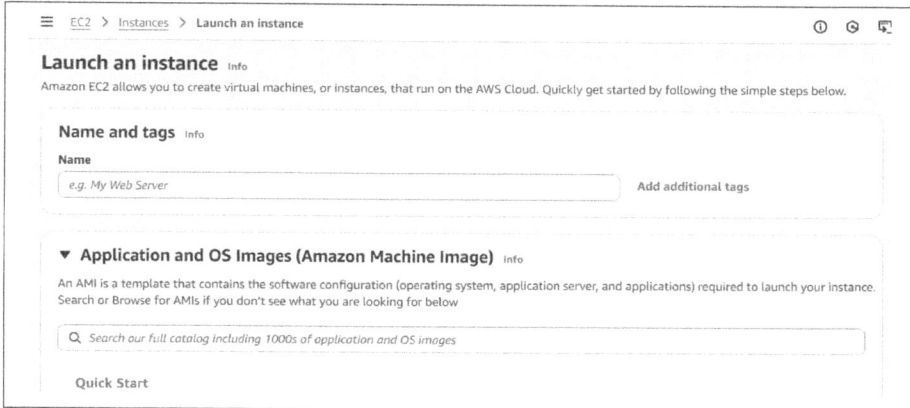

Figure 9-1. The dashboard for setting up an EC2 instance

5. Enter a name for the EC2 instance.
6. You will select a base image for the EC2 instance, which is the OS. Some of the main ones include Windows, Amazon Linux, macOS, Red Hat, and SUSE Linux.
7. You will select an instance type. For example, if you choose Amazon Linux, there are dozens available. You will select the one that will meet your performance needs, such as in terms of the CPU, memory, and costs. If you select "Compare instance types," you can see the differences.
8. You can use a key pair to securely connect to your instance using SSH. When launching your EC2 instance, select "Create key pair" to generate the credentials needed for secure login.

   Figure 9-2 shows the screen for this.

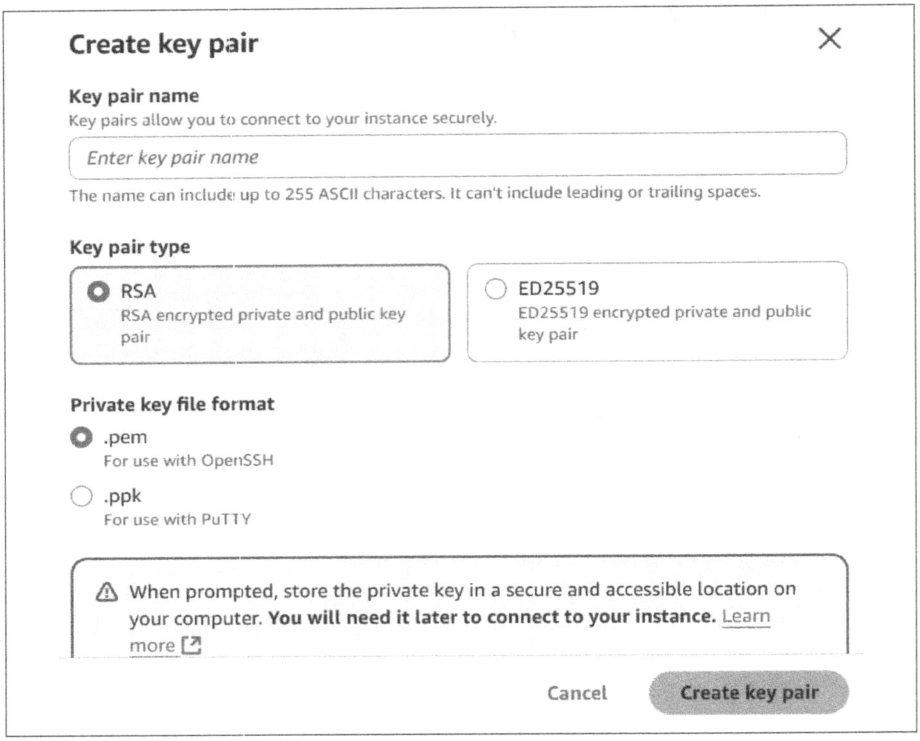

Figure 9-2. The setup for a key pair

You will enter a name for the key pair and select an encryption type, such as RSA or ED25519. (RSA stands for Rivest, Shamir, and Adleman, who described the algorithm that supports the cryptosystem.) You will also select a file format.

9. For "Network settings," you'll choose the VPC where the instance will reside. If you don't have a custom VPC, you can use the default one provided by AWS. Next, you select a subnet, which defines the Availability Zone and IP address range. You'll also decide whether to enable "Auto-assign public IP," which allows the instance to be reachable from the internet. For security, you can create or select an existing security group.

10. In "Configure storage," you'll define the size and type of the root volume, which is the main disk attached to your VM. By default, EC2 uses EBS for this purpose. You can increase the size from the default (usually 8 GB or more) based on your application's needs.

11. Select "Launch instance." It will take 10 to 20 seconds for it to be activated.

In addition to manually managing Spot Instances for batch jobs, AWS also provides AWS Batch. This is a fully managed service designed for batch processing workloads.

AWS Batch takes care of provisioning and scaling compute resources—including both On-Demand and Spot Instances—so you don't have to manage the underlying infrastructure. It handles job scheduling, cost optimization, and workload orchestration. This makes it well-suited for tasks like large-scale data processing, scientific simulations, and rendering. Since AWS Batch is considered a key compute-related service, it's important to be familiar with it for the CLF-C02 exam.

Container Services

Building an application rarely starts with a blank slate. Developers lean heavily on external libraries, frameworks, and modules to accelerate the process. Some examples include routing tools, model–view–controller (MVC) frameworks, or backend helpers that come preloaded with security and async capabilities. One framework might handle cross-platform frontend work, while another streamlines API development in C# or whatever your stack calls for.

In addition to frameworks, many teams use containers to package code and dependencies together. Containers ensure consistent environments across development, testing, and production. This helps to reduce the classic "works on my machine" problem. Compared to VMs, containers start up faster, use fewer resources, and provide improved portability. These benefits make them a natural fit for microservices architectures and CI/CD pipelines, where speed, scalability, and reliability are critical.

But pulling in those dependencies can be challenging for the following reasons:

Steep learning curves
Every library comes with its own way of doing things: configs, syntax, and patterns you have to learn from scratch.

Rigid structures
Some tools are so opinionated that they box you into their way of thinking, which limits how much you can tweak or customize.

Code bloat
Dependencies often pack in more features than you actually use, which can drag down your application's performance.

Version whiplash
Updates can break applications. One change in a third-party package can leave you scrambling to patch things up.

Security blind spots
When you rely on someone else's code, you're also trusting that they're handling security properly. That's not always a safe bet, especially with smaller, less-maintained projects.

Containers can make a lot of these problems easier to manage. When you use something like Docker to bundle your code, configs, and dependencies into a single container image, you create a clean, portable unit that works the same whether it's running on Windows, Linux, your laptop, or the cloud. This consistency means fewer unpleasant surprises when moving between environments.

Once your app lives inside a container, an orchestration layer—like Kubernetes or AWS ECS—can take over. It'll handle the nitty-gritty of scaling, load balancing, rolling updates, and keeping your services healthy without much hand-holding.

AWS brings a full toolbox for running containers at scale. Whether you're after control, managed simplicity, or something in between, AWS has a container service that fits.

Amazon Elastic Container Service (ECS)

ECS makes it easier to run containers on AWS. It's fully managed and built to scale, so you don't have to worry about spinning up servers, patching them, handling networking, or keeping track of cluster health. You define your containers, and ECS handles the rest. One key advantage with ECS is how well it integrates with other AWS services. It ties into IAM, VPC, CloudWatch, and load balancers.

At the core of ECS is the concept of a task definition. This is a JSON script that tells ECS what container images to run, how much CPU allocation and memory to give them, which ports to expose, and what roles or volumes they need. You can launch these as tasks or long-running services inside ECS clusters.

Clusters themselves are logical groups of compute resources. You can use EC2 instances if you want direct control over the underlying infrastructure and OS configuration. ECS schedules, launches, stops, and monitors your containers automatically to keep things running smoothly.

If managing EC2 instances sounds like too much, Fargate is a good option. You specify your app's requirements—CPU, memory, network settings—and Fargate figures out the infrastructure part. You don't see or manage the servers at all.

ECS also supports Fargate Spot, which uses spare capacity for lower cost. It's a good option for flexible workloads that can handle the occasional interruption (you'll get a two-minute heads-up when it happens). Every task runs in its own isolated environment, with built-in monitoring and load balancing support.

ECS has auto-scaling features. If you're using EC2-backed clusters, it watches metrics like how full your capacity providers are and adjusts your Auto Scaling groups to match demand. That way, you don't end up overpaying for idle resources or running short when traffic spikes.

For running services, ECS can scale the number of tasks based on CPU and memory usage, scheduled rules, or predictive patterns. This helps you keep costs in check while maintaining performance.

Amazon Elastic Kubernetes Service (EKS)

Kubernetes has become a popular platform for running containers at scale. It handles everything from deploying and scaling applications to managing their entire lifecycle. Under the hood, it groups containers into pods (essentially units of work) and spreads them across a cluster of nodes. This setup gives you high availability, built-in fault tolerance, and the ability to describe your infrastructure using clean, declarative configs.

However, managing Kubernetes can be complicated. That's where EKS comes in. It handles the control plane for you and spreads it across three Availability Zones for better resilience. If anything fails, EKS quietly replaces it behind the scenes.

You get a fully managed, single-tenant Kubernetes endpoint that's 100% compatible with upstream Kubernetes. This means you can plug in all your favorite community tools and use the same patterns you're already familiar with.

EKS also ties into key AWS services. You can route traffic through ELB, manage access with IAM, and set up fine-grained networking for your pods using the AWS Container Network Interface (CNI) plugin and your VPC.

EKS also offers Auto Mode, where AWS goes even further by managing the data plane too. It handles everything from networking and storage to patching and auto-scaling.

AWS Lambda

The term "serverless" can throw people off. It doesn't mean there are no servers. Instead, it means you don't have to manage them. With serverless, you write code, and the cloud provider takes care of the rest: provisioning, scaling, maintenance, and uptime. Everything runs behind the scenes, so you can focus on building and shipping features. Your application scales automatically as demand changes, and you're only billed for the exact time your code runs. That makes serverless a good choice for projects that need to move fast, stay flexible, and use resources efficiently.

In this book, we've already seen a variety of serverless systems:

- Amazon S3 gives you serverless file storage. You upload files, and it scales automatically. No need to think about disk space or servers.

- Amazon DynamoDB offers a serverless NoSQL database. You define your table, and AWS handles throughput, replication, and scaling.

Another popular one is Lambda. It is Amazon's implementation of function as a service (FaaS), which is a cloud computing model where you run code in response to events without managing servers or infrastructure. Instead of provisioning a VM like you would with EC2, you upload your function and define a trigger (such as an HTTP request or a file upload), and AWS takes care of the rest. This includes running your code when needed, scaling automatically, and stopping when the job is done.

Lambda supports many popular programming languages like Node.js, Python, Java, C# (via .NET Core or PowerShell), and Ruby. And thanks to the custom runtime API, you can use languages like Rust or Go. If you prefer working with containers, Lambda has support for that too, although ECS or Fargate might be a better fit for full-fledged container workloads.

Monitoring is baked in through CloudWatch, so you can track what your functions are doing without bolting on extra tools.

Here are a couple of real-world examples of how Lambda is used:

Serverless image processing
> Let's say someone uploads a photo to S3. That upload can trigger a Lambda function to create a thumbnail, save it back to S3, and optionally log some metadata—like file size or upload time—to DynamoDB.

Automated cron jobs
> Instead of writing a cron job on a Linux box, you can schedule a Lambda function using EventBridge. It can run hourly, daily, weekly—whatever you need—without you having to maintain a server.

API backends
> You can pair Lambda with API Gateway to create scalable, cost-efficient web or mobile backends. Each incoming request triggers a function execution.

Let's now see how to create a Lambda function.

1. Log into AWS. Search for Lambda. Select it.

2. Choose "Create function." You will be taken to the setup screen, which you can see in Figure 9-3.

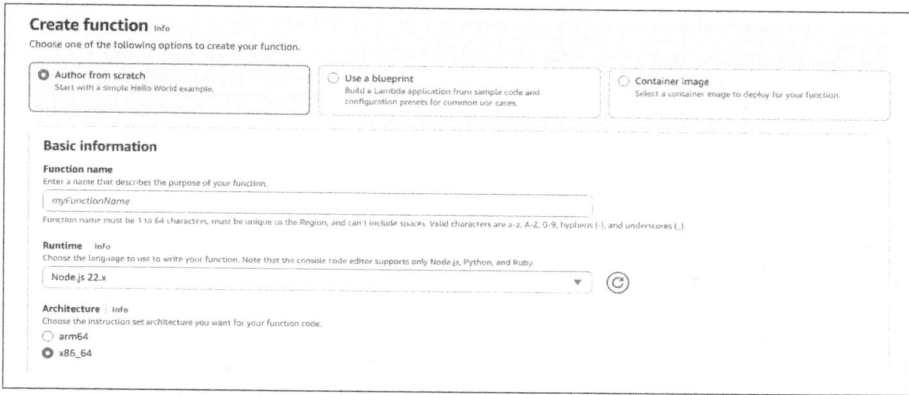

Figure 9-3. Dashboard for creating a Lambda function

3. You'll see three options: "Author from scratch," "Use a blueprint," and "Container image." Select "Author from scratch."

4. Enter a description name for the Lambda function. It can be from 1 to 64 characters, but it can only have letters, numbers, hyphens, and underscores.

5. Select a language.

6. Choose the architecture, which is either x86_64 (default) or arm64 (Graviton2).

7. Use the default option to allow Amazon to collect logs using CloudWatch Logs.

8. Choose "Create function." You will be taken to a screen that allows for managing the Lambda function, which you can see in Figure 9-4.

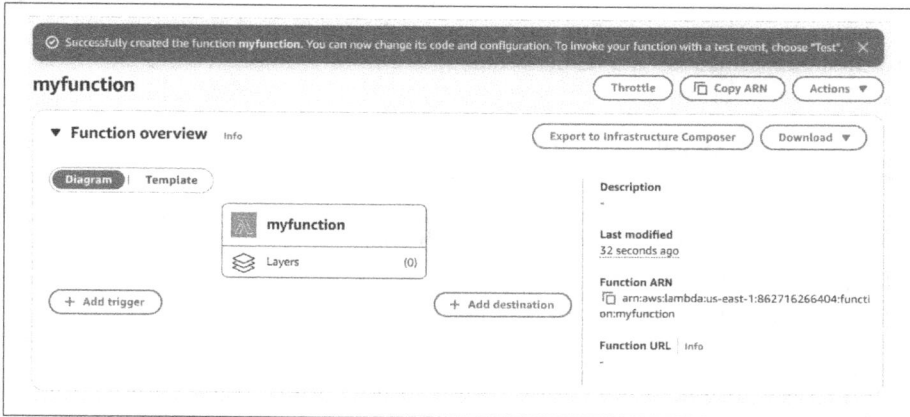

Figure 9-4. Management screen for a Lambda function

9. Scroll down and you'll see a menu. The Code option shows a "Hello world" Lambda function. Here, you can enter your own code. You can also upload code from a *.zip* file or an S3 bucket.

10. You can select "Test to run the Lambda function."

11. When you are finished testing the function, you can select Deploy to put it into production.

AWS Compute Elasticity

Compute elasticity in AWS refers to a cloud system's ability to automatically scale compute resources up or down in response to changing workload demands. Whether it's a predictable sales spike or unexpected viral traffic, AWS can dynamically adjust infrastructure to match the load. This elasticity is a key architectural advantage of cloud computing. Two AWS services help make it happen: Auto Scaling and ELB.

Auto Scaling is AWS's mechanism for right sizing compute capacity in real time. You define parameters like minimum, maximum, and desired EC2 instance counts within an Auto Scaling Group (ASG), and then set policies based on metrics such as CPU utilization or request rate. As demand increases, Auto Scaling adds instances; when demand drops, it removes them. While this is most often thought of as horizontal scaling (adding or removing instances), modern automation tools can also adjust instance sizes in some scenarios, enabling limited vertical scaling.

Beyond reactive scaling, AWS also offers predictive scaling, which uses ML models to anticipate demand and proactively adjust capacity. This helps applications stay ahead of traffic spikes rather than simply reacting to them. Auto Scaling also improves fault tolerance by continuously monitoring instance health and automatically replacing any that fail. You can fine-tune behavior using scheduled scaling (for predictable loads), target tracking (for specific metrics), or step scaling (for gradual changes).

ELB complements Auto Scaling by distributing incoming traffic across multiple healthy compute targets—like EC2 instances, containers, or IP addresses—spanning multiple Availability Zones. ELB ensures high availability and fault tolerance by routing traffic only to resources that pass health checks and scaling itself to handle varying traffic volumes.

There are multiple types of ELBs:

- Application Load Balancer (ALB) for advanced HTTP/HTTPS routing
- Network Load Balancer (NLB) for ultra-low-latency Transmission Control Protocol (TCP) traffic
- Gateway Load Balancer (GWLB) for integrating third-party network appliances

---

Each type offers features like SSL/TLS termination, session stickiness, and integration with AWS WAF (Web Application Firewall) for enhanced performance and security.

To extend elasticity beyond servers, AWS also offers Lambda Layers, which let developers package and share dependencies, libraries, or custom code across multiple Lambda functions. This reduces duplication, simplifies updates, and makes serverless applications more efficient—an increasingly common topic on AWS exams.

When used together, Auto Scaling and ELB create a robust and cost-effective architecture. New instances launched by Auto Scaling are automatically registered with the load balancer; those terminated are cleanly removed. ELB continuously directs traffic only to healthy instances, while Auto Scaling ensures there's enough capacity to meet demand without overspending.

Conclusion

In this chapter, we learned how AWS approaches compute, from the flexibility of EC2 instances to the streamlined deployment of containers and the hands-off simplicity of serverless functions like Lambda. We also touched on critical features like Auto Scaling and ELB, which help your applications adapt to demand without burning through your budget.

In the next chapter, we'll take a look at storage and database services for AWS.

Chapter Quiz

To check your answers, please refer to the "Chapter 9 Answer Key" on page 207.

1. Which Elastic Compute Cloud (EC2) instance type is best suited for compute-heavy workloads?

   A. T series

   B. R series

   C. C series

   D. M series

2. Which service allows Kubernetes orchestration in a fully managed environment?

   A. EC2

   B. Lambda

   C. Amazon Elastic Kubernetes Service (EKS)

   D. AWS Outposts

3. What AWS service would you use to scale EC2 instances automatically?

   A. Route 53

   B. Auto Scaling

   C. Amazon Virtual Private Cloud (VPC)

   D. CloudFront

4. What is the primary function of Elastic Load Balancing (ELB)?

   A. To back up data across Regions

   B. To distribute incoming traffic across multiple resources

   C. To encrypt files in Simple Storage Service (S3)

   D. To provide caching for EC2 instances

5. In Amazon EKS, what is the smallest deployable unit?

   A. Container

   B. Node

   C. Pod

   D. Task

CHAPTER 10

AWS Storage Services

Storing today's massive amounts of data takes more than just traditional solutions. Companies need storage that scales, maintains reliability, and doesn't pressure the budget.

That's where AWS storage services prove their worth. There's Amazon S3 for object storage, EBS for block storage, Elastic File System (EFS) and FSx for shared file storage, Storage Gateway for bridging on-premises and cloud data, and AWS Backup for data protection. Together, these services form a solid toolkit for almost any workload.

And yes, these are all topics that frequently appear on the AWS Certified Cloud Practitioner exam. It's important to understand what these services do, their use cases, and how they integrate with the rest of AWS.

Overview

By 2025, Edge Delta projects (*https://oreil.ly/v9Ul0*) that the world will generate about 175 zettabytes (ZB) of data (this is one billion terabytes). This is a massive jump from the 33 ZB produced in 2018. Nearly half of this massive volume will live in the cloud.

Here are some of the main drivers for the growth:

Artificial intelligence
Training cutting-edge models like those from OpenAI, Microsoft, and Amazon takes enormous amounts of data. Some models crunch through massive datasets that span much of the internet. And as training moves beyond text to images and video, the appetite for data only grows.

Mobile devices
Billions of people carry smartphones, and they're streaming, uploading, and browsing constantly.

Internet of Things
> These include sensors for smart homes and connected factories. Each one gathers a steady stream of data.

Streaming services
> Platforms like Netflix, Peacock, and Disney+ attract millions of viewers who watch content online every day.

All this data has to go somewhere. Storing it isn't cheap, and the scale requires advanced systems like direct-attached storage, network-attached storage (NAS), or storage area networks (SANs). These setups can be powerful but also complex and expensive to manage.

Under the AWS Shared Responsibility Model, AWS takes care of the infrastructure that powers its storage services. This is known as security of the cloud. Customers, however, are responsible for security in the cloud: configuring encryption, setting access controls, and managing backup policies. This division ensures that while AWS provides a secure, reliable foundation, customers must still take proactive steps to safeguard their own data.

Let's take a look at the Amazon storage services you'll likely see on the exam.

Amazon S3

Simple Storage Service (S3) is AWS's service for object storage. This is available through the AWS console, the CLI, SDKs, or REST APIs.

Behind the scenes, S3 runs on a massively scalable infrastructure. There's no cap on how much you can store overall, and each individual object can be as large as 5 terabytes.

Durability is one of S3's biggest advantages. It's built to keep your data safe with 99.999999999% durability referred to as "11 nines" durability by automatically distributing copies of your files across multiple Availability Zones. You also get 99.99% availability, which is backed by a service-level agreement (SLA). This is a contract between a service provider and a customer, which sets the levels of service for a system.

It's important to note, however, that not all S3 storage classes replicate data across multiple AZs. For example, S3 One Zone-Infrequent Access (IA) and S3 Express One Zone store data in a single Availability Zone, which reduces redundancy and results in lower durability compared to multi-AZ storage classes. Customers should select a storage class based on their specific durability, availability, and cost requirements.

In terms of security, S3 supports encrypted data in transit (using SSL/TLS) and at rest (server-side or client-side encryption). You can also control who has access with IAM roles, bucket policies, and features like Object Lock, which is useful for compliance needs like write-once-read-many (WORM) storage.

Here are common use cases for S3:

Primary storage for cloud apps
> S3 is useful for hosting website assets, mobile app backends, gaming content, and files for distribution.

Data lakes and analytics
> S3 integrates with AWS tools like Athena, Redshift, and Elastic MapReduce (EMR) for large-scale data analysis.

Backup and disaster recovery
> S3 has features such as lifecycle policies that can be used for off-site backups. Lifecycle policies consist of rules that shift older backups to cheaper storage tiers or delete them when they're no longer needed.

Serverless and event-driven workflows
> You can trigger Lambda functions on file uploads, integrate with the API Gateway, or route messages through SNS and Simple Queue Service (SQS) for automation.

Amazon S3 allows you to balance cost and performance with its tiered storage system. Instead of treating all your data the same, you can pick a storage class that matches how often you need to access the data, how quickly you need to retrieve it, and how much availability you want.

Let's take a look at S3's storage classes.

General Purpose

If you need fast, reliable access to your data, S3 Standard is your best starting point. It's the default storage class in S3. Your data is spread across at least three Availability Zones, so even if one zone has issues, your files stay safe and available.

This class is suitable for cloud native applications, dynamic websites, content delivery, and analytics workloads. You get low latency and high throughput.

Unpredictable or Changing Access

S3 Intelligent-Tiering is designed for when access to your data is unpredictable. The service automatically moves your data between five access tiers: Frequent Access, Infrequent Access, Archive Instant Access, Archive Access, and Deep Archive Access. The last two tiers—Archive Access and Deep Archive Access—require opt-in but provide additional cost savings for rarely accessed data.

You still get the same multi-AZ durability and millisecond-level latency of S3 Standard.

High-Performance, Single-AZ Access

For workloads where speed is critical and cross-AZ resilience isn't required, S3 Express One Zone is optimized for sub-millisecond latency and high throughput. This makes it ideal for applications that demand ultra-fast data access without the overhead of multi-AZ replication.

S3 Express is for use cases like running real-time analytics, ML training, or tightly coupled workloads near compute resources (like AWS Local Zones or Outposts).

Infrequent Access

When data persists for long durations and does not get accessed much, Amazon S3 offers two storage classes that can save you money without sacrificing durability.

S3 Standard-IA is designed for infrequently accessed data that still needs to be readily available when accessed. It provides the same 11 nines of durability as S3 Standard and stores data across multiple AZs, but with slightly lower availability at 99.9%. The trade-off is lower storage costs, balanced by retrieval fees. This makes it a good fit for backups, disaster recovery plans, and older datasets that don't change often.

S3 One Zone-IA is a lower-cost option that stores your data in one AZ. You still get the same high durability, but availability drops to 99.5%, and there's no cross-AZ redundancy.

Archive

When you need to store data long-term but access it rarely, S3's archive classes provide flexible retrieval options depending on how fast you need the data back. There are AWS services for this:

S3 Glacier Instant Retrieval
   You get millisecond-level access, multi-AZ durability, and much lower storage costs compared to active storage classes. It's a good choice for things like archived media, medical imaging, or compliance records that need to be available on demand.

S3 Glacier Flexible Retrieval (formerly called "Glacier")
   This gives you a range of retrieval speeds, from minutes for expedited requests to several hours for bulk jobs. It's built for long-term data that you access occasionally. This class is good for backups or archives that need to stay safe but aren't time-sensitive.

S3 Glacier Deep Archive

This option is built for data you rarely, if ever, need to access, such as legal records or regulatory data that you have to keep for years. You'll wait 12 to 48 hours for retrieval, but you'll pay significantly less to store it.

Data Residency and Isolation

When data needs to stay within a specific geographic boundary—whether for compliance, sovereignty, or performance—Amazon S3 offers options designed to meet those strict requirements.

S3 on Outposts brings the familiar S3 interface to your on-premises environment using AWS Outposts hardware. Your data stays local, stored on redundant devices within the Outposts rack, but it's managed using the same S3 API you'd use in the cloud.

Directory buckets in Dedicated Local Zones anchor your data inside a tightly controlled perimeter. These buckets support classes like Express One Zone and One Zone-IA. They allow you to keep data physically within a jurisdiction while still using S3's robust API, access controls, and security features.

Global Data Transfers

For scenarios where data must move quickly across regions, S3 Transfer Acceleration uses Amazon CloudFront's globally distributed edge locations to speed up uploads to S3 buckets. This is especially valuable for transferring large files or datasets over long distances, helping reduce latency and improve performance for globally distributed teams.

Using S3

Let's see how to create an S3 bucket:

1. Log in to AWS.
2. In the search box, enter S3. Select it.
3. Click "Create bucket."
4. Enter a name for the bucket. Figure 10-1 shows the setup screen for this.

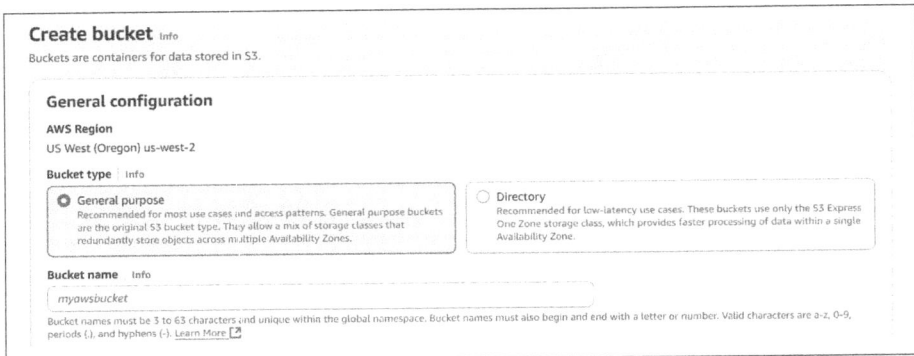

Figure 10-1. Setup for an S3 bucket

5. Choose an AWS region. Select the one closest to you so as to reduce latency.

6. Use the default bucket type of "General purpose," which is the standard for multiple AZs.

7. Enter a name for the S3 bucket.

8. You will select the object ownership settings. The recommended option is to disable access control lists (ACLs) by choosing "Bucket owner enforced." This makes your account the owner of all objects in the bucket and simplifies access management.

9. You can set whether your files are publicly accessible. But the recommended option is to block all public access.

10. Select Disable for "Public versioning." This means there will not be any versions maintained for your objects.

11. You can set the encryption settings. Select "Amazon S3 managed Keys."

12. Select "Create bucket." Figure 10-2 shows your S3 bucket.

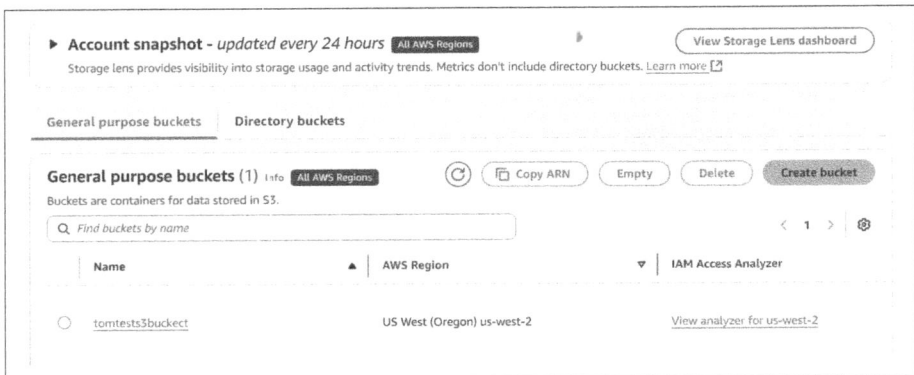

Figure 10-2. Summary of your S3 buckets

13. Click the name of your bucket. Select Upload, and you can choose one or more files or folders to upload.

Amazon Elastic Block Store (EBS)

Amazon EBS is the main boot storage for your EC2 instances. It's a durable, high-performance block storage system that automatically replicates data within its Availability Zone. This means if the underlying hardware fails, your data remains protected. AWS reports annual failure rates (AFRs) of 0.1–0.2% for standard EBS volumes, which makes them reliable for everything from development workloads to production databases. Different volume types offer varying levels of performance and resilience, letting you balance cost, throughput, and availability based on your needs.

Performance remains consistently low in latency. You can also adjust volume size, performance, and type dynamically using Elastic Volumes. You can do this without needing to stop your instance or experiencing downtime.

EBS offers several volume types tuned for different needs:

General Purpose SSD (solid-state drive) (gp2 and gp3)
These work well for boot volumes, development environments, and most general-purpose applications. Gp3, in particular, provides a baseline performance of 3,000 IOPS and 125 MiB/s throughput at any volume size, with the ability to provision additional performance up to 80,000 IOPS and 2,000 MiB/s throughput for an additional cost. This delivers a strong balance of predictable performance, flexibility, and cost efficiency.

Provisioned IOPS SSD (io1, io2, io2 Block Express)
If you're running mission-critical database workloads, these volumes are a good option. They scale up to 256,000 IOPS and 4,000 MB/s throughput, with sub-millisecond latency and sizes up to 64 terabytes. This combination supports heavy database transactions without bottlenecks.

Throughput Optimized HDD (hard disk drive) (st1)
This is suitable for big data workloads and data warehouses where high throughput (MB/s) is more important than IOPS.

Cold HDD (sc1)
This is built for infrequently accessed data with moderate throughput requirements.

For security, EBS volumes support encryption both at rest and in transit. They use Advanced Encryption Standard (AES)-256 encryption with AWS KMS.

Snapshots in EBS act as point-in-time backups. These are incremental, meaning only changed data blocks are stored. This reduces both backup time and storage costs.

You can use snapshots to create new volumes, replicate data across AZs or regions, share data between AWS accounts, or enable fast restores. Other advanced snapshot features include locking for compliance, cross-region copies, archiving, and automated lifecycle management with Data Lifecycle Manager.

When you attach an EBS volume to an EC2 instance, it functions like a native block device. You can format it with any file system your OS supports and treat it like a local disk. The data remains persistent across reboots and detachments.

Multi-Attach for io2 Block Express lets you attach one EBS storage volume to multiple EC2 instances at the same time (as long as they are in the same Availability Zone). This is useful for high-availability applications that need multiple servers to access the same data. Instead of making several copies of the same storage, all the servers can read/write to the same volume. This feature is designed for very high-performance and mission-critical workloads, but the application must be written to handle multiple servers writing to the same storage safely.

AWS Elastic File System (EFS)

AWS Elastic File System (EFS) is a plug-and-play file storage system in the cloud. It can also connect to on-premises servers.

One of its most helpful features is how it scales automatically. If your storage needs grow, EFS expands to keep up, scaling to petabytes without any interruptions. When your needs shrink, it scales down just as easily.

Here are some of its other key features:

- EFS supports standard NFS (Network File System) protocols, versions 4.0 and 4.1. Multiple EC2 instances, or even your Linux servers running on-premises, can read from and write to the same file system at the same time. This makes it a good choice for workloads that need shared file access.

- Similar to S3's tiering, EFS can move files you don't use often into lower-cost storage classes like Infrequent Access or Archive. This happens automatically.

- You can set up multiple entry points into the same file system. Each access point can have its own root directory and enforce specific POSIX (Portable Operating System Interface) user and group permissions (POSIX is a set of standards to maintain compatibility between operating systems). This approach makes it easy to secure different applications that share the same EFS.

- When you create a regional file system, EFS stores your data redundantly across multiple AZs. It offers 11 nines' (99.999999999%) durability and up to four nines' (99.99%) availability. Throughput and IOPS scale automatically to meet your workload demands.

AWS FSx

Amazon FSx is a fully managed, high-performance file system that offers multiple options to fit different workload needs:

- FSx for Windows File Server is built specifically for Windows environments. It supports the Server Message Block (SMB) protocol, integrates smoothly with Active Directory, and includes features like file restore, quotas, access controls, and automatic backups. All of this is done with enterprise-grade security and scalability.

- FSx for Lustre is designed for compute-heavy workloads such as high-performance computing (HPC) and big data processing. It delivers ultra-fast, scalable storage with millions of IOPS and high throughput. It supports POSIX access for Linux-based applications and integrates directly with Amazon S3 for durable data storage.

- FSx for NetApp ONTAP brings the popular enterprise-grade NetApp ONTAP file system to AWS. It provides advanced features like multiprotocol access (NFS; SMB; Internet Small Computer Systems Interface, or iSCSI), inline data deduplication, compression, thin provisioning, and SnapMirror replication for disaster recovery. It's well-suited for enterprise applications needing flexible, shared storage.

- FSx for OpenZFS offers a fully managed Zettabyte File System (ZFS) with strong data integrity, snapshots, and cloning capabilities. It's a good choice for Linux-based workloads that need robust data protection and efficient storage management.

Deployment and scaling are straightforward across all FSx variants. You can adjust capacity or performance levels, choose between single or multi-AZ setups, and integrate these file systems with other AWS services to meet diverse workload requirements.

AWS Storage Gateway

AWS Storage Gateway allows you to connect your on-premises data center to AWS storage without having to rip and replace your existing setup. You deploy it as a virtual appliance, running on VMware, Hyper-V, or Kernel-based Virtual Machine (KVM). You can also launch it as an EC2 instance. Once deployed, it securely connects your local applications to AWS storage. It also caches frequently accessed data locally, so your users get low-latency performance.

There are four types of Storage Gateway:

S3 File Gateway

> This gateway lets you present Amazon S3 as a file share via NFS or SMB protocols. Files are stored in S3 as objects, so you can apply S3 lifecycle policies for archiving or tiering. It's a good choice for backups, archives, and hybrid data workflows.

FSx File Gateway

> This type gives your on-premises users access to Amazon FSx file shares—typically FSx for Windows File Server—using SMB. It caches files locally and keeps them synchronized with FSx. This option is good for scenarios where teams in multiple locations need to share files seamlessly.

Volume Gateway

> If you need block storage, Volume Gateway provides it using iSCSI, a network protocol that allows you to send commands for local hard drives over IP networks. You can run it in cached mode, where your main data sits in S3 and frequently accessed data is cached locally, or in stored mode, where your full data set remains on-premises and backups are sent to S3. This flexibility makes it a good option for hybrid storage needs and disaster recovery plans.

Tape Gateway

> This replaces physical tape libraries with a virtual tape library (VTL). Your existing backup software treats it like a normal tape system, but behind the scenes, virtual tapes are stored in S3 and can be archived to Glacier tiers.

Setting up Storage Gateway is straightforward. You install the appliance, activate it through the AWS console or API, choose the gateway type you need, and connect it to the appropriate AWS storage service. Your applications continue using standard file or block protocols without realizing that the data now lives in the cloud.

AWS Backup

AWS Backup is a fully managed service that centralizes backup management across your AWS resources and hybrid environments. Instead of juggling separate scripts or tools for each service, you can set up everything from a single console, the CLI, or APIs.

With AWS Backup, you can create backup plans that define what gets backed up, how often, and for how long. You can set schedules, retention rules, and lifecycle transitions to cold storage, and specify vault locations.

One of its strengths is policy-based backup. You can assign backups to resources using tags, automate lifecycle management, and run incremental backups to cut down on storage costs. All backups are encrypted with KMS by default.

If you need to replicate backups for disaster recovery or compliance, AWS Backup makes that straightforward too. You can copy backups across regions or accounts, ensuring you have resilient copies in different locations. For example, you might schedule DynamoDB or RDS backups to be retained and restored in another region to meet your recovery time objectives (RTOs) and recovery point objectives (RPOs).

Vaults in AWS Backup are immutable. This means that data can't be changed once it's written.

For hybrid environments, AWS Backup integrates with Storage Gateway and VMware workloads, giving you a centralized way to manage backups across on-premises and cloud data.

Table 10-1 summarizes the different AWS storage services.

Table 10-1. AWS storage services

AWS service	Key points
Amazon S3	• Object storage with unlimited scalability and 11 nines durability • Multiple storage classes for cost and performance optimization • Supports encryption, access controls, and event-driven workflows
Amazon EBS	• Block storage for EC2 with consistent low latency • Offers SSD, provisioned IOPS, and HDD volume types • Supports snapshots, encryption, and Multi-Attach for io2 Block Express
Amazon EFS	• Fully managed, scalable file storage with NFS support • Shared access across multiple EC2 or on-premises servers • Automatic tiering to lower-cost storage and strong durability (11 nines)
AWS FSx	• Managed file systems for Windows (SMB) and Lustre (HPC) • Supports enterprise features like Active Directory integration • High-performance, scalable storage with simple deployment
AWS Storage Gateway	• Connects on-premises environments to AWS storage • Offers File Gateway (S3, FSx), Volume Gateway, and Tape Gateway • Caches frequently accessed data locally for low-latency access
AWS Backup	• Centralized, policy-based backup for AWS and hybrid workloads • Supports scheduling, retention, and lifecycle transitions to cold storage • Enables cross-region/account backups with encryption and vault lock

Conclusion

In this chapter, we learned about the key AWS storage services that power modern cloud applications. We looked at Amazon S3 for scalable object storage, Amazon EBS for reliable block storage with flexible performance options, and Amazon EFS for seamless file storage with shared access. We also covered specialized services like AWS FSx for Windows and HPC needs, Storage Gateway for hybrid environments, and AWS Backup for centralized, policy-based data protection.

In the next chapter, we'll take a look at AWS services for databases.

Chapter Quiz

To check your answers, please refer to the "Chapter 10 Answer Key" on page 207.

1. What is the main advantage of Amazon Simple Storage Service (S3)'s durability model?

   A. It automatically distributes copies across multiple Availability Zones.

   B. It uses local redundant array of inexpensive/independent disks (RAID) storage for durability.

   C. It relies on customer-managed backups.

   D. It only stores data in one Availability Zone.

2. What is the retrieval time for S3 Glacier Deep Archive?

   A. Milliseconds

   B. Minutes

   C. Hours

   D. 12 to 48 hours

3. Which AWS service enables tape-based backup applications to store data in Amazon S3 or Glacier?

   A. FSx File Gateway

   B. Volume Gateway

   C. Tape Gateway

   D. S3 File Gateway

4. Which AWS storage service supports Multi-Attach to connect a volume to multiple Elastic Compute Cloud (EC2) instances simultaneously?

   A. Amazon S3

   B. Amazon Elastic File System (EFS)

   C. Amazon Elastic Block Store (EBS) io2 Block Express

   D. AWS Backup

5. What type of storage is Amazon EBS categorized as?

   A. Object storage

   B. Block storage

   C. File storage

   D. Archive storage

CHAPTER 11

AWS Database Services

A self-managed EC2-hosted database is where you handle tasks like installing the operating system, configuring the database engine, applying security patches, setting up backups, and replicating data. You will also need to set up the systems for availability, scaling, and monitoring. However, a key advantage of this type of database is that you have full control and flexibility. This can certainly be important for mission-critical databases.

AWS also offers a number of managed database services so that you don't have to manage all these tasks yourself. Services like Amazon RDS, Aurora, DynamoDB, ElastiCache, and DocumentDB handle the heavy lifting for you.

That said, running your own database on EC2 might look cheaper if you only compare instance costs, especially when using Reserved Instances. But don't overlook the hidden costs. Your team will spend significant effort on upkeep and troubleshooting.

For the AWS Certified Cloud Practitioner exam, make sure you understand these trade-offs clearly. You'll also need to know the different types of managed database options AWS provides, which we'll cover in this chapter.

Relational Database Services—RDS and Aurora

A relational database stores data in tables made up of rows and columns. Each row represents an individual record, while each column defines what type of data goes into that record.

A major benefit of a relational database is that it can connect different tables together. This is done using something called primary keys and foreign keys. A primary key is a unique identifier in one table, and when another table references it as a foreign key, you can easily pull related data across both tables in your queries.

Another major strength of relational databases lies in their strict adherence to ACID principles. ACID stands for atomicity, consistency, isolation, and durability. This means every transaction either completes fully or doesn't happen at all (atomicity), keeps data valid according to rules you've set (consistency), prevents operations from interfering with each other (isolation), and ensures data stays safe even if the system crashes (durability). These properties protect your data's integrity, which is why relational databases are a good choice for use cases like financial records, inventory systems, or user account management.

In AWS, you'll mainly work with two types of relational databases: Amazon RDS and Amazon Aurora. You can then compute analytics on the data using Amazon Redshift.

Amazon RDS

Amazon Relational Database Service (RDS) simplifies setting up, operating, and scaling relational databases. It supports multiple database engines, including PostgreSQL, MySQL, MariaDB, Oracle, Microsoft SQL Server, and IBM Db2.

In addition, Amazon Aurora is available as a high-performance, fully managed database service that is compatible with MySQL and PostgreSQL. Aurora offers enhanced scalability, reliability, and performance compared to traditional engines, making it a popular choice for demanding workloads.

Through the AWS Management Console, the CLI, or API calls, you can create a fully functioning database within minutes. RDS is also highly scalable. You can increase your database's compute power and storage capacity quickly with minimal downtime, which is useful when your applications grow.

Let's see how to create an RDS instance using the AWS Management Console:

1. Log in to AWS.
2. Search for RDS and select it.
3. On the left sidebar, choose Databases.
4. Select "Create database." You will be taken to the setup form, which you can see in Figure 11-1.
5. You will choose a database engine. Select MySQL.
6. Choose a use case template. The choices include a free tier (for learning and testing), Dev/Test (for development use), and production (for high availability and performance).
7. Select the deployment option, which depends on what you want for the availability and durability.
8. Create a unique name for your database.

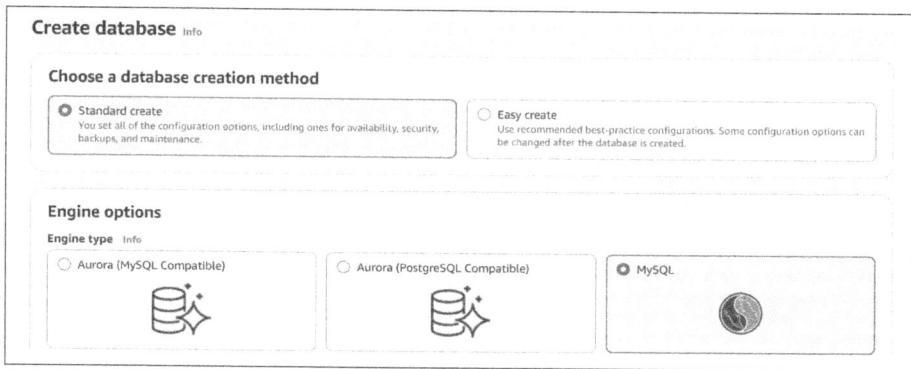

Figure 11-1. Setup screen for an RDS database

Besides these settings, there are additional configurations you can make, such as for networking (e.g., VPC, subnet groups, IPv6, or Internet Protocol version 6), security groups (firewall-style access control), and monitoring tools (like CloudWatch, Performance Insights, and Enhanced Monitoring). These settings can improve performance, visibility, security, and connectivity. However, for creating a basic database, the steps we have covered are sufficient.

Amazon Aurora

Amazon Aurora combines the speed and reliability of high-end commercial databases with the simplicity and lower cost of open source options. It is compatible with both MySQL and PostgreSQL. In terms of performance, Aurora delivers up to 5× the throughput of standard MySQL and up to 3× that of standard PostgreSQL on similar hardware, making it well-suited for high-performance relational workloads.

Security is another strong point for Aurora. It offers network isolation within your VPC, encrypts data at rest using AWS KMS, and encrypts data in transit with SSL. It also scales easily. You can choose instance sizes ranging from smaller setups with 2 vCPUs to powerful configurations with 32 vCPUs and 244 GB of memory.

Aurora is also built for high availability and durability. It maintains six copies of your data spread across three Availability Zones, aiming for an uptime of over 99.99%.

Amazon Redshift

Amazon Redshift is a fully managed cloud data warehouse service designed to handle massive, petabyte-scale datasets. It allows organizations to run complex analytical queries using standard SQL without the need to manage infrastructure. With Redshift, data can be quickly ingested from multiple sources—such as operational databases, data lakes, and streaming services—and then transformed into a format optimized for analytics. By leveraging columnar storage and parallel query execution, Redshift ensures high performance for large-scale workloads, making it well-suited for BI, reporting, and data-driven decision making.

A key strength of Amazon Redshift is its integration with AWS services and BI tools. It works seamlessly with Amazon QuickSight for visualization, supports connections with popular third-party tools like Tableau and Looker, and integrates with Amazon S3 through Redshift Spectrum for querying data directly in data lakes. Its managed nature also means automatic scaling, backups, patching, and security features like encryption and network isolation are handled by AWS, reducing the operational burden.

NoSQL Databases—DynamoDB, Neptune, and Timestream

A NoSQL database does not have a traditional table-and-row design. Instead, it stores data as documents, key-value pairs, graphs, or wide-column tables. This flexibility makes NoSQL especially useful when dealing with data that changes frequently or comes in mixed formats.

Another strength of NoSQL systems is their ability to scale horizontally, spreading data across many servers. As applications grow and attract more users, NoSQL databases can expand without bottlenecks. This is why you'll often find them powering social media feeds, IoT telemetry, fraud detection, and real-time analytics platforms.

Let's take a look at the NoSQL databases on AWS.

Amazon DynamoDB

One of the most widely used NoSQL databases on AWS is Amazon DynamoDB, a fully managed key-value and document database. It delivers single-digit millisecond response times even at massive scale. For example, during Amazon Prime Day, DynamoDB processed trillions of API calls, peaking at nearly 90 million requests per second, while maintaining consistent low latency.

Key capabilities include the following:

Flexible data modeling
Supports both key-value and document-style schemas, including nested data such as lists and maps.

Consistency and transactions
DynamoDB supports ACID transactions for multi-item operations, providing strong consistency for critical workloads like order processing or financial systems.

Supports PartiQL, a SQL-compatible query language for reading, updating, and inserting data without requiring DynamoDB's native API syntax.

Caching

For read-heavy workloads, DynamoDB Accelerator (DAX) offers in-memory caching that delivers sub-millisecond performance.

Amazon Neptune

Amazon Neptune is AWS's fully managed graph database, designed for workloads where relationships between data points are critical.

This makes Neptune a strong choice for applications such as fraud detection, knowledge graphs, recommendation engines, and social networking platforms.

Amazon Timestream

Amazon Timestream is a fully managed time-series database, built to efficiently store and analyze trillions of time-stamped events each day at low cost. It automatically manages the data lifecycle, moving recent data into memory for fast access and archiving older data to lower-cost storage.

Typical use cases include the following:

- IoT sensor data
- Operational monitoring
- Real-time analytics for applications like DevOps or industrial telemetry

Memory-Based Databases—ElastiCache

In-memory databases hold their data entirely in a system's RAM, bypassing the slower access times of disk-based storage. This approach enables fast read and write operations. Such databases are good for use cases like real-time analytics, high-frequency trading, telecommunication systems, gaming leaderboards, or fraud detection platforms.

The trade-off, however, is volatility. If the system crashes or loses power, all stored data vanishes, although some systems address this by periodically writing snapshots to disk, appending transaction logs, replicating across servers, or leveraging nonvolatile memory.

Amazon ElastiCache is a fully managed in-memory caching and database service designed to simplify deploying, operating, and scaling high-speed data layers in the cloud. It supports two open source engines: Redis and Memcached, letting you plug into existing tools.

Redis-powered ElastiCache supports advanced structures, such as sorted sets for leaderboards, hash maps for user sessions, the publish/subscribe pattern (pub/sub) for messaging, and atomic counters. This enables real-time processing. Meanwhile, Memcached provides a straightforward, scalable key-value caching layer compatible with most existing codebases.

Database Migration Tools—DMS and SCT

A database migration tool moves your data, schemas, and database-specific behaviors from one system to another. You might use it when shifting from on-premises infrastructure to the cloud, switching to a different database engine, or consolidating several databases into a single system.

One of the key benefits of these tools is that they minimize downtime. They keep your source database running while syncing changes over to the target, so your users do not notice the transition. Most tools also handle schema conversion, continuous data replication, and migration monitoring to keep the process smooth and reliable.

For AWS, there are two main migration tools.

AWS Database Migration Service (AWS DMS)

AWS Database Migration Service (DMS) is a fully managed service that automates database migration and replication with minimal disruption. It uses change data capture (CDC) to continuously grab updates from the source while your migration runs.

You can use DMS for both one-time migrations and continuous replication. This makes it useful not only for replatforming but also for consolidating multiple databases or syncing data into data warehouses like Amazon Redshift, Aurora, or S3.

DMS runs on a replication instance, which is an EC2 server that connects to both your source and target databases. You set up your endpoints and migration tasks through the AWS Management Console or APIs. The service scales with your workloads, minimizes downtime, copies schemas, and lets you monitor progress in real time. It also offers features like multi-AZ deployments for high availability, flexible on-demand pricing, and a serverless mode that scales automatically to your needs.

AWS Schema Conversion Tool (AWS SCT)

While AWS DMS handles moving your data, the AWS Schema Conversion Tool (SCT) takes care of transforming your schemas and database code. The SCT generates a detailed report highlighting what it converted automatically and what requires manual adjustments, which can save months of work compared to rewriting everything by hand.

DMS is a fully managed AWS service that you configure through the AWS Management Console or CLI. It enables both homogeneous and heterogeneous database migrations with minimal downtime.

The SCT, on the other hand, is a desktop application. Beyond just schema conversion, it can also transform extract, transform, load (ETL) workflows and embedded SQL in applications, making modernization and migration projects more efficient.

You can also use DMS and SCT together, such as with this workflow:

1. Run AWS SCT to assess your source database and transform the schema into the target engine's format.

2. Review the report, fix any components needing manual changes, and apply the converted schema to your target database.

3. Use AWS DMS to transfer the data, starting with a full load and then continuously replicating updates using CDC.

4. Switch over your application to point to the new database when you're ready.

This combined approach ensures minimal downtime and a smooth migration, so you can focus on delivering features rather than worrying about data transfer complexity.

Table 11-1 shows a summary of the different type of AWS database services.

Table 11-1. AWS database services

AWS database service	Description and key points
EC2 self-managed database	• You install, configure, patch, and manage everything yourself • Full control and flexibility • Requires significant expertise and operational effort
Amazon RDS	• Managed relational database service • Supports MySQL, PostgreSQL, MariaDB, Oracle, SQL Server, and Aurora • Handles backups, patching, scaling, and high availability
Amazon Aurora	• High-performance managed relational database • MySQL- and PostgreSQL-compatible • Up to 5× throughput of standard MySQL, 2× of PostgreSQL; built for high availability with replication across three AZs
Amazon DynamoDB	• Fully managed NoSQL key-value and document database • Single-digit millisecond latency at massive scale • Supports ACID transactions and horizontal scaling
Amazon ElastiCache	• Managed in-memory caching service • Supports Redis (advanced data structures) and Memcached (simple key-value caching) • Enables microsecond read/write performance for real-time applications

AWS database service	Description and key points
AWS Database Migration Service (DMS)	• Fully managed database migration and replication service • Uses change data capture for continuous updates • Supports one-time migrations and ongoing replication
AWS Schema Conversion Tool (SCT)	• Converts database schemas and application SQL code for new engines • Generates conversion reports highlighting automatic versus manual changes • Often used with DMS for end-to-end migrations

Conclusion

In this chapter, we looked at the various AWS database services and tools. We learned about self-managed EC2-hosted databases that offer maximum control but require extensive operational effort. However, much of the chapter was focused on fully managed options like Amazon RDS, Aurora, DynamoDB, and ElastiCache. We also covered database migration solutions such as AWS DMS and the SCT, which simplify moving and transforming databases with minimal downtime.

In the next chapter, we'll take a look at networking in AWS.

Chapter Quiz

To check your answers, please refer to the "Chapter 11 Answer Key" on page 207.

1. What is a key advantage of using a self-managed database on Elastic Compute Cloud (EC2)?

    A. Full control and flexibility over configuration and management

    B. Automated backups and patching

    C. Managed scaling with minimal downtime

    D. Single-digit millisecond latency at scale

2. What does Amazon DynamoDB primarily provide?

    A. Managed relational database

    B. In-memory caching

    C. Fully managed NoSQL key-value and document database

    D. Schema conversion

3. What type of scaling does DynamoDB support to handle massive workloads?

   A. Horizontal scaling

   B. Vertical scaling only

   C. No scaling capabilities

   D. Manual scaling with downtime

4. What are Redis and Memcached supported by?

   A. Amazon Relational Database Service (RDS)

   B. Amazon DynamoDB

   C. Amazon ElastiCache

   D. Amazon Aurora

5. Which tool would you use to convert embedded SQL in applications during migration?

   A. Amazon RDS

   B. Amazon DynamoDB

   C. AWS Database Migration Service (DMS)

   D. AWS Schema Conversion Tool (SCT)

CHAPTER 12

AWS Networking Services

In this chapter, you'll learn about AWS networking services. You'll see how virtual private clouds create isolated networks, enabling your resources to stay secure and organized. You'll also learn what makes Route 53 work, from directing global traffic with resilience to keeping your applications available through routing policies and health checks. And if you need to connect your on-premises environments to AWS, services like Site-to-Site VPN and Direct Connect come into play.

In the AWS Certified Cloud Practitioner exam, the focus is on what each networking service does, its key features, and when to use it.

Networking in a Data Center

In a data center, networking systems allow servers, applications, storage and other systems to talk to each other—both internally and across the internet.

At the core of networking are protocols. These are agreed-upon rules that govern how data moves back and forth. Here are some of the most common protocols you'll see in a data center:

Ethernet
> Created in the 1970s, this technology remains a workhorse protocol today. It uses physical cables to connect devices and delivers high-speed data transfers while ensuring the information arrives accurately.

Transmission Control Protocol/Internet Protocol (TCP/IP)
> This set of protocols connects systems to the internet as well as private networks, managing the complex interactions required to deliver data packets reliably. While most networks today use Internet Protocol version 4 (IPv4), IPv6 adoption is growing due to its vastly expanded address space. To support both current and

future networking needs, AWS enables dual-stack mode—supporting both IPv4 and IPv6—across services like VPCs, EC2, and load balancers, ensuring flexibility and scalability for modern architectures.

Data center bridging (DCB)
Developed by the IEEE (Institute of Electrical and Electronics Engineers), DCB enhances Ethernet performance and reliability. One key feature is priority-based flow control, which helps balance and manage heavy traffic loads in the data center.

Fibre Channel
Designed for high-speed networking, this protocol can reach speeds up to 256 Gbps. It's often used to connect servers to shared storage systems that need rapid and consistent data access.

Inside an organization, you'll find different types of networks serving specific needs. These are examples:

Local area networks (LANs)
These cover small areas like an office or a single building. Because of their limited reach, LANs usually deliver faster speeds.

Wide area networks (WANs)
WANs span larger areas, connecting multiple cities or even entire countries. In many ways, cloud platforms are advanced WANs. Whether public or private, they provide networking and compute resources on demand.

Software-defined WANs (SD-WANs)
SD-WANs take a virtual approach, letting you configure and manage the network through software rather than relying only on hardware. This flexibility makes it easier to adapt to changing traffic demands.

At the hardware level, networking relies on switches and routers. Switches manage internal communication within the data center, directing data packets efficiently between servers and storage. Routers, on the other hand, handle communication between the data center and external networks, such as the internet, always aiming to find the best route for data to travel.

To keep everything secure, data centers deploy firewalls. These combine hardware and software to control incoming and outgoing traffic based on pre-established security rules.

As for networking architectures, there are two types:

Client-server
> A server provides resources like storage, processing power, and data, whereas the client (the end user) consumes these services. Each client connects to the server, but they don't share resources with each other.

Peer-to-peer (P2P) networks
> Here, all computers in the network have equal privileges. There's no central server controlling access. Instead, each machine can share resources directly with the others.

Now, let's look at AWS's networking services in more detail.

Virtual Private Cloud (VPC)

A virtual private cloud (VPC) allows for full control over your network setup. Figure 12-1 shows an example of how this works.

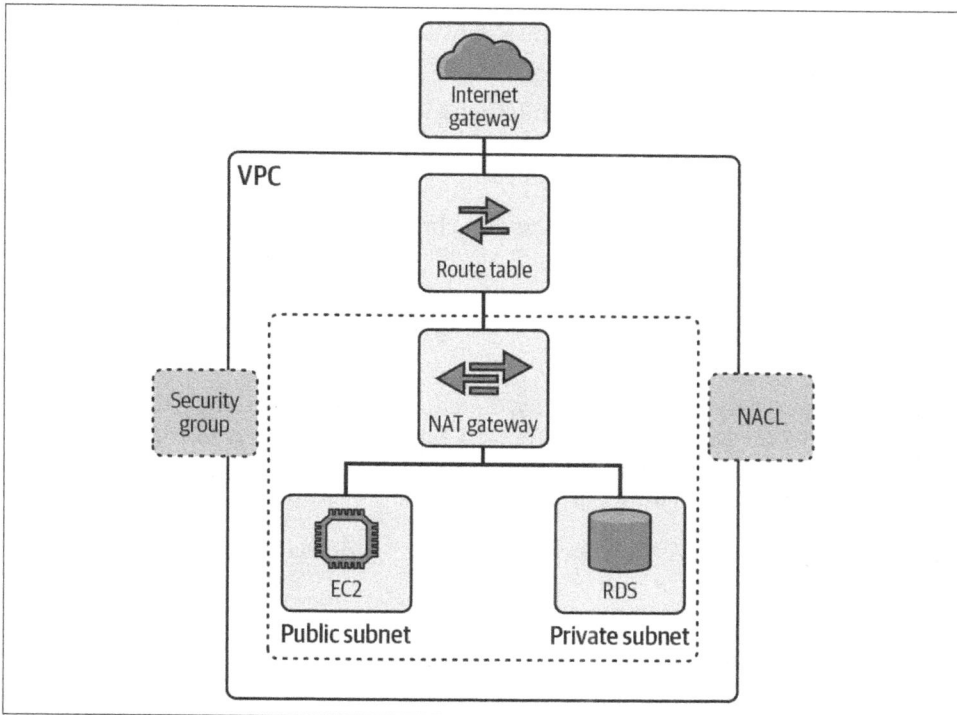

Figure 12-1. The setup of a VPC

With a VPC, you decide your IP address ranges, create subnets to organize resources into logical groups, and set up routing and security rules that fit your architecture. A subnet is a segmented portion of a VPC's IP address range that allows you to organize and isolate resources within your virtual network for better security and efficient routing.

For example, suppose you're running a web application. You might place your public-facing web servers in a subnet that connects to the internet, while your sensitive database servers sit in a private subnet without internet access. That way, customers can browse your website freely, but your database remains tucked away from direct exposure.

When it comes to securing your VPC, AWS gives you multiple layers of defense. At the instance level, you have Security Groups. For example, you might configure one to only allow HTTP and HTTPS traffic into your web server and permit database connections only from the web server's IP.

Then there are network access control lists (NACLs), which provide an additional layer of security at the subnet level. Unlike Security Groups, which are stateful (if traffic is allowed in, the response is automatically allowed out), NACLs are stateless. You have to define both inbound and outbound rules explicitly.

Another key piece of a VPC is the internet gateway (IGW). This is what connects your VPC to the internet. If your EC2 instance needs to download software updates, it uses the IGW to reach external servers.

But what if you have resources that shouldn't be accessible from the internet but still need to initiate outbound connections? That's where a network address translation (NAT) gateway comes in. For example, your database server might need to download security patches without exposing itself to inbound connections from the outside world.

Route tables tie everything together by directing traffic within your VPC. Think of them like a GPS for your network traffic. If a user sends a request to your web server, the route table makes sure the reply goes back out through the IGW or to another subnet, depending on its destination.

Here are some common AWS services you'll deploy inside your VPC:

- EC2 for virtual servers to run applications
- Amazon RDS for managed relational databases like MySQL or PostgreSQL
- ELB to distribute incoming traffic across multiple servers, which boosts reliability
- EFS for scalable shared storage between instances

Finally, your VPC doesn't operate in isolation. AWS offers services like VPC peering, which enables two VPCs to communicate privately, even across regions. Keep in mind that while this is useful for setups such as separate development, staging, and production environments, data transfer charges apply for cross-region traffic.

For larger or more complex environments, AWS also provides Transit Gateway. This acts as a scalable hub to connect multiple VPCs, on-premises networks, and VPNs. Unlike full-mesh peering, Transit Gateway simplifies network architecture by centralizing routing and control, making it especially valuable for enterprises managing dozens or hundreds of interconnected networks.

Setting Up a VPC

Let's set up a VPC in AWS. Here are the steps:

1. Log in to AWS.

2. Enter VPC in the search box.

3. Select Create VPC. You will see the setup screen shown in Figure 12-2.

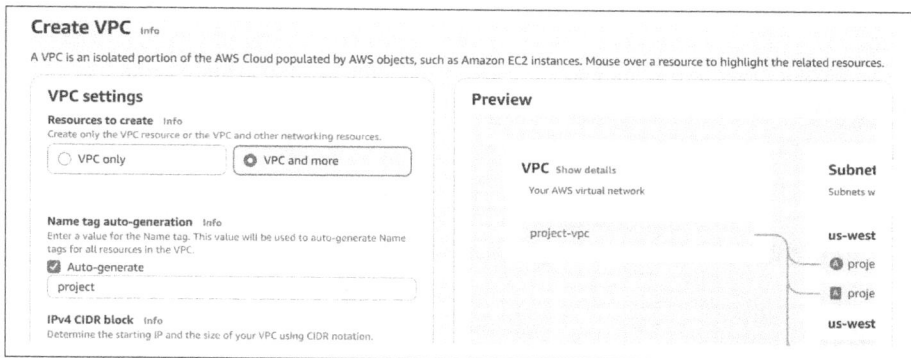

Figure 12-2. The setup screen to create a VPC

4. Enter a name for the VPC.

5. For "Resources to create," select "VPC and more." This will create the VPC along with subnets, route tables, and gateways.

6. Enter an IPv4 Classless Inter-Domain Routing (CIDR) block. Use the default 10.0.0.0/16, which gives you plenty of IP addresses.

7. Leave the IPv6 CIDR block field set to "No IPv6 CIDR block" unless you require IPv6 connectivity.

8. For Tenancy, keep the default option selected.

9. Choose the number of Availability Zones. Select 2 to provide high availability across data centers.

10. For "Number of public subnets," select 2. These will host resources like web servers that need internet access.

11. For "Number of private subnets," select 2. These are for backend resources such as databases that should not be exposed to the internet.

12. For "NAT gateways ($)," choose "In 1 AZ" to allow private subnets to initiate internet connections securely.

13. Leave VPC endpoints as None. You can add endpoints like S3 File Gateway later if needed.

14. Ensure DNS hostnames and DNS resolution are both enabled so your resources can use domain names easily.

15. Select Create VPC.

Route 53

In Chapter 8, we talked about Route 53's global DNS architecture and how it anchors name resolution at the edge. But let's dig deeper into how this system weaves itself into AWS networking to boost resiliency, performance, security, and hybrid-cloud flexibility.

Amazon Route 53 can act as a traffic director, sending users to where they need to go. That could be an EC2 instance, an S3 bucket, a server in your data center, or a third-party endpoint. If you're running a hybrid setup with resources split between AWS and on-premises, Route 53 routes traffic to the right place.

One of its most useful features is health checks. Every minute, Route 53 sends out quick probes using HTTP, HTTPS, TCP, or CloudWatch alarms to check that each endpoint is up and running. These results feed straight into CloudWatch, giving you near-real-time visibility. And if a server fails, Route 53 automatically reroutes traffic to a healthy endpoint.

Route 53 gives you various options for routing traffic. You can steer users to the endpoint with the lowest latency, send them based on their geographic location, or split traffic evenly to run A/B tests. You can combine these routing rules however you need. Plus, Domain Name System Security Extensions (DNSSEC) adds an extra layer of security by cryptographically signing your DNS records to protect against tampering.

If you operate in both AWS and your own network, Route 53 Resolver bridges them. It lets your AWS applications resolve internal data center records. It uses inbound and outbound Resolver endpoints along with forwarding rules sent over AWS VPN or

AWS Direct Connect. This setup ensures the DNS works smoothly whether your resources live in the cloud or on-premises.

AWS also offers PrivateLink, which lets you securely access AWS services (like S3 or DynamoDB) and third-party SaaS applications directly through VPC endpoints. With PrivateLink, traffic never traverses the public internet, which reduces latency and significantly improves security for sensitive workloads.

Finally, Route 53 keeps detailed logs of every DNS query. You'll see what was queried, when it happened, where it came from, and which firewall rule or policy applied.

Network Connectivity Options to AWS

Connecting your office network or data center to AWS might feel daunting at first, but AWS gives you two options to make it straightforward: Site-to-Site VPN and Direct Connect. Both create secure links between your on-premises environment and AWS resources, but they differ in speed, reliability, cost, and setup complexity. Let's break down what each one brings to the table.

AWS Site-to-Site VPN

AWS Site-to-Site VPN sets up an encrypted tunnel over the public internet to link your network to a VPC. It's like driving on a public highway in an armored car. Your data stays protected, but the ride quality depends on internet traffic conditions.

Here are the factors to consider for this option:

Setup and cost
> You can get a VPN connection up and running within minutes using the AWS Management Console, with no extra physical hardware needed. It's budget-friendly and comes with two automatically provisioned tunnels for redundancy, so if one drops, traffic switches to the other.

Performance
> Speeds can reach up to 4 Gbps, but performance varies depending on internet conditions.

Security
> VPN connections use industry-standard Internet Protocol Security (IPsec) encryption, keeping data safe as it travels across public networks.

AWS Direct Connect

AWS Direct Connect provides a dedicated, private fiber link from your premises directly into AWS, skipping the public internet altogether. These are some of the main factors to consider:

Setup and cost

Direct Connect requires physical setup, either in your own facility or through a co-location partner. It usually takes anywhere from 4 to 12 weeks to establish, and upfront costs are higher compared to a VPN.

Performance

Because it's a private line, you get consistent bandwidth ranging from 1 Gbps up to 100 Gbps or more, with stable low latency and no fluctuations from internet congestion.

Security

The connection is private, and you can enhance security further with MACsec encryption (a network security standard that operates at the medium access control layer), though this option is only available at select locations and for speeds of 10 Gbps or higher. For broader compatibility, you can also overlay an IPsec VPN for end-to-end encryption when needed.

It's common for organizations to choose to use both. They may rely on Direct Connect for its stable, high-performance backbone and add a VPN either as an extra encryption layer over Direct Connect or as a failover path if Direct Connect goes down. This hybrid setup ensures maximum reliability, redundancy, and secure connectivity across your environments.

Table 12-1 shows a summary of the different types of AWS networking services.

Table 12-1. Summary of AWS networking services

Service	Description and features
Virtual Private Cloud (VPC)	• Provides full control over your virtual network setup • Allows creation of subnets, route tables, IGWs, and NAT gateways • Enhances security with Security Groups and NACLs
Route 53	• Acts as a DNS service and traffic director for routing • Includes health checks and DNSSEC for security and resiliency • Supports hybrid DNS resolution with Route 53 Resolver
AWS Site-to-Site VPN	• Creates an encrypted tunnel over the public internet • Quick setup with redundant tunnels for failover • Uses IPsec encryption for secure connectivity
AWS Direct Connect	• Provides dedicated private fiber connection to AWS • Offers consistent high bandwidth with low latency • Requires physical setup with higher upfront costs

Conclusion

In this chapter, we learned about the core networking services that AWS offers to build secure, scalable, and reliable cloud architectures. We saw how VPCs provide full control over your network setup with subnets, route tables, security groups, and NAT gateways. We also examined Route 53's role as a global DNS and traffic routing service with features like health checks and DNSSEC for security and resiliency. Finally, we covered connectivity options, comparing Site-to-Site VPN's quick, encrypted internet tunnels with Direct Connect's dedicated private links offering consistent high bandwidth and low latency.

In the next chapter, we'll take a look at AI services for AWS.

Chapter Quiz

To check your answers, please refer to the "Chapter 12 Answer Key" on page 208.

1. What does a virtual private cloud (VPC) allow you to do in AWS?

    A. Control your virtual network setup, including subnets and route tables

    B. Automatically encrypt all data at rest

    C. Create EC2 instances without security groups

    D. Connect directly to on-premises data centers without any setup

2. What is a function of a network address translation (NAT) gateway in a VPC?

    A. It provides inbound internet access to private subnets.

    B. It acts as a firewall.

    C. It allows outbound internet connections from private subnets.

    D. It stores database snapshots.

3. What is the purpose of a subnet in a VPC?

    A. It provides Domain Name System (DNS) services.

    B. It encrypts traffic in transit.

    C. It segments IP ranges to organize resources.

    D. It creates virtual private network (VPN) tunnels.

4. What is the primary use of AWS Site-to-Site VPN?

A. Creating an encrypted tunnel between on-premises and AWS

B. Direct physical fiber connection

C. Hosting DNS services

D. Caching web content globally

5. What is the purpose of an internet gateway in a VPC?

A. It encrypts traffic in transit.

B. It creates private subnets.

C. It allows resources to connect to the internet.

D. It provides DNS resolution.

CHAPTER 13

Artificial Intelligence and Data Analytics Tools

Artificial intelligence (AI) is reshaping industries faster than ever. International Data Corporation (IDC) predicts that by 2027, global spending on AI systems will reach $500 billion, more than double what organizations spent in 2023 (*https://oreil.ly/ 3xBGs*). Companies are investing heavily in AI to automate tasks, improve customer experiences, and innovate across their products and services.

You see AI at work every day, whether it's the personalized recommendations on your favorite streaming app, an intelligent chatbot that answers your banking questions, or real-time systems that detect fraud before it impacts customers. As AI capabilities continue to grow, so does the demand for people who know how to build and deploy these solutions in the cloud. This is also a key reason that AI is covered in the AWS Certified Cloud Practitioner exam.

In this chapter, we'll break down the core ideas behind AI, machine learning (ML), deep learning (DL), and generative AI (GenAI), and see how each fits into the broader AI landscape. We'll also look at key AWS services that support these workloads. They include Amazon SageMaker for building and deploying ML models, AWS Lex for creating conversational interfaces like chatbots, and Amazon Kendra for enterprise search.

Finally, we'll touch on AWS data analytics services such as Athena, Glue, Kinesis, and QuickSight.

Artificial Intelligence, Machine Learning, Deep Learning, and Generative AI

AI covers a wide range of technologies. But at the core, it's about building machines and systems that can act in ways we usually associate with human intelligence. This means they can learn, reason, perceive their environment, and make decisions.

Within this broad field is ML. It is about teaching machines to learn from data without explicitly programming every rule. Instead, these systems rely on statistical models and algorithms, such as regression, decision trees, clustering, and reinforcement learning. You see ML in many applications like email spam filters and recommendations for ecommerce systems.

DL is a subset of ML. It uses artificial neural networks with many layers (this is where "deep" comes from). These networks can extract and build features from raw, unstructured data such as images, audio, or text. For instance, DL powers capabilities like tagging people in photos, translating languages, or powering chatbots.

GenAI is a part of DL. It uses models such as generative adversarial networks (GANs) and large language models (LLMs) to create entirely new content, such as text, images, audio, video, and code. Today, you see GenAI in tools like ChatGPT and Claude, as well as those from Amazon Bedrock.

Figure 13-1 shows how AI, ML, DL, and GenAI relate to each other.

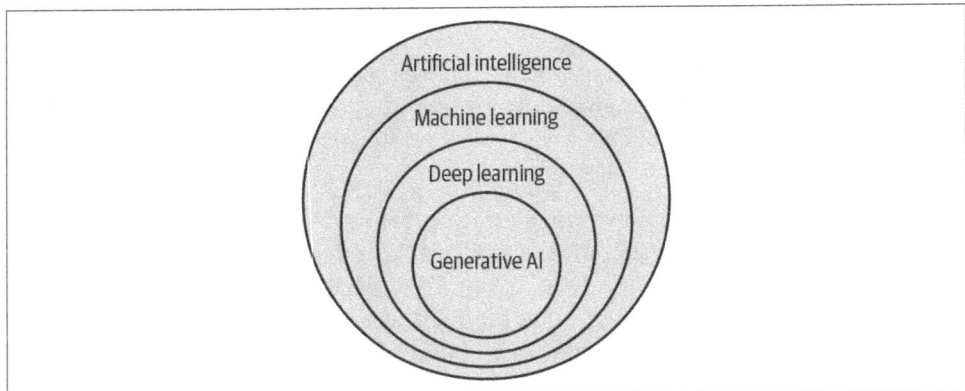

Figure 13-1. The relationships between AI, ML, DL, and GenAI

Running modern AI, ML, DL, and GenAI workloads often requires large amounts of compute, memory, and storage. AWS offers a myriad of services to meet these demands.

Amazon SageMaker AI

Amazon SageMaker is a platform for building AI, ML, DL, and GenAI solutions. It covers the entire development lifecycle, from bringing in and preparing data to experimenting with models, deploying them, and monitoring their performance. For generative AI projects, SageMaker integrates with Bedrock, which lets you design GenAI applications, knowledge bases, and agents.

A key feature in SageMaker is its notebooks, which are built on the Jupyter platform. They let you write and run code, visualize data, and document your workflows all in one place. This setup makes it easy to experiment with different approaches, build and refine models, and share your findings with your team.

When your models are ready for production, SageMaker simplifies deployment at scale, whether you're running real-time predictions or processing data in batches. It does this through MLOps pipelines. They are automated workflows that bring AI, ML, DL, and GenAI models into production environments. SageMaker also supports CI/CD. This automates the building, testing, and rollout of models or applications. This allows you to release updates quickly with minimal manual work.

SageMaker integrates with ETL pipelines as well. This means you can pull data from different sources, transform it into the format you need, and load it into storage or analytics systems for use in your ML projects.

Here are a few other key features of Amazon SageMaker:

Unified Studio
SageMaker brings together AI, ML, DL, and GenAI workflows alongside data engineering and analytics tasks. It connects easily to AWS services like EMR, Glue, Athena, and Redshift.

Data and AI governance
Built on AWS DataZone, SageMaker helps organizations securely discover, share, and manage data assets and AI artifacts. It offers unified metadata tracking, fine-grained access controls, asset lineage, and policy enforcement across your analytics and AI projects. These governance tools support responsible AI practices, such as detecting model bias, implementing toxicity safeguards, and monitoring models throughout their lifecycle.

Lakehouse architecture

SageMaker Lakehouse creates an open, unified data layer that combines data from Amazon S3 data lakes, S3 Tables, Amazon Redshift, and other external sources. You can query this data in place using engines like Athena, Spark, and SQL, and it supports federated queries along with zero-ETL ingestion from various databases.

Amazon CodeWhisperer

This uses AI to generate code suggestions within integrated development environments (IDEs) like Visual Studio Code and JetBrains. There is support for various languages, like Python, Java, and JavaScript.

AWS Lex

AWS Lex allows you to build virtual assistants and conversational interfaces for your applications. It combines advanced natural language understanding (NLU) with automatic speech recognition (ASR). In simple terms, Lex acts as the brain behind chatbots. This allows them to understand what users say or type, pull out key details (known as slots), and respond in an intelligent way. Lex also works with both text and voice inputs.

This service comes with built-in integrations for services like Amazon Connect. This streamlines the process of creating interactive voice response (IVR) systems for customer service. You can also connect your Lex bots to mobile apps, websites, or messaging platforms such as Facebook Messenger.

Since Lex uses the same deep learning technology that powers Amazon Alexa, it delivers strong speech recognition and NLU right out of the box. It also integrates with AWS Lambda, which means your bots can execute business logic behind the scenes, like booking an appointment or looking up user information.

Let's see how to use Lex:

1. Log in to AWS.
2. Enter Lex into the search box. Select it.
3. Choose "Create bot." You will see the bot setup screen in Figure 13-2.

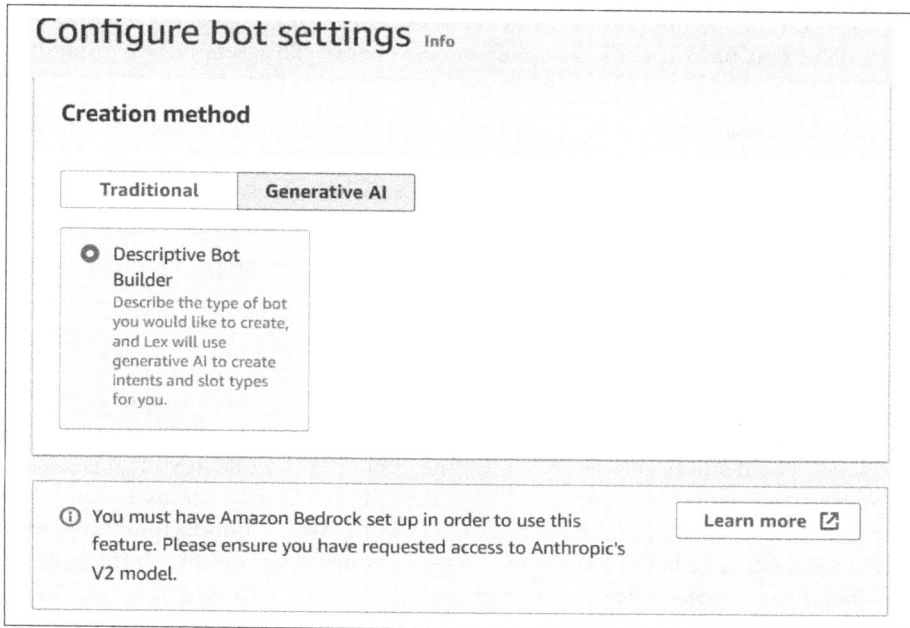

Figure 13-2. The setup screen to create a bot in Amazon Lex

4. For "Creation method," select Traditional. This lets you manually define intents and slot types.

5. Enter a name for your bot.

6. Under IAM permissions, choose a Runtime role. Select "Create a role with basic Amazon Lex permissions" to automatically create a role.

7. Under "Bot error logging," select Enabled to allow Lex to log errors for debugging.

8. Under the Children's Online Privacy Protection Act (COPPA), choose No unless your bot is subject to COPPA compliance.

9. For "Idle session timeout," leave it at the default of 5 minutes, or adjust to your needs (between 1 and 1,440 minutes).

10. Select Next.

11. For Language, select English (US) or your preferred language from the drop-down list.

12. Under "Voice interaction," you can choose a text-to-speech voice. To hear how each voice sounds, click Play next the voice sample, and then choose the one you like.

13. For "Intent classification confidence score threshold," leave it at the default 0.40 unless you have specific accuracy requirements. This sets how confidently Lex must match user inputs to intents (range is 0.00 to 1.00).

14. Under "Describe your use case," enter a description of what your bot should do. For example, you can enter something like this: "We want a bot to help customers order food (using item id, quantity, size), check order status, and cancel an order. Use Order ID for indexing orders."

15. Select the model you want to use for GenAI features. For example, choose Claude V2 under Anthropic if enabled in your account.

16. Select Done.

By building this bot with GenAI, you start off with a basic set of intents and slot types. These are the building blocks that define what your bot can understand and ask users. But you'll still need to review and fine-tune them to match your business goals. For example, if your bot needs to place orders or check order statuses, you'll have to connect them to your backend services, like with AWS Lambda functions, to carry out those tasks. The benefit is speed. GenAI sets up the groundwork for you, so you can spend more time polishing the user experience and wiring up the workflows that make your bot useful.

Amazon Kendra

Amazon Kendra is an AI-powered enterprise search service that leverages natural language processing and deep learning. It enables users to ask questions in conversational language (like "What are my 2025 healthcare benefits?") and returns the most relevant snippets, answers, or documents by understanding the context and intent behind the query.

This is how it works:

Indexing and ingestion
Kendra connects to your data sources like SharePoint, S3, Salesforce, ServiceNow, Google Drive, or custom repositories. It then crawls, parses, and indexes the documents to make them searchable.

Query processing
When a user enters a query, Kendra uses NLP to determine intent, expands with synonyms, and performs both semantic and keyword searches.

Ranking and retrieval
Kendra ranks the results using relevance models based on document metadata and user feedback. It can deliver short factoid answers, long-form descriptive passages, or FAQ-style matches extracted directly from indexed content.

With its GenAI Index, Kendra supports retrieval augmented generation (RAG) workflows. This improves the results of LLMs by retrieving relevant information from the documents.

Kendra also helps to mitigate the issue of data silos, such as by consolidating content from diverse repositories. This centralized approach allows teams and customers to search FAQs, wikis, tables, and full documents quickly and accurately. Plus, its built-in ML continuously refines result relevance by learning from user interactions.

Data Analytics

Data analytics tools help companies make sense of their data. They collect, process, analyze, and visualize information so that teams can spot trends, find patterns, and make decisions backed by evidence. Whether you're looking at customer buying habits, operational metrics, or website traffic, these tools turn raw data into useful insights. Most of them come with features for preparing data, running queries, and generating reports.

We'll look at the data analytics services AWS offers.

Amazon Athena

Amazon Athena lets you run SQL queries directly against data stored in Amazon S3. You only pay for the data you scan, so it's an affordable way to explore massive datasets, run ad hoc analyses, or build dashboards and reports on the fly.

Athena integrates with file formats like CSV, JSON, Optimized Row Columnar (ORC), Avro, and Parquet. Under the hood, it uses Presto, a powerful open source SQL engine designed for fast, distributed queries. This means you can run complex joins and window functions and handle arrays.

Athena is useful for quick log analysis, exploring data lakes, or feeding results into BI tools.

Amazon Kinesis

Amazon Kinesis is a set of services built to handle real-time streaming data at massive scale. You can bring in data from sources like website clicks, financial transactions, social media feeds, server logs, or IoT devices, and make that data instantly available for analysis. Use cases include detecting fraud in transactions as it happens, personalizing content in real time, or monitoring the performance of your applications.

Kinesis comes with several key components. There's Kinesis Data Streams for ingesting data in real time; Amazon Data Firehose for delivering streaming data into destinations like Amazon S3, Redshift, or Elasticsearch; and Kinesis Data Analytics, which lets you run SQL queries on streaming data for immediate insights. It also includes Kinesis Video Streams for securely streaming and processing video.

Amazon Glue

Amazon Glue is a data integration service that helps you discover, prepare, and combine data for analytics, ML, or application development. It scales automatically to handle anything from a few gigabytes to petabytes of data, and you only pay for the compute time your jobs use.

With Glue, connecting to different data sources is straightforward. You can pull in data from Amazon S3, RDS, DynamoDB, and streaming sources like Kinesis or Kafka. Glue uses crawlers to scan these sources, determines their schemas, and organizes everything in the Glue Data Catalog.

Glue also helps to simplify ETL processes. You can build data transformation jobs using a visual interface in AWS Glue Studio or write scripts in Python or Scala. It supports both batch processing for large datasets and streaming processing for real-time data.

Amazon QuickSight

Amazon QuickSight is a BI service that helps you share insights across your organization. You can connect it to different data sources, run fast and scalable analyses, and build interactive dashboards that anyone can access from their laptop, tablet, or smartphone.

One of QuickSight's most useful features is embedded analytics. This lets you integrate interactive dashboards and visualizations directly into your apps or internal portals, giving users the data they need right where they need it. QuickSight also uses ML to deliver features like anomaly detection and forecasting. Even if you're not a data scientist, you can easily spot trends, outliers, or future projections with just a few clicks.

Conclusion

In this chapter, we looked at the foundations of AI, including ML, DL, and GenAI, and learned how these technologies allow systems to perform tasks that mimic human intelligence. We examined AWS services like Amazon SageMaker for building and deploying AI solutions, Amazon Lex for creating conversational interfaces, and Amazon Kendra for enterprise search with NLU. We also covered data analytics services such as Athena, Kinesis, Glue, and QuickSight, which help organizations transform raw data into actionable insights.

In the next chapter, we'll take a look at AWS developer tools and other essential services.

Chapter Quiz

To check your answers, please refer to the "Chapter 13 Answer Key" on page 208.

1. What does machine learning (ML) enable systems to do?

   A. Perform only pre-programmed tasks

   B. Store relational data in databases

   C. Learn from data without explicit programming of rules

   D. Encrypt data automatically

2. Deep learning (DL) is a subset of which technology?

   A. Generative AI

   B. Natural language processing

   C. Data analytics

   D. Machine learning

3. What AWS service is used for building and deploying ML models?

   A. Amazon Kinesis

   B. AWS Lex

   C. Amazon SageMaker

   D. Amazon Athena

4. What is retrieval-augmented generation (RAG) used for in Amazon Kendra?

   A. Running extract, transform, load (ETL) jobs faster

   B. Improving large language model (LLM) results with retrieved document context

   C. Generating SQL queries automatically

   D. Creating business dashboards

5. What is the primary function of Amazon Bedrock?

   A. Building ML models from scratch

   B. Providing managed access to foundation models

   C. Running SQL queries on Simple Storage Service (S3)

   D. Managing Internet of Things (IoT) devices

CHAPTER 14

AWS Developer Tools and Other Essential Services

This chapter looks at the types of AWS tools that can help organizations to build, integrate, and manage applications efficiently. You will find some of these tools mentioned in the AWS Certified Cloud Practitioner exam.

In this chapter, you'll learn about application integration tools like Amazon Event-Bridge, which routes events between services; SNS, a messaging service for notifications; and SQS, a managed message queue for decoupling systems. It also covers business applications such as Amazon Connect, a cloud contact center, and Simple Email Service (SES), an email sending service.

Key developer and DevOps tools are also introduced. They include CodeBuild for building code, CodePipeline for automating deployments, and AWS X-Ray for application tracing. What's more, the chapter covers services for delivering client-facing applications and desktops, such as AppStream 2.0 and WorkSpaces, as well as AWS IoT Core, which connects and manages Internet of Things devices securely at scale.

Application Integration Tools

Application integration services include connectors that help keep different parts of an IT system working smoothly. They allow for managing messages, alerts, and events automatically. That way, every piece can do its job on its own and only reach out to others when necessary. By doing this, the system stays reliable even if one part fails, making it easy to expand or maintain down the line.

For developers, this toolkit lets you build systems where components talk to each other seamlessly without being locked together in complex ways. In the end, you get solutions that are strong, flexible, and ready to adapt as needs change.

We'll now discuss three AWS integration tools.

Amazon EventBridge

Amazon EventBridge works like a central traffic hub for your IT systems. For example, it takes in events from AWS services, your own applications, or SaaS tools. Then, it checks each event against rules you define, and it decides where it should go next. If an event matches a rule, EventBridge routes it to a target. That target could be a Lambda function, an SQS queue, an SNS topic, or an HTTP endpoint using API destinations. With this setup, you can build workflows that are scalable.

Here are a few ways teams commonly use EventBridge:

- This tool triggers serverless functions, workflows, or batch jobs when something changes, such as a new file in S3 or an update in your database.

- EventBridge shares events across AWS accounts or Regions, which is helpful for centralized monitoring or orchestration when multiple teams work together.

- You can use EventBridge for advanced rule matching, including wildcards or exclusions, to ensure only the right events get processed. This helps improve performance and manage costs effectively.

Amazon Simple Notification Service (SNS)

Think of Amazon Simple Notification Service (SNS) as a real-time broadcasting system for your applications and users. You send a message to a topic, and it instantly pushes that message out to everyone subscribed. These subscribers can be anything from applications and AWS services (like Lambda or SQS queues), to email addresses and mobile devices, which receive messages via SMS or push notifications.

For app-to-app communication, SNS helps keep your systems decoupled. That means one part of your system can announce something—like a new order placed in your ecommerce store—without needing to know who's listening. Inventory services, shipping workflows, and analytics pipelines can all subscribe to that topic and react independently from that single notification.

SNS also handles app-to-person messaging. You can send SMS messages, emails, or push notifications across more than 200 countries. Use cases include order confirmations, security alerts, and promotional messages.

A few features make SNS especially practical in real-world setups:

Message filtering and fan-out
    You can choose which subscribers get which messages, avoiding unnecessary traffic and processing.

Durability and retries

SNS stores messages redundantly and retries deliveries on failures. You can also route failed messages to a dead-letter queue for later analysis.

Strong security controls

With encryption at rest through AWS KMS, VPC endpoint support via Private-Link, and fine-grained access controls using IAM policies, you can keep communication secure and compliant.

Targeted campaigns

Amazon Pinpoint complements SNS by providing personalized push notifications, email, and SMS with analytics and A/B testing for customer engagement.

Amazon Simple Queue Service (SQS)

Amazon Simple Queue Service (SQS) is a to-do list for your systems. It lets one part of your application send messages to a queue, where they wait safely until another part is ready to process them. This approach keeps your systems responsive by buffering tasks when things get busy, and it prevents messages from getting lost, even if there's an outage or a sudden traffic spike.

SQS stores messages redundantly across multiple servers to ensure durability. You can choose between standard queues, which offer almost unlimited throughput, or first-in-first-out (FIFO) queues, which guarantee that messages are processed in order and without duplication. This flexibility lets you pick the right option based on your speed and precision needs.

Beyond basic queuing, SQS includes useful features like automatic retries if something fails, and dead-letter queues to catch messages that couldn't be processed for later inspection and debugging.

Table 14-1 summarizes these different application integration services.

Table 14-1. AWS application integration services

Service	Features and use cases
Amazon EventBridge	• Routes events from AWS services, custom applications, or SaaS tools based on defined rules • Supports advanced filtering, content-based routing, and event transformation • Useful for event-driven orchestration, complex workflows, and loosely coupled system integration
Amazon SNS (Simple Notification Service)	• Publishes messages that are sent immediately to all subscribers (apps, email, SMS, mobile push, Lambda, SQS, etc.) • For real-time broadcasting, such as alerts and notifications • Includes features like content-based filtering, retries, message durability, and encryption
Amazon SQS (Simple Queue Service)	• A pull-based queue, where messages are stored until a consumer retrieves and processes them • Strong durability and reliability

Business Applications

Companies need strong cloud services to keep customers engaged and operations running smoothly. AWS provides a toolkit designed for exactly that. Here's a look at two popular systems.

Amazon Connect

Amazon Connect is a cloud-based contact center. It manages calls, chats, and SMS. It has a drag-and-drop Contact Flow Editor that makes it easy to build customer journeys visually, whether you're designing IVR menus or routing chats with AI. It integrates tightly with AWS Lambda for serverless workflows, Lex for chatbots, and S3 for call recordings. Connecting it to your customer relationship management (CRM) system is straightforward. This brings customer data directly into each interaction.

Connect supports video calls, screen sharing, and persistent context across channels. Human agents can pick up conversations without forcing customers to repeat themselves. Amazon Connect integrates with AI services like Amazon Lex for chatbots, Amazon Transcribefor call transcription, and Amazon Comprehend for sentiment analysis, enhancing customer interactions. These features translate into real-world benefits: shorter call times, faster agent onboarding, better first-contact resolution, and measurable return on investment (ROI) improvements. Supervisors gain live insights through key performance indicators (KPIs), sentiment tracking, and workforce forecasting tools.

Amazon Simple Email Service (SES)

If your team sends a lot of emails—such as for password resets, order confirmations, newsletters, and marketing campaigns—Amazon Simple Email Service (SES) can simplify that work. SES is AWS's cloud-based email platform built to handle everything from a handful of messages to billions per month.

Because it's fully managed, SES takes care of the complex parts of email delivery, like maintaining server health and protecting sender reputation.

SES supports both transactional emails (like receipts or password resets) and bulk marketing campaigns. It can also handle incoming mail. For example, you can store inbound emails in S3, process them with Lambda functions, or publish events to SNS to trigger workflows like automated ticket creation.

SES includes various forms of authentication, along with reputation dashboards and the Virtual Deliverability Manager. Together, these tools ensure that your emails avoid spam folders and maintain high trust with recipients. Dedicated IP addresses and automated warm-up processes further protect sender reputation.

Integration is easy. SES supports Simple Mail Transfer Protocol (SMTP), APIs, and AWS SDKs. You can connect it with other AWS services to build robust workflows, using CloudWatch for monitoring, Lambda for custom logic, SNS for bounce and complaint notifications, and S3 for archiving. SES even provides a mailbox simulator to test bounces and complaints without risking your actual reputation scores.

Developer Tools and DevOps

Building, testing, and deploying software quickly and reliably has become table stakes in modern development. That's where developer tools and DevOps services come in. They automate repetitive tasks, streamline workflows, and boost collaboration between development and operations teams.

AWS offers a suite of tools to make this happen, such as CodeBuild, CodePipeline, and AWS X-Ray. Together, they help developers deliver new features rapidly while keeping performance, security, and stability in check throughout the software lifecycle.

AWS CodeBuild

CodeBuild compiles source code, runs tests, and produces deployable software packages. It automatically provisions and scales compute resources to run multiple builds in parallel. This eliminates bottlenecks and keeps your development workflow moving smoothly. You define your build instructions using buildspec files in your repository or directly in the AWS Management Console. A buildspec is a collection of build commands and related settings, in YAML format, that CodeBuild uses to run a build. It supports a wide range of programming languages and frameworks.

CodeBuild integrates with other AWS services like CodePipeline for CI/CD workflows, and it works with source control tools such as GitHub and Bitbucket.

AWS CodePipeline

Continuous integration and continuous delivery or deployment (CI/CD) has become the backbone of efficient software releases. These practices automate the steps of integrating code changes (CI) and deploying them to production (CD). This helps to reduce manual errors and provide for reliable, rapid updates.

AWS CodePipeline is AWS's fully managed CI/CD service. It models workflows as stages with actions such as source (e.g., CodeCommit), build (CodeBuild), test, deploy (e.g., ECS, Lambda), and manual approvals. Each time you commit code, CodePipeline triggers the entire workflow. This ensures new features, bug fixes, and enhancements make their way to production quickly and consistently.

CodePipeline integrates with CodeBuild to compile and test your code, and with deployment services like Elastic Beanstalk, ECS, and Lambda for rollouts. It also connects to third-party tools like GitHub and Jenkins. This makes it flexible enough for almost any development environment.

AWS X-Ray

With X-Ray, you get visual maps of your application's architecture. These maps highlight slow services, failed dependencies, and inefficient database queries. This visibility is invaluable for diagnosing production issues quickly, optimizing performance, and ensuring a smooth user experience.

X-Ray integrates with services like Lambda, ECS, and EC2. If you instrument your code correctly, it can trace requests across on-premises systems and external APIs.

Client-Facing Application and Desktop Delivery on AWS

AWS offers various solutions for delivering rich application experiences, whether your users work on traditional desktops or modern web and mobile platforms. At a high level, these services fall into two categories:

End user computing (EUC)
> This includes services like AppStream 2.0, WorkSpaces, and WorkSpaces Secure Browser. They provide managed virtual desktops and streamed applications, letting users run full desktop software from almost any device.

Frontend web and mobile
> Tools like Amplify and AppSync help developers build, deploy, and manage responsive applications with integrated backend services, real-time data, and authentication.

Together, these offerings allow organizations to create seamless digital experiences.

Amazon AppStream 2.0

AppStream 2.0 streams desktop applications from the cloud to any device running an HTML5 browser or a native Windows client. This means software vendors, schools, and enterprises can deliver their desktop apps as scalable SaaS offerings without rewriting code.

Here's how it works: only encrypted pixels travel over the network, keeping applications and data secure within your VPC and reducing endpoint exposure. You can choose among deployment models—Always-On, On-Demand, or Elastic fleets—depending on whether you prioritize instant access, cost optimization, or usage spikes.

Amazon WorkSpaces

Amazon WorkSpaces is a desktop-as-a-service (DaaS) platform. It lets you provision Windows or Linux desktops in minutes, accessible from PCs, Macs, tablets, and Chromebooks. Data stays securely within your VPC, encrypted both at rest and in transit. Moreover, Amazon WorkSpaces Secure Browser streams browser sessions from AWS. This isolates browsing from local devices to prevent data leakage and enhance security for web-based applications.

WorkSpaces integrates with Active Directory, Security Assertion Markup Language (SAML), and Entra ID, and supports BYOL (Bring Your Own License) for Windows and Microsoft 365 applications. GPU-enabled bundles are available for high-performance use cases, such as for sophisticated AI applications.

WorkSpaces Secure Browser

WorkSpaces Secure Browser streams an AWS-hosted Chrome browser session to a local device. It sends only encrypted pixels, never HTML or Document Object Model (DOM) content. It also doesn't require VPNs or specialized clients.

Admins can enforce URL allow/block lists, manage clipboard and file transfer restrictions, and limit access by IP. Sessions run in fresh, patched containers each time, which minimizes attack surfaces and helps to prevent data leaks.

AWS Amplify

AWS Amplify accelerates full-stack web and mobile application development. It provides CLI tools, libraries, UI components, and Amplify Studio so that frontend developers can build features like authentication, storage, real-time data sync, and AI-powered services (such as image recognition and translation).

Amplify also offers a Git-based CI/CD pipeline with CloudFront hosting for automatic deployments, pull-request previews, and zero-downtime updates.

AWS AppSync

AWS AppSync connects data from DynamoDB, Aurora, Elasticsearch, Lambda, and external APIs under a single endpoint. It handles query parsing, authorization, subscriptions, and caching. This allows applications to fetch only the data they need with predictable performance.

AppSync supports WebSockets for real-time updates, server-side caching for faster responses, and offline sync for applications that operate intermittently. This is a good option for field service, logistics, or note-taking.

Table 14-2 summarizes the different types of AWS services for client-facing applications and desktop delivery.

Table 14-2. AWS services for client-facing applications and desktop delivery

AWS services	Description and key points
Amazon AppStream 2.0	• Streams desktop apps from AWS to any device with an HTML5 browser or native Windows client • Keeps apps and data secure within your VPC by sending only encrypted pixels • Offers Always-On, On-Demand, and Elastic fleets to balance instant access and cost efficiency
Amazon WorkSpaces	• Desktop-as-a-service for Windows or Linux, accessible from PCs, Macs, tablets, and Chromebooks
WorkSpaces Secure Browser	• Streams a secure AWS-hosted Chrome browser session to local devices with only encrypted pixels • Enforces URL filtering, clipboard/file transfer restrictions, and IP-based access controls • Uses fresh, patched containers per session to minimize attack surfaces and data leaks
AWS Amplify	• Provides tools, libraries, and UI components for fast full-stack web/mobile app development • Includes features like authentication, storage, real-time data sync, and AI services
AWS AppSync	• Aggregates data from DynamoDB, Aurora, Elasticsearch, Lambda, and external APIs under one endpoint • Supports WebSockets for real-time updates, caching for faster responses, and offline sync

Managing IoT Devices with AWS IoT Core

The Internet of Things (IoT) is a network of physical objects that connect to the internet to share data. These "things" include everything from smart thermostats and fridges in your kitchen to industrial machines monitoring production lines. They come embedded with sensors, software, and connectivity features that let them communicate without human intervention.

AWS IoT Core is Amazon's managed cloud service that helps you securely connect your IoT devices to the AWS ecosystem. Some of the key features include the following:

Device gateway and protocols
> Devices connect via MQTT (a lightweight messaging protocol commonly used in IoT devices for communication), HTTPS, WebSockets, and LoRaWAN, which is a low-power, wide-area network protocol that wirelessly connects battery-operated devices to the internet, for long-range low-power setups. This flexibility supports everything from tiny sensors to heavy industrial machinery.

Security
> AWS IoT Core uses mutual authentication (both the device and AWS verify each other) and end-to-end encryption to keep communications safe. Tools like Device Advisor help test setups before production to catch issues early.

Managed MQTT Broker

This is a lightweight messaging protocol popular in IoT. AWS manages the broker for you.

Rules engine

This filters, transforms, and routes data in real-time to other AWS services like Lambda or DynamoDB. You can set up automated actions without running separate servers.

Device software development kits (SDKs)

These are available for languages like C, JavaScript, and Arduino. They allow for connecting devices, authenticating them, and managing their communication.

Conclusion

In this chapter, we looked at a range of AWS services that help organizations build, integrate, and manage their applications efficiently. They include EventBridge, SNS, and SQS to keep systems scalable, Amazon Connect for customer engagement, and SES for email communications. We also looked at developer and DevOps tools, such as CodeBuild, CodePipeline, and AWS X-Ray. Finally, we covered services for delivering client-facing applications and desktops, along with AWS IoT Core for connecting and managing IoT devices.

In the next chapter, we'll cover billing, budgeting, and cost management in AWS.

Chapter Quiz

To check your answers, please refer to the "Chapter 14 Answer Key" on page 208.

1. What does Amazon EventBridge allow you to do?

    A. Store files in the cloud

    B. Route events from AWS services, apps, or software as a service (SaaS) tools based on rules

    C. Host virtual desktops for remote teams

    D. Automatically compile source code

2. Which Amazon Simple Queue Service (SQS) feature ensures that messages are not lost if processing fails repeatedly?

    A. First-in-first-out (FIFO) queues

    B. Dead-letter queues

    C. Encryption at rest

    D. Event-based filtering

3. What does AWS CodePipeline automate?

   A. Server provisioning only

   B. The entire continuous integration and continuous delivery or deployment (CI/CD) process from source to deploy

   C. Database backups

   D. Identity and Access Management (IAM) user management

4. What does AWS AppSync aggregate?

   A. Data from multiple sources under a single GraphQL endpoint

   B. Virtual machines for compute scaling

   C. Messages from different queues

   D. Virtual desktops across accounts

5. What protocol is commonly used with AWS Internet of Things (IoT) Core for lightweight messaging?

   A. HTTPS only

   B. WebSockets only

   C. LoRaWAN only

   D. MQTT

CHAPTER 15

Billing, Budgeting, and Cost Management in AWS

In this chapter, we'll start by reviewing AWS's pricing models, including On-Demand, Reserved Instances, Savings Plans, and Spot Instances.

But picking the right pricing model is just the beginning. AWS gives you solid tools to help track and manage your costs. Tools like Cost Explorer, AWS Budgets, and the AWS Pricing Calculator give you visibility into where your money's going, and help you make smarter decisions about resource usage.

This chapter will also show how cost allocation tags can categorize expenses by team, project, or environment. When you combine these tags with AWS Organizations and the right support plans, you will have a strong foundation for managing cloud spend across different parts of your business.

These topics represent the smallest proportion of the questions on the AWS Certified Cloud Practitioner exam, at 12%. But this certainly does not diminish their importance. In this chapter, we'll look at what you need to know.

AWS Pricing Models

AWS pricing works much like your electricity bill. That is, you pay for what you use. Instead of shelling out sums up front for servers and infrastructure, you're only charged based on your consumption.

Pricing for services falls into three main categories: compute, storage, and outbound data transfers. You generally won't pay anything for data coming into AWS or moving between services in the same region.

Each AWS service has its own pricing factors. For EC2, costs depend on factors like how many hours you run instances, the types of instances you choose, whether you enable detailed monitoring, and any cross-region data transfers. For S3, pricing varies based on storage class, number of requests, and how often you retrieve data. EBS pricing takes into account your volume type, performance requirements, and snapshots for backups. RDS costs reflect database runtime, storage size, setup complexity, and your deployment architecture.

For many organizations, compute resources make up the biggest slice of their AWS bill. That's why Amazon has rolled out so many pricing models over the years: to give you as many tools as possible to optimize and control these costs without sacrificing performance.

Let's take a look at these pricing models.

On-Demand Instance Pricing

When you launch a VM in Amazon EC2, you'll usually end up using On-Demand pricing by default. This option is straightforward and flexible. With On-Demand, you only pay for the compute time you use.

The billing is precise. It's calculated per second with a 60-second minimum for Linux instances. So whether your instance runs for a couple of minutes or several hours, you pay only for that exact usage.

The On-Demand instance pricing model is a good choice for when you have workloads with sudden spikes in demand or for applications where resource needs fluctuate unpredictably. On-Demand pricing is also useful for testing, experimenting, or running proof-of-concept projects. You can spin up an instance in minutes, test your ideas, and shut it down without worrying about ongoing commitments.

Reserved Instance Pricing

Reserved Instances provide up to 72% savings for three-year All Upfront commitments on specific instance types in a Region, though savings vary by term, payment option, and instance family. Although AWS often recommends Savings Plans for more flexibility, Reserved Instances pricing remains popular. The savings come from your commitment, which helps AWS plan its capacity better. You get to choose how you pay:

- All Upfront
- Partial Upfront (you pay a smaller initial payment and then reduced hourly rates)
- No Upfront (skips the initial payment but still offers discounted hourly charges compared to On-Demand pricing)

Reserved Instances work best when you have predictable, steady workloads and you know you'll need those resources for a long time. They're good for if you're running mature applications with consistent usage, and you want both lower costs and predictable budgeting.

Savings Plan Pricing

The Savings Plan pricing option is similar to Reserved Instances pricing. Both save up to 72% compared to On-Demand pricing, so long as there is a commitment of between one and three years. So what are the differences? First, the Savings Plan pricing option tends to be easier to manage across a wider range of services.

For example, if you have a Compute Savings Plan, you'll get the same discount whether you switch from C4 to C6g instances, move workloads between EU (Ireland) and EU (London), or migrate from EC2 to services like Fargate or Lambda.

AWS currently offers three types of Savings Plans:

Compute Savings Plan
> The most flexible option, covering EC2, Fargate, and Lambda usage regardless of instance family or region.

EC2 Instance Savings Plan
> Offers deeper discounts but requires you to stick with specific instance families within a region.

SageMaker Savings Plan
> Designed specifically for ML workloads, giving you cost savings on SageMaker usage.

Savings Plans make the most sense for organizations with steady, predictable workloads that still want the freedom to adjust architectures or adopt new AWS services over time.

Spot Instance Pricing

Spot Instance pricing provides unused EC2 capacity at discounts of up to 90% compared to the On-Demand model. But the pricing is dynamic. The cost goes up or down based on long-term trends in supply and demand for unused capacity. Moreover, if AWS needs that capacity back for On-Demand customers, it can reclaim your Spot Instances with little notice.

Spot Instances work best for workloads that are fault-tolerant and can handle being interrupted. Think of stateless applications that don't rely on persistent in-memory data. They're also a good fit for batch processing, data analysis jobs, and ML model training.

When using Spot Instances, you should build your applications to handle sudden termination smoothly.

Dedicated Host Pricing

Dedicated Host pricing is where you get an entire physical server. This setup gives you full control over the system.

While Dedicated Host pricing usually comes with higher upfront costs than shared infrastructure, it can save you money in the right situations. For instance, if you already own licenses for software like Windows Server, SQL Server, or SUSE Linux Enterprise Server, you can bring those licenses to your dedicated hosts.

AWS offers dedicated hosts through both On-Demand pricing and Savings Plans. This gives you flexibility in how you manage costs. You can pay as you go if you need short-term dedicated infrastructure or commit to longer terms for lower rates if you have predictable, ongoing needs.

Dedicated Instance Pricing

Both Dedicated Instances and Dedicated Hosts provide your own physical servers. However, they work differently.

Dedicated Instances don't give you full control of the system. AWS manages the underlying servers for you.

A disadvantage of the Dedicated Instance pricing model is that you cannot get the savings from server-bound licenses. The reason is that AWS cannot guarantee that your instances will stay on the same physical server.

Another drawback is with compliance. Since there is uncertainty about the location of the physical servers, this could mean violating sovereign residency requirements.

Then why use the Dedicated Instance pricing model? A major advantage is the simplicity. AWS only charges you for the instances you launch, not for the entire physical server.

On-Demand Capacity Reservation Pricing

On-Demand Capacity Reservation pricing gives you a way to lock in EC2 capacity within a specific Availability Zone. It guarantees that the compute resources you need will be there when you need them, even during peak demand, without requiring a long-term commitment.

When you create a capacity reservation, you're securing compute resources in advance. This means your instances can launch without delay, even if other users are competing for the same capacity in that AZ. For organizations that can't afford downtime, this assurance is critical.

These reservations are suitable for business-critical and time-sensitive workloads where availability isn't negotiable. For example, if you're about to launch a major ecommerce promotion, run financial end-of-day processing, or host a live-streamed event, you don't want to risk your instances failing to launch because capacity isn't available.

They're also useful for compliance. Organizations with strict uptime and failover requirements can use reservations to meet their high availability standards reliably.

Another important use case is disaster recovery. During regional outages or emergencies, many businesses scramble to spin up additional resources, which can lead to shortages. By reserving capacity in advance, you make sure your backup systems work as planned, keeping your operations running smoothly even when demand surges. On-Demand Capacity Reservations secure EC2 capacity in a specific Availability Zone but charge for reserved capacity whether used or not. But you can use Reserved Instances or Savings Plans for discounts on usage.

Table 15-1 summarizes the different AWS pricing models.

Table 15-1. AWS pricing models

Models	Description and key points
On-Demand Instance pricing	• Pay only for compute time used (per second, 60-sec minimum for Linux) • Flexible for unpredictable workloads, testing, or proofs of concept (POCs)
Reserved Instance pricing	• Up to 72% discount for one- or three-year commitments • Options: All Upfront, Partial Upfront, or No Upfront payments
Savings Plan pricing	• Similar savings to Reserved Instances with more flexibility • Types: Compute, EC2 Instance, SageMaker Savings Plans
Spot Instance pricing	• Up to 90% discount on unused capacity • Best for fault-tolerant, interruptible workloads like batch jobs
Dedicated Host pricing	• Entire physical server dedicated to you • Supports BYOL (Bring Your Own License) for certain software
Dedicated Instance pricing	• Instances run on hardware dedicated to you but managed by AWS • Simpler billing; cannot use server-bound licenses
On-Demand Capacity Reservation pricing	• Reserve capacity in a specific AZ without long-term commitment • Ensures availability for critical or time-sensitive workloads

AWS Billing and Cost Management

The AWS Billing Console is a financial dashboard for your AWS account. It gives you a clear view of both current and historical usage and costs. This makes it easier to spot trends, catch unexpected charges early, and plan ahead.

Figure 15-1 shows the dashboard. You can find this by first going to the AWS Management Console and searching for Billing and Cost Management.

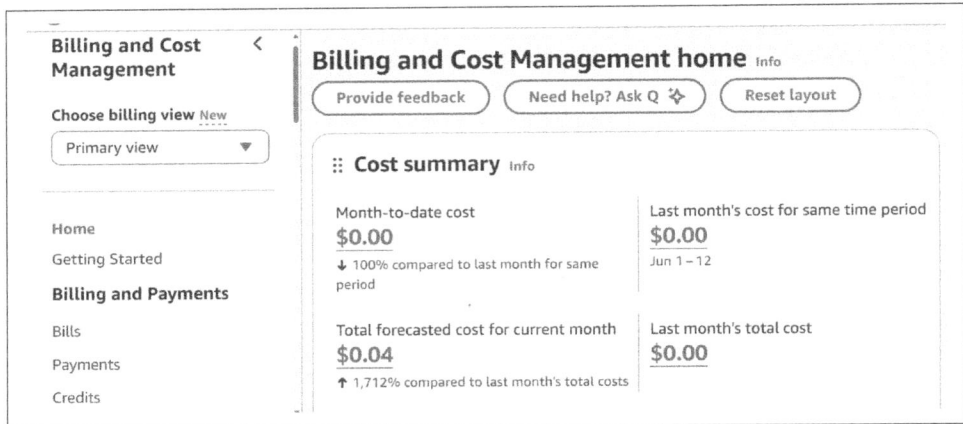

Figure 15-1. Dashboard for AWS Billing and Cost Management

A key advantage of this dashboard is centralized billing. If you manage multiple AWS accounts—say, for different teams or departments—you can pull all the costs into one place. This makes internal accounting simpler and helps keep everyone on the same page.

For this, you can use AWS Organizations. They allow for grouping accounts into different units. This makes it easier to apply policies, allowing for stronger governance and improved security.

The service also simplifies billing. Instead of managing invoices for every account, you get one consolidated bill. This makes it easier to track overall spending, divide costs by team or project, and take advantage of AWS volume discounts.

Regardless of whether you use AWS Organizations, the dashboard provides various options for cost analysis, which you can find on the left sidebar. We'll take a look at some of the main ones.

AWS Cost Explorer

AWS Cost Explorer gives you a clear, visual way to track your cloud spending over time.

Once you turn it on through the AWS Billing and Cost Management Dashboard, it automatically pulls in up to 13 months of historical data and can project up to a year into the future. The data refreshes daily.

To turn on this service, you click Cost Explorer and select Enable Cost Explorer. AWS may take a few minutes to prepare your historical cost and usage data.

With the Cost Explorer, you can break down your costs by month or day, and if you need more detail, there's an option to view hourly usage for the past two weeks.

The Cost Explorer comes with a set of helpful reports, such as those showing monthly spend by service, or daily EC2 usage. But you can also create customized reports, using up to 18 filters, such as for tags, services, regions, resource types, and accounts.

The Cost Explorer uses ML to forecast your future spending for up to 12 months.

If you're using Reserved Instances (RIs) or Savings Plans, Cost Explorer helps you keep track of utilization and coverage. It flags upcoming expirations and suggests new commitments based on your actual usage.

AWS Pricing Calculator

The AWS Pricing Calculator helps you plan costs before you spin up any infrastructure, such as for configuring services like EC2, S3, RDS, and Lambda. For larger projects, you can group services into logical units, so it's easier to manage complex estimates. Each estimate shows a clear breakdown of upfront and ongoing costs.

Once you're done, you can save your estimate as a shareable link, or export it to PDF or CSV. If you sign in with your AWS account, the calculator can factor in your existing usage patterns, discounts, and purchase commitments to produce more realistic, personalized estimates.

However, the AWS Pricing Calculator is a planning tool, not a quote. Real-world costs can vary depending on your usage, pricing region, discounts, taxes, and more.

AWS Budgets

AWS Budgets provides tools to set spending limits, track usage, and get alerts before things spiral out of control. The budgets can run on a schedule that fits your needs: daily, monthly, quarterly, or annually. And you can slice them by service, tag, account, or region.

What really sets AWS Budgets apart is its ability to act—not just alert you—when thresholds are hit. You can tie a budget to an automated response, like denying new resource provisioning by applying IAM.

AWS Cost Allocation Tags

AWS cost allocation tags help you make sense of your cloud bill by adding context to your resources. They are labels in the form of key-value pairs, which you attach to services like EC2 instances, S3 buckets, or RDS databases. Cost allocation tags are included with tools like the Cost Explorer and Budgets. AWS supports both built-in system tags (like `aws:createdBy`) and fully custom, user-defined tags.

It's worth noting that tags only start affecting cost reports after you activate them. They don't apply retroactively, and not every AWS service supports tagging. You'll want to think about tag enforcement early, especially if you're planning to use them for cost allocation.

AWS Technical Resources and AWS Support Options

AWS has a wide range of technical resources and support options. Let's start with the basics. AWS Documentation (at *docs.aws.amazon.com*) is packed with useful information. You'll find everything from EC2 Linux and Windows user guides to detailed API references, CLI instructions, and tutorials covering services like Auto Scaling, Lambda, and Nitro Enclaves. It's comprehensive, well-organized, and kept up to date.

Alongside the documentation, AWS offers FAQs, whitepapers, and architecture guides that provide best practices for security, compliance, and cloud design patterns. The AWS Blog is also a great place to stay current. It features service announcements, technical walkthroughs, and real-world case studies.

When you're looking for more than documentation, AWS has specialized resources to help solve real-world challenges. AWS Prescriptive Guidance offers curated strategies and reference implementations from AWS experts and partners. This is helpful for cloud adoption, migration, and modernization.

For quick troubleshooting, there's the AWS Knowledge Center, and if you prefer a community-driven approach, AWS re:Post has a Q&A platform.

AWS support is based on tiers:

Basic Support (free)
    Covers billing issues, access to community forums, and basic health data.

Developer Support
    Adds business-hours access to Cloud Support Associates. This is a good option for early-stage or test environments.

Business Support
    Designed for production use. It includes 24/7 access to senior engineers, the full Trusted Advisor toolkit, third-party software support, and optional event support through Infrastructure Event Management (IEM).

Enterprise On-Ramp
    Built for critical workloads. It includes a pool of Technical Account Managers (TAMs), prioritized case handling (e.g., 30-minute SLA for critical issues), architectural reviews, and AWS Countdown planning for major events.

Enterprise Support

The top tier. You get a dedicated TAM, a Concierge billing team, faster SLAs (as low as 15 minutes), ongoing proactive reviews, and advanced automation tools to keep everything running smoothly at scale.

There is also the AWS Partner Network (APN), which includes independent software vendors (ISVs), system integrators, and consultants. Through the AWS Marketplace, customers can discover vetted tools for cost tracking, governance, security, and more.

And when your team needs direct, hands-on help, AWS Professional Services and Solutions Architects are available to collaborate on architecture design, deployment, and optimization.

Conclusion

In this chapter, we looked at the key concepts and tools related to AWS billing, budgeting, and cost management. From understanding the various pricing models to leveraging tools such as AWS Cost Explorer, Budgets, and the Pricing Calculator, we've seen how AWS provides a helpful framework for tracking and optimizing costs. We also covered resource tagging, centralized billing with AWS Organizations, and available support options to help ensure both financial control and operational efficiency.

We have now reached the point of this book where we have covered all the main topics you may see on the exam. In the next chapter, we'll look at tips and strategies for how to study for it.

Chapter Quiz

To check your answers, please refer to the "Chapter 15 Answer Key" on page 208

1. What is a key benefit of AWS On-Demand Instance pricing?

   A. You pay only for compute time used without long-term commitments.

   B. You receive up to a 72% discount with a three-year commitment.

   C. It automatically scales based on traffic.

   D. It requires upfront payment for cost optimization.

2. Which AWS service provides a visual breakdown of costs over time?

   A. AWS Pricing Calculator

   B. AWS Budgets

   C. AWS Cost and Usage Report

   D. AWS Cost Explorer

3. What is the key feature of On-Demand Capacity Reservation pricing?

    A. It requires a one-year commitment.

    B. It automatically migrates instances.

    C. It guarantees capacity in a specific Availability Zone.

    D. It offers the cheapest Elastic Compute Cloud (EC2) rates.

4. What is the purpose of cost allocation tags?

    A. To encrypt resources

    B. To track AWS resource costs based on project or department

    C. To predict usage trends

    D. To enable data replication

5. What is the role of AWS Organizations in billing?

    A. It hosts your EC2 instances.

    B. It consolidates billing across multiple accounts.

    C. It encrypts billing data.

    D. It migrates workloads between accounts.

Strategies and Techniques for Successfully Taking the AWS Certified Cloud Practitioner Exam

We've covered a lot in this book. So how much study time should you set aside for the AWS Certified Cloud Practitioner exam? That really comes down to your background. If you're new to this category, budget around 15–20 hours. If you've already had some hands-on experience, you may only need 5–10 hours to get ready.

To help you gauge where you stand, I've included a practice exam. It's a good gut check. Also, don't skip the glossary. Definitions come up often on the test, and having those locked in can help you rack up points.

In this chapter, we'll start off with strategies to help you walk into the exam room feeling confident. Then we'll dig into the core topics, so you'll have a clear plan for your study sessions.

Tips for Taking the Exam

Strategy can make a big difference between barely passing and getting a solid score. Good time management, clear focus, and a few smart habits can give you an edge. In this section, you'll find practical tips to help you stay sharp from start to finish.

Manage Your Time

Time is one of your biggest assets on exam day. You'll get 90 minutes to answer 65 questions. So you've got a little over a minute per question.

Start with the questions you know cold. Knock those out early to build momentum. When you hit something tough, don't freeze. Mark it, move on, and circle back later. Focus on getting all the easier questions out of the way first. That clears space and stress for the trickier ones when you loop back through them.

Read Questions Carefully

It's easy to skim when you're in a hurry, but don't. Take a breath and carefully read what each question is asking. Small words like *not*, *only*, or *except* can completely flip the meaning.

Here's a common trap: "Which of the following is not a benefit of using AWS AI services?" That tiny *not* changes everything. Now you're hunting for the odd one out—not picking the best feature.

Slowing down just a touch helps you catch what's really being asked.

Use the Process of Elimination

Multiple choice questions aren't just about spotting the right answer. Often, they're about spotting the wrong ones first. If you're unsure, start by ruling out anything that's clearly off base.

This trick works especially well when none of the answers jump out. Nix the ones that don't make sense, and your odds go up. Say you've got four choices. Eliminate one, and your chances jump from 25% to 33%. Knock out two, and you're at 50/50.

Besides improving your odds, trimming the options saves mental energy. Fewer choices means less second-guessing, which helps you stay focused and make faster decisions as you move through the test.

Stay Calm and Double-Check Your Answers

Staying calm matters a lot. It's easy to tense up, especially when the clock is ticking or a tough question throws you off.

That stress is normal. But if you let it take over, it can derail your performance. Instead, pause. Take a few deep breaths. It sounds simple, but those few seconds can reset your mind, slow the swirl of thoughts, and help you get back on track with a clear head.

If you've paced yourself well and have time at the end, don't rush out. Use those last minutes to review. Go back to anything you flagged, especially the ones that gave you pause the first time around.

This final check can really pay off. Sometimes, fresh eyes help you spot something you missed or rethink an answer you rushed through.

Crash Course: What to Know Before Exam Day

The following is a crash course, not a full review. The focus is on a rundown of the key concepts, tools, and services most likely to show up on test day.

This is broken into four sections, which are based on the official AWS study guide domains.

Cloud Concepts

Cloud computing is about getting IT resources on demand, over the internet, and paying only for what you use. AWS offers a flexible, scalable alternative to an on-premises setup. Instead of paying for expenses up front for hardware—and then dealing with ongoing maintenance—you can spin up what you need, when you need it.

One of AWS's biggest advantages is its global footprint. With Regions and Availability Zones around the world, you can place your services closer to users. This helps cut down latency and makes it easier to meet data residency requirements.

Another key advantage is elasticity. You can scale resources up or down automatically based on real-time demand. This not only keeps systems running smoothly during traffic spikes but it also helps control costs. Agility comes with it. You can provision resources in minutes, which means teams can move fast, experiment more, and ship applications quicker.

AWS also offers high availability by spreading workloads across isolated AZs. And thanks to its massive user base, AWS achieves economies of scale that bring costs down for everyone.

You'll also want to get familiar with the AWS Well-Architected Framework. It lays out core design principles built around six pillars: operational excellence (improving through automation), security (keeping data safe and intact), reliability (bouncing back from failure), performance efficiency, cost optimization, and sustainability. For example, breaking your application into loosely coupled components supports both scalability and reliability.

Cloud migration is another important area. AWS offers the Cloud Adoption Framework (CAF) to help organizations manage the cultural and technical shifts involved. There are different strategies for migrating workloads, including rehosting (lift-and-shift), replatforming, and refactoring.

As for cloud economics, understand how AWS moves spending from CapEx (capital expenditure) to OpEx (operational expenditure). You'll also see cost-saving strategies like rightsizing, automation, and smart use of reserved or spot instances.

Security and Compliance

Under the Shared Responsibility Model, AWS manages the security of the cloud, such as the physical hardware, software, networking, and facilities. You're responsible for what happens in the cloud, like setting up permissions, encrypting data, and locking down your applications. The exact split depends on the service you're using. For instance, with EC2, you manage the operating system and updates. But with AWS Lambda, AWS handles more of the stack.

To help you meet compliance standards—whether global or industry-specific—AWS includes tools for governance and reporting. AWS Artifact gives you access to audit reports and other compliance documents. AWS also supports a long list of frameworks like HIPAA, GDPR, FedRAMP, and PCI DSS. You can automate controls using services such as AWS Config, CloudTrail, and Audit Manager. On the encryption front, AWS supports encryption both at rest and in transit, with key management handled through AWS KMS. Logging and monitoring give you visibility into what's happening in your environment.

One of the most important parts of cloud security is identity and access management. AWS IAM lets you control access using users, groups, roles, and policies.

You should also use the principle of least privilege. This means only granting the permissions that are absolutely necessary. And take special care with the root user: turn on MFA and avoid using that account for day-to-day tasks. If you're managing multiple AWS accounts, IAM Identity Center can help you handle permissions from a central place, with support for external identity providers.

For active protection, AWS offers services like GuardDuty (which scans for threats), AWS Shield (DDoS defense), AWS WAF (a firewall for web apps), and Security Hub, which pulls together alerts across your accounts. Trusted Advisor also checks for weak points like open ports or loose permissions. You'll get monitoring through CloudWatch and audit logs via CloudTrail to track changes and access.

Many customers also use third-party security tools from the AWS Marketplace. AWS keeps its best practices and guidance up to date through blogs, documentation, and services like Security Hub.

Cloud Technology and Services

AWS gives you several methods for deploying and managing workloads in the cloud. You can use the AWS Management Console for manual tasks, or the CLI and SDKs when you want more control or need to script actions. For repeatable infrastructure, tools like AWS CloudFormation let you define your setup as code, such as for automation and consistency.

You'll also encounter different cloud deployment models. Cloud native means building directly on AWS using its services. Hybrid lets you blend on-premises systems with cloud infrastructure.

As for the global infrastructure for AWS, this includes Regions, AZs, and Edge Locations. Each Region holds multiple isolated AZs, which help boost availability and fault tolerance. If one AZ goes down, others keep the systems running. Edge Locations support Amazon CloudFront, caching content closer to users to cut down latency. Some companies go multi-Region to meet compliance rules, improve global application performance, or build strong disaster recovery plans.

When it comes to compute services, AWS has various options. Amazon EC2 gives you VMs with a wide range of instance types, such as those optimized for compute, memory, or storage. You can scale them up and down automatically with Auto Scaling. For container workloads, AWS offers ECS(its native container service) and EKS (managed Kubernetes). If you prefer not to deal with the complexities of servers, AWS Lambda runs your code in response to events, and AWS Fargate handles containers without you managing the infrastructure. To keep everything performing smoothly, ELB spreads traffic across your instances or containers.

For databases, AWS supports different data models. Use Amazon RDS or Aurora for traditional relational databases. Go with DynamoDB if you need a fast, scalable NoSQL option. Amazon ElastiCache supports Redis and Memcached for in-memory caching. If you're migrating from another system, you can use tools like AWS DMS.

Networking in AWS starts with Amazon VPC (Virtual Private Cloud), which lets you create isolated networks in the cloud. Inside your VPC environment, you set up subnets, IGWs, and NAT gateways. You control security using security groups and NACL.

Amazon Route 53 handles DNS and domain registration. If you need to connect your on-premises data center to the cloud, AWS Direct Connect or VPN options support hybrid networking.

On the storage side, AWS covers major use cases. Amazon S3 offers scalable object storage, with storage classes that balance cost and access needs. For block storage, there is Amazon EBS. For shared file storage, Amazon EFS or FSx are good choices. Storage Gateway helps bridge your on-premises storage systems with AWS. To manage backups and data lifecycle efficiently, AWS Backup and lifecycle policies are built in.

AWS also includes tools for AI/ML and analytics. Amazon SageMaker handles everything from building to deploying ML models. Other AI tools include Comprehend (text analysis), Lex (chatbots), and Rekognition (image and video).

On the analytics side, Athena lets you query data in S3, while Kinesis supports real-time streaming. Glue handles ETL jobs, and QuickSight turns your data into interactive dashboards.

Rounding things out, AWS offers services across dozens of categories. SQS (message queues), SNS (notifications), and EventBridge (event bus) help you build event-driven systems. Amazon Connect supports cloud call centers, while SES takes care of sending emails.

Developers can use tools like CodeBuild, CodePipeline, and X-Ray for CI/CD and debugging. And as for end-user computing, you have options like Amazon WorkSpaces, AppStream 2.0, and WorkSpaces Secure Browser. For IoT, there's AWS IoT Core. Finally, when it comes to mobile or web apps, you have AWS Amplify and AppSync.

Billing, Pricing, and Support

AWS gives you a range of pricing models designed to fit different workloads, budgets, and business needs. For compute services, you've got several options. On-Demand Instances let you pay as you go, with no long-term commitment. This is a good option for unpredictable usage. Reserved Instances lock in lower rates if you commit to a one- or three-year term, making them suitable for steady-state workloads. Spot Instances let you bid on unused capacity at steep discounts, which works well for flexible, interruption-tolerant jobs. Savings Plans offer a broader discount model based on committed usage, not tied to specific instance types. For specific compliance or licensing needs, Dedicated Hosts and Dedicated Instances give you physical isolation. And if you need guaranteed capacity in a particular Availability Zone, On-Demand Capacity Reservations can secure it in advance.

On the storage side, AWS gives you multiple pricing tiers depending on how often you access your data. Amazon S3 includes Standard, Intelligent-Tiering, and Glacier options—each balancing cost and performance in different ways. Amazon EBS (block storage) and Amazon EFS or FSx (file storage) are priced based on both capacity and throughput. It's worth noting that AWS doesn't charge for inbound data (ingress), but outbound data (egress), especially across regions or to the public internet, does incur fees.

To stay on top of spending, AWS offers several built-in tools. The AWS Pricing Calculator helps you estimate monthly costs. AWS Budgets lets you set limits and receive alerts when you're approaching them. AWS Cost Explorer gives you visual reports to track usage trends. Use cost allocation tags to break down expenses by team, project, or department.

If your company uses multiple AWS accounts, AWS Organizations makes cost management easier. You get consolidated billing, which combines usage across accounts for volume discounts. You can also share Reserved Instances and Savings Plans across accounts to reduce unused capacity.

On the support side, AWS offers several tiers: Developer, Business, Enterprise On-Ramp, and Enterprise Support. Each plan comes with different response times, support access, and guidance levels. You'll also have tools like AWS Support, Health Dashboard, and Trusted Advisor to monitor your environment and get actionable recommendations.

Outside of paid support, AWS offers extensive self-service content. There are whitepapers, technical blogs, the AWS Knowledge Center, and AWS re:Post (a community Q&A site). AWS Prescriptive Guidance gives step-by-step advice for common use cases. And for hands-on help, you can work with AWS Professional Services or find a certified partner through the AWS Marketplace.

Conclusion

In this chapter, we started off by covering hands-on exam strategies. From there, we looked into the four main domains: cloud concepts, security and compliance, cloud technology and services, and billing, pricing, and support. Each section laid out the essentials, such as the definitions, examples, and practical tips. With a solid grip on these core topics and a game plan for how to approach the exam, you'll be prepared to succeed.

Practice Exam

To check your answers, please refer to the "Practice Exam Answer Key" on page 209.

1. Where do you go in the AWS console to see your spending forecast?

    A. Billing Console

    B. Identity and Access Management (IAM) Role Manager

    C. Elastic Compute Cloud (EC2) Dashboard

    D. AWS Health widget

2. What is the purpose of setting an AWS budget?

    A. To receive promotional credits

    B. To enable new AWS services

    C. To enforce usage quotas

    D. To get alerts when spending approaches or exceeds a defined amount

3. Which AWS service is best suited for storing media files and backup archives?

    A. Amazon Relational Database Service (RDS)

    B. Amazon Simple Storage Service (S3)

    C. Amazon EC2

    D. AWS CloudTrail

4. What does Amazon CloudWatch primarily help with?

    A. Setting budgets for cost tracking

    B. Monitoring logs and performance metrics

C. Creating user access policies

D. Running relational databases

5. What is a key characteristic of the public cloud deployment model?

   A. Everything, including compute, storage, and networking, lives in the cloud provider's infrastructure.

   B. It gives maximum control over hardware, which is owned by the user.

   C. It is only suitable for applications that cannot be migrated.

   D. It requires users to manage physical data centers.

6. Which cloud service model provides users with access to the fundamental building blocks of computing, such as virtual machines, storage, and networking, without managing physical servers?

   A. IaaS (infrastructure as a service)

   B. SaaS (software as a service)

   C. PaaS (platform as a service)

   D. DaaS (database as a service)

7. A team wants to develop web and mobile applications quickly and needs a service model that handles provisioning, scaling, and patching so that they can focus solely on writing code. Which model is most suitable?

   A. PaaS

   B. IaaS

   C. SaaS

   D. On-premises

8. Which cloud service model offers the highest level of control over the operating system and installed software?

   A. SaaS

   B. PaaS

   C. FaaS (function as a service)

   D. IaaS

9. What is a key characteristic of the AWS operating expenditure (OpEx) pricing model?

   A. It is a pay-as-you-go model.

   B. It requires upfront licensing.

   C. It requires dedicated hardware.

   D. It charges annual subscription fees.

10. What is the goal of rightsizing in AWS?

    A. Increase redundancy

    B. Automate patching

    C. Maximize security layers

    D. Eliminate underutilized resources

11. What AWS migration strategy involves fully redesigning applications for cloud native capabilities?

    A. Rehost

    B. Replatform

    C. Retire

    D. Refactor

12. What migration strategy involves keeping an application in its current environment temporarily due to constraints or dependencies?

    A. Repurchase

    B. Retain

    C. Refactor

    D. Replatform

13. Which AWS tool helps automate the setup of a secure, governed multi-account environment?

    A. AWS Config

    B. AWS Organizations

    C. AWS Control Tower

    D. AWS License Manager

14. What AWS tool helps you prepare for audits by collecting evidence?

    A. AWS IAM

    B. AWS Shield

    C. AWS Audit Manager

    D. AWS Control Tower

15. What is a key benefit of using AWS Organizations?

    A. It encrypts all stored data.

    B. It automates resource scaling.

    C. It centralizes multi-account management.

    D. It detects malicious activity.

16. What does the AWS Compliance Center provide?

    A. EC2 usage reports

    B. Whitepapers, checklists, and legal resources for compliance

    C. IAM user configurations

    D. Real-time DDoS alerts

17. Which service is used to create policies that define access in AWS?

    A. IAM

    B. CloudTrail

    C. Shield

    D. CloudWatch

18. What is a key benefit of using IAM roles instead of IAM users for EC2 instance access?

    A. It is faster to create users.

    B. It reduces risk by not using access keys.

    C. Roles provide higher billing priority.

    D. Roles allow root-level access.

19. Which of the following is a benefit of using the AWS Command Line Interface (CLI) with IAM?

    A. It bypasses permission checks.

    B. It enables automation of IAM tasks.

    C. It encrypts user passwords.

    D. It grants access to AWS Marketplace.

20. Why is IAM considered foundational in AWS security?

    A. It creates billing dashboards.

    B. It controls identity and permissions across services.

    C. It provides virtual private network (VPN) encryption.

    D. It manages virtual machines.

21. What is the purpose of Amazon Inspector?

    A. To automatically scan AWS resources for vulnerabilities

    B. To configure IAM policies

    C. To distribute global web content

    D. To manage encryption keys

22. What is a zero-day exploit?

   A. Malware disguised as antivirus software

   B. An attack on a software vulnerability not yet patched

   C. An attack that requires physical access

   D. A brute-force password attack

23. What is a key benefit of Amazon Route 53 for security?

   A. It encrypts stored data.

   B. It blocks access to known malicious domains using the Domain Name System (DNS) Firewall.

   C. It scans images for vulnerabilities.

   D. It monitors HTTP request headers.

24. What is the role of AWS Certificate Manager (ACM)?

   A. It detects threats.

   B. It manages IAM users.

   C. It stores database passwords.

   D. It issues and manages Transport Layer Security (TLS) certificates.

25. What are AWS Availability Zones (AZs) designed to prevent?

   A. Single points of failure within a Region

   B. Unauthorized physical access to data

   C. Overuse of compute resources

   D. Budget overruns from network transfer

26. What AWS feature provides localized compute and storage capacity for low-latency use cases in cities?

   A. Wavelength Zone

   B. Local Zone

   C. Edge Location

   D. Availability Zone

27. What tool is most commonly used to write and manage infrastructure as code (IaC) in AWS?

   A. AWS Shield

   B. Route 53

   C. AWS Software Development Kit (SDK)

   D. AWS CloudFormation

28. What AWS service allows launching compute resources at telecom provider data centers?

   A. Local Zones

   B. CloudFront

   C. Wavelength Zones

   D. Outposts

29. What does AWS Fargate eliminate the need for?

   A. Data encryption

   B. Server provisioning

   C. IAM role creation

   D. Load balancing

30. What benefit do EC2 Spot Instances provide?

   A. Up to 90% cost savings

   B. Longer uptime guarantees

   C. Reserved compute availability

   D. Managed scaling for RDS

31. What is an example use case for AWS Lambda?

   A. Launching EC2 backup scripts

   B. Running code after an S3 upload

   C. Hosting a long-running server

   D. Building a custom virtual private cloud (VPC)

32. What is the primary function of the AWS Compute Optimizer?

   A. Distributing traffic across instances

   B. Optimizing EC2, Lambda, and Fargate resources

   C. Managing container orchestration

   D. Providing DNS resolution

33. Which S3 storage class automatically moves data between tiers based on usage patterns?

   A. S3 Standard

   B. S3 Express One Zone

   C. S3 Intelligent-Tiering

   D. S3 Glacier Deep Archive

34. Which AWS service allows your on-premises applications to access cloud storage as local files via Server Message Block (SMB) or Network File System (NFS) protocols?

    A. AWS Backup

    B. AWS Storage Gateway

    C. Amazon Elastic Block Store (EBS)

    D. Amazon FSx

35. What is a key characteristic of Amazon S3 Glacier Instant Retrieval?

    A. Retrieval times of 12–48 hours

    B. Retrieval takes minutes to hours

    C. Millisecond-level retrieval for archived data

    D. It stores data only in one AZ

36. What is AWS Backup's primary benefit?

    A. It provides block-level storage.

    B. It offers direct file sharing services.

    C. It enables compute scaling for applications.

    D. It centralizes backup management across AWS services.

37. Which AWS service offers MySQL and PostgreSQL compatibility with up to 5× throughput compared to standard MySQL?

    A. Amazon RDS

    B. Amazon DynamoDB

    C. Amazon Aurora

    D. Amazon ElastiCache

38. Which service helps convert database schemas and application SQL code for new engines?

    A. Amazon DynamoDB

    B. Amazon Aurora

    C. AWS Database Migration Service (DMS)

    D. AWS Schema Conversion Tool (SCT)

39. Which Amazon service provides microsecond read/write performance?

    A. Amazon Aurora

    B. Amazon RDS

    C. Amazon DynamoDB

    D. Amazon ElastiCache

40. Which database option is best suited for order processing requiring consistency?

    A. Amazon ElastiCache

    B. Amazon DynamoDB

    C. Amazon SCT

    D. Amazon DMS

41. What is a main benefit of AWS Direct Connect compared to Site-to-Site VPN?

    A. It has lower upfront costs.

    B. It has a faster setup time.

    C. It uses the public internet.

    D. It provides consistent high bandwidth and low latency.

42. What does AWS Route 53 Resolver do?

    A. It provides direct fiber connectivity to AWS.

    B. It allows DNS queries between on-premises and AWS.

    C. It creates VPC subnets.

    D. It sets up edge caching for content delivery.

43. Which service enables low-latency and high-throughput dedicated connectivity to AWS?

    A. AWS VPN

    B. Amazon Virtual Private Cloud (VPC)

    C. Amazon Route 53

    D. AWS Direct Connect

44. Which protocol is commonly used for high-speed connections to storage systems?

    A. Transmission Control Protocol/Internet Protocol (TCP/IP)

    B. Ethernet

    C. Data center bridging (DCB)

    D. Fibre Channel

45. What type of models does generative AI commonly use?

    A. Generative adversarial networks (GANs) and large language models (LLMs)

    B. Only regression models

    C. Only clustering algorithms

    D. Traditional relational database models

46. Which AWS service is specifically designed for enterprise search with natural language queries?

    A. Amazon Athena

    B. Amazon Kendra

    C. Amazon Redshift

    D. AWS Lambda

47. Which AWS service simplifies extract, transform, load (ETL) work with a visual interface or Python/Scala scripts?

    A. Amazon Glue

    B. Amazon Kendra

    C. Amazon SageMaker Notebooks

    D. Amazon QuickSight

48. What is AWS Glue Data Catalog used for?

    A. Creating ML models

    B. Building chatbots

    C. Organizing and cataloging data schemas

    D. Delivering dashboards

49. What is a common use of Amazon Simple Notification Service (SNS)?

    A. Broadcasting real-time messages to multiple subscribers

    B. Running serverless compute functions directly

    C. Hosting static websites

    D. Storing structured relational data

50. What does AWS CodeBuild do?

    A. It manages DNS services.

    B. It monitors applications for errors.

    C. It creates virtual private networks.

    D. It compiles code, runs tests, and produces software packages.

51. What does Amazon AppStream 2.0 provide?

    A. It streams desktop applications from AWS to devices.

    B. It runs serverless functions.

    C. It manages event routing.

    D. It hosts GraphQL APIs.

52. Which AWS service provides message durability with retry mechanisms?

    A. Amazon SNS

    B. AWS Amplify

    C. AWS X-Ray

    D. Amazon AppStream 2.0

53. Which pricing model offers the greatest flexibility across AWS compute services?

    A. Reserved Instance

    B. Compute Savings Plan

    C. Spot Instance

    D. Dedicated Host

54. Which pricing model provides an entire physical server to you?

    A. On-Demand Instance

    B. Dedicated Instance

    C. Dedicated Host

    D. EC2 Spot

55. What tool helps create cost estimates before launching services?

    A. Cost Explorer

    B. AWS Budgets

    C. AWS Pricing Calculator

    D. AWS Organizations

56. Which support plan includes a Concierge billing team?

    A. Business

    B. Developer

    C. Enterprise On-Ramp

    D. Basic

Answer Key

Chapter 2 Answer Key

1. C: The Free Tier helps users try AWS without incurring costs—within usage limits.

2. C: The AWS root user has full access and poses a security risk if compromised.

3. A: IAM is used to manage users and permissions.

4. A: EC2 provides scalable virtual machines in the cloud.

5. C: AWS CloudTrail provides API activity logs.

Chapter 3 Answer Key

1. B: A private cloud refers to an organization hosting everything in its own data center, sometimes called on-premises when using virtualization and cloud-style management.

2. C: Scalability, or whether workloads spike seasonally or need rapid scaling, is a key technical and business need when choosing a model.

3. B: With SaaS, no setup or maintenance is required, and it's always the latest version.

4. D: Hybrid setups offer flexibility and scalability while maintaining control where you need it, especially useful for legacy systems or when regulations require certain data to stay in-house.

5. C: High availability aims for minimal downtime by distributing workloads and adding redundancy.

Chapter 4 Answer Key

1. D: The TCO includes reduced hardware, maintenance, and staffing costs.
2. B: Repackage is not part of the 6 Rs.
3. B: Sustainability promotes energy efficiency and environmental care.
4. B. Governance focuses on risk, compliance, and business alignment.
5. D: SaaS like Salesforce replaces old tools.

Chapter 5 Answer Key

1. D: Governance is about setting and enforcing rules.
2. B: The Federal Risk and Authorization Management Program (FedRAMP) is for federal cloud security.
3. B: AWS Config evaluates configuration changes.
4. C: Amazon Inspector scans EC2 for risks.
5. A: SCPs enforce permission boundaries.

Chapter 6 Answer Key

1. A: IAM is used to securely manage access and permissions for AWS resources.
2. C: Groups assign permissions to users with similar responsibilities.
3. D: Temporary credentials are short-lived and safer.
4. B: IAM Access Advisor highlights permissions that have not been used.
5. C: Condition allows contextual restrictions like IP.

Chapter 7 Answer Key

1. C: AWS manages infrastructure-level security.
2. B: WAF filters HTTP/HTTPS requests to block threats like SQL injection.
3. D: Firewall Manager enforces WAF and Shield rules centrally.
4. A: KMS handles encryption key management.
5. B: Security Hub aggregates and prioritizes findings from GuardDuty, Inspector, Config, and other sources into a single view.

Chapter 8 Answer Key

1. D: Multi-Region deployment helps reduce latency and improve resilience.
2. D: Data centers are the foundational physical units.
3. A: AWS Shield defends against DDoS attacks.
4. C: Amazon CloudFront uses multilevel caches.
5. B: Each Region includes multiple fault-isolated AZs.

Chapter 9 Answer Key

1. C: C series are compute-optimized for CPU-intensive tasks.
2. C: Amazon EKS is a managed Kubernetes service.
3. B: Auto Scaling adjusts EC2 instances to demand.
4. B: ELB ensures availability and performance by distributing traffic.
5. C: Pods are the smallest deployable unit in Kubernetes.

Chapter 10 Answer Key

1. A: S3 achieves 11 nines of durability by replicating data across multiple AZs.
2. D: Deep Archive retrieval times range between 12 and 48 hours.
3. C: Tape Gateway emulates virtual tape libraries stored in S3/Glacier.
4. C: io2 Block Express supports Multi-Attach to 16 Nitro instances.
5. B. EBS provides block-level storage for EC2.

Chapter 11 Answer Key

1. A: Self-managed EC2 databases give you full control of configuration and management.
2. C: DynamoDB is a managed NoSQL database.
3. A: DynamoDB scales horizontally.
4. C: ElastiCache supports Redis and Memcached.
5. D: AWS SCT converts schemas and embedded SQL code.

Chapter 12 Answer Key

1. A: A VPC allows full control over networking setup.
2. C: A NAT Gateway enables outbound connections.
3. C: Subnets organize and isolate resources.
4. A: AWS VPN creates secure tunnels.
5. C: An internet gateway connects to the internet.

Chapter 13 Answer Key

1. C: ML enables systems to learn from data patterns.
2. D: Deep learning is a subset of machine learning.
3. C: SageMaker builds ML models.
4. B: RAG combines retrieval and generation.
5. B: Amazon Bedrock provides access to many foundation models.

Chapter 14 Answer Key

1. B: EventBridge routes events based on rules.
2. B: Dead-letter queues store failed messages.
3. B: AWS CodePipeline automates CI/CD workflows.
4. A: AppSync unifies data sources via GraphQL.
5. D: MQTT is the lightweight messaging protocol.

Chapter 15 Answer Key

1. A: On-Demand pricing is designed for flexibility and short-term or unpredictable workloads.
2. D: AWS Cost Explorer offers charts and graphs to view and analyze historical and forecasted costs.
3. C: Reservations ensure that capacity in a specific Availability Zone is available when needed.
4. B: Cost allocation tags provide metadata to break down costs across services or teams.
5. B: AWS Organizations allows consolidated billing for easier cost tracking.

Practice Exam Answer Key

1. A: The Billing Console shows charges and forecasts.
2. D: Budgets provide alerts to help track and manage spending.
3. B: Amazon S3 is designed to be used for object storage.
4. B: CloudWatch monitors and collects performance data.
5. A: In a public cloud setup, the whole stack, including compute, storage, networking, and databases, lives in the cloud.
6. A: IaaS gives access to virtual machines, storage, and networking without asking you to manage physical servers.
7. A: PaaS is ideal for developers who want to move fast and focus on writing code, as the platform handles provisioning, scaling, patching, and so on.
8. D: IaaS provides virtual machines where you can choose your operating system, install whatever software you need, and configure things exactly how you like, offering full control.
9. A: OpEx reflects operational, usage-based expenses.
10. D: Rightsizing optimizes costs by matching resource size to demand.
11. D: Refactor rebuilds apps for cloud native features.
12. B. Retain means holding off on migration due to valid reasons.
13. C: AWS Control Tower sets up landing zones and enforces guardrails.
14. C: AWS Audit Manager automates compliance evidence collection.
15. C: AWS Organizations centralizes multi-account management.
16. B: The Compliance Center supports compliance professionals.
17. A: IAM is responsible for identity and access control, including policies.
18. B: It reduces risk by not using access keys
19. B: AWS CLI allows scripted IAM operations.
20. B: IAM manages access control across AWS.
21. A: Inspector scans compute resources for security flaws.
22. B: Zero-day exploits target unknown or unpatched flaws.
23. B: DNS Firewall can block known malicious lookups.
24. D: ACM handles certificate lifecycles.
25. A: AZs are isolated to prevent shared failure.
26. B: Local Zones provide AWS services to users in cities.
27. D: AWS CloudFormation is built for IaC.

28. C: Wavelength Zones are embedded within 5G networks.

29. B: Fargate abstracts infrastructure, eliminating server management.

30. A: Spot Instances offer deep discounts for interruptible workloads.

31. B. Lambda can trigger on S3 events.

32. B: Compute Optimizer analyzes usage patterns and recommends optimal configurations for EC2, Lambda, and Fargate resources, helping improve cost efficiency and performance.

33. C: Intelligent-Tiering optimizes cost by moving between four access tiers.

34. B: AWS Storage Gateway bridges on-premises to AWS storage.

35. C: Instant Retrieval provides fast access to archived data.

36. D: AWS Backup consolidates backup management.

37. C: Aurora is MySQL- and PostgreSQL-compatible with high throughput.

38. D: AWS SCT converts schemas and application SQL code.

39. D: ElastiCache delivers microsecond performance.

40. B: DynamoDB supports ACID (atomicity, consistency, isolation, and durability) transactions for consistency.

41. D: AWS Direct Connect offers stable dedicated connectivity.

42. B: AWS Resolver bridges the DNS between environments.

43. D: Direct Connect provides dedicated connectivity.

44. D: Fibre Channel is high-speed for storage.

45. A: GANs and LLMs are core to generative AI.

46. B: Kendra is designed for enterprise search with NLP.

47. A: Amazon Glue is for ETL.

48. C. Glue Data Catalog organizes data for analysis.

49. A: SNS is a publish-subscribe notification service.

50. D. CodeBuild handles builds and tests.

51. A: AppStream 2.0 streams apps from AWS to devices.

52. A: SNS stores and retries failed messages.

53. B:. Compute Savings Plans apply across EC2, Fargate, and Lambda with fewer restrictions.

54. C: Dedicated Hosts give you full visibility and control of the physical server.

55. C: The Pricing Calculator models and estimates future AWS costs.

56. C: Enterprise On-Ramp includes access to a Concierge for billing/account issues.

Glossary

ACID

A set of principles (atomicity, consistency, isolation, and durability) that relational databases adhere to. They ensure data integrity during transactions.

Amazon Virtual Private Cloud (VPC)

A logically isolated section of the AWS Cloud where users can launch AWS resources in a virtual network that they define and control.

Application Load Balancer (ALB)

A type of Elastic Load Balancer used for advanced HTTP/HTTPS routing.

Artificial intelligence (AI)

A broad field focused on building machines and systems that can perform tasks typically associated with human intelligence, such as learning, reasoning, and decision making.

Auto Scaling group (ASG)

A collection of EC2 instances that are treated as a logical grouping for automatic scaling and management.

Availability Zone (AZ)

A geographically distinct and isolated location within an AWS Region, designed to be independent of other AZs to provide fault tolerance and high availability.

AWS Amplify

A set of tools, libraries, and UI components that accelerate full-stack web and mobile app development, including features like authentication, storage, and real-time data sync.

AWS AppSync

A service that aggregates data from various sources under a single GraphQL endpoint, supporting real-time updates, caching, and offline sync.

AWS Artifact

A centralized repository that provides instant access to AWS compliance reports, such as SOC, PCI DSS, and ISO certifications, and legal agreements like HIPAA Business Associate Addenda.

AWS Audit Manager

A tool that automates evidence collection for audits, mapping AWS resource activity to control requirements from various compliance frameworks.

AWS Auto Scaling

A service that automatically adjusts the number of compute resources (like EC2 instances) in response to changing workload demands to maintain performance and optimize costs.

AWS Backup

A fully managed service that centralizes and automates backup management across diverse AWS resources and hybrid environments based on defined policies.

AWS Budgets

A tool that allows users to set custom spending limits and receive alerts when costs or usage approach or exceed predefined thresholds.

AWS Certificate Manager (ACM)

A service that automates the provisioning, management, and deployment of Secure Sockets Layer SSL/TLS certificates for secure network connections.

AWS Cloud Adoption Framework (CAF)

A comprehensive guide that helps organizations assess and build the strategic, organizational, and operational capabilities required for successful cloud transformation.

AWS CloudFormation

An infrastructure-as-code (IaC) tool that allows users to define and provision AWS infrastructure resources using code or configuration files.

AWS CloudShell

A browser-based shell environment built into the AWS Management Console that provides a terminal for interacting with AWS services using the AWS CLI.

AWS CodeBuild

A fully managed continuous integration service that compiles source code, runs tests, and produces deployable software packages.

AWS CodePipeline

A fully managed continuous delivery service that automates release pipelines for fast and reliable application and infrastructure updates.

AWS Command Line Interface (CLI)

A text-based interface that allows users to interact with AWS services by running commands in a terminal or command prompt.

AWS Config

A service that tracks and records configuration changes for AWS resources, evaluates them against defined rules, and helps ensure continuous compliance.

AWS cost allocation tags

Labels in the form of key-value pairs that are attached to AWS resources to categorize expenses by criteria such as team, project, or environment for cost tracking.

AWS Cost Explorer

A tool that provides a visual interface to analyze and manage AWS costs and usage over time, allowing users to identify trends and forecast future spending.

AWS Database Migration Service (DMS)

A fully managed service that facilitates the migration and replication of databases to AWS with minimal downtime.

AWS Direct Connect

A networking service that provides a dedicated, private fiber optic connection from an on-premises environment directly to AWS, bypassing the public internet.

AWS Elastic File System (EFS)

A scalable, fully managed file storage service that supports the Network File System (NFS) protocol, allowing multiple EC2 instances or on-premises servers to access shared files.

AWS Fargate

A serverless compute engine for containers that eliminates the need to provision, manage, and scale servers or clusters.

AWS Firewall Manager

A security management service that centralizes the administration and auditing of firewall rules across multiple AWS accounts and organizations.

AWS Global Accelerator

A networking service that improves the availability and performance of applications for global users by directing traffic through the AWS global network using static anycast IP addresses.

AWS Glue

A fully managed extract, transform, and load (ETL) service that helps discover, prepare, and combine data for analytics, machine learning, and application development.

AWS IAM Identity Center

A service that allows users to sign in with their existing corporate credentials to access AWS accounts and cloud applications.

AWS Identity and Access Management (IAM)

A web service that helps you securely control access to AWS resources by managing users, groups, roles, and permissions.

AWS IoT Core

A managed cloud service that allows securely connecting and managing IoT devices at scale.

AWS Key Management Service (KMS)

A managed service that simplifies the creation and control of encryption keys used across various AWS services.

AWS Lambda

A serverless compute service that allows you to run code without provisioning or managing servers, executing functions in response to events.

AWS Lex

An AI service that enables the building of conversational interfaces, such as chatbots, by combining natural language understanding (NLU) and automatic speech recognition (ASR).

AWS License Manager

A service that helps manage and track software licenses from various vendors across AWS and on-premises environments.

AWS Management Console

A web-based interface for managing and accessing AWS services and resources.

AWS Marketplace

A curated digital catalog where customers can discover, purchase, and deploy third-party software, services, and data.

AWS Network Firewall

A managed firewall service that provides network traffic filtering, intrusion prevention, and deep packet inspection at the edge of a virtual private cloud (VPC).

AWS Organizations

A service that helps centralize the management of multiple AWS accounts, enabling consolidated billing, account grouping, and policy enforcement across the organization.

AWS Outposts

A fully managed service that extends AWS infrastructure, services, APIs, and tools to virtually any on-premises data center or co-location facility.

AWS Pricing Calculator

A web-based tool that helps estimate the costs of AWS services for planning purposes before deploying resources.

AWS Schema Conversion Tool (SCT)

A tool that converts existing database schemas and application code from one database engine to another.

AWS Secrets Manager

A service that helps securely store, manage, and rotate sensitive credentials such as database passwords, API keys, and other secrets.

AWS Security Hub

A service that provides a comprehensive view of security alerts and compliance status across multiple AWS accounts, aggregating findings from various AWS security services and third-party tools.

AWS Shared Responsibility Model

A framework that defines the security responsibilities shared between AWS and its customers, where AWS is responsible for the security *of* the cloud and the customer is responsible for security *in* the cloud.

AWS Shield

A managed DDoS protection service that safeguards applications running on AWS.

AWS Site-to-Site VPN

A networking service that creates an encrypted tunnel over the public internet to connect an on-premises network securely to an Amazon VPC environment.

AWS Snowball

A ruggedized data migration and edge computing device that comes in two versions (Storage Optimized and Compute Optimized) for transferring large amounts of data to and from AWS.

AWS Snowcone

The smallest, ultra-portable device in the AWS Snow Family, designed for edge computing and data transfer in environments with limited space, power, or connectivity.

AWS Snowmobile

A large-scale data transfer service that uses a shipping container-sized truck to move exabytes of data to AWS.

AWS Storage Gateway

A hybrid cloud storage service that connects on-premises applications to AWS cloud storage, providing local caching and efficient data transfer.

AWS Systems Manager

A unified management service that helps automate operational tasks across AWS resources and on-premises environments, including patching, inventory, and configuration management.

AWS Trusted Advisor

A service that acts as a virtual consultant, providing real-time recommendations to help optimize AWS resources for cost, performance, security, and fault tolerance.

AWS Wavelength Zones

Infrastructure deployments embedded within 5G telecom providers' data centers, designed to deliver ultra-low-latency applications to mobile devices and edge use cases.

AWS Web Application Firewall (WAF)

A web application firewall that helps protect web applications from common web exploits that could affect application availability, compromise security, or consume excessive resources.

AWS Well-Architected Framework

A set of guiding principles for designing and operating reliable, secure, efficient, and cost-effective workloads in the cloud.

Bring Your Own License (BYOL)

A licensing model where organizations use their existing software licenses on AWS, often leveraging dedicated hosts or specific software assurance programs to maintain compliance and reduce costs.

Brute-force attacks

Cyberattack techniques that involve guessing login credentials using automated tools.

Capital expenditure (CapEx)

Upfront investments made to acquire physical assets like buildings, data centers, servers, and perpetual software licenses.

Change data capture (CDC)

A technology used by AWS DMS to continuously track and replicate changes from a source database to a target database.

Client-server model

A network architecture where a client requests resources or services from a server, which then processes the request and sends back a response.

Cloud computing

The on-demand delivery of IT resources (such as compute power, storage, and databases) over the internet with pay-as-you-go pricing, rather than owning and maintaining physical infrastructure.

Cloud-based deployment (public cloud)

A cloud deployment model where all IT infrastructure and applications are hosted entirely within a third-party cloud provider's data centers and accessed over the internet.

CloudFront

AWS's content delivery network (CDN) service that securely delivers static and dynamic content to users globally with low latency by caching it at edge locations.

CloudHSM

A managed hardware security module (HSM) service that allows customers to generate and manage their own encryption keys.

CloudWatch

A monitoring and observability service that collects metrics, logs, and events from AWS resources and applications, enabling users to track performance, set alarms, and visualize operational data.

Compliance

The adherence to external regulations, industry standards, and internal policies related to data handling, security, and risk management.

Container

A lightweight, portable, and executable software package that bundles an application along with its dependencies, libraries, and configuration files, ensuring consistent operation across different environments.

Data center bridging (DCB)

An Institute of Electrical and Electronics Engineers (IEEE) standard that enhances Ethernet performance and reliability within data centers, particularly through features like priority-based flow control.

Data lakes

Centralized repositories designed to store large amounts of raw data in its native format, often for big data analytics and machine learning.

Deep learning (DL)

A subset of machine learning that uses artificial neural networks with multiple layers to learn complex patterns from large amounts of data, often used for tasks like image recognition and natural language processing.

Defense-in-depth

A security philosophy and strategy that involves implementing multiple layers of security controls and safeguards to protect systems and data from various angles of attack.

Desktop as a service (DaaS)

A cloud computing offering that provides virtual desktop environments to users over the internet, accessible from various devices.

DevOps

A set of practices that combines software development (Dev) and IT operations (Ops) to shorten the systems development life cycle and provide continuous delivery with high software quality.

Digital certificates

Electronic documents used to prove the ownership of a public key and to verify the identity of individuals, applications, or devices in digital communications.

Distributed denial-of-service (DDoS) attacks

Cyberattacks that flood a website or application with excessive traffic, overwhelming its resources and making it unavailable to legitimate users.

DNS spoofing

A type of cyberattack where attackers redirect users to fake websites by manipulating Domain Name System (DNS) responses, making the fake site appear legitimate.

Elastic Block Store (EBS)

The main boot storage for EC2 instances. It's a durable, high-performance block storage system that automatically replicates data within its Availability Zone.

Elastic Compute Cloud (EC2)

A web service that provides resizable compute capacity in the cloud, allowing users to launch and manage virtual servers (instances) with various operating systems and configurations.

Elastic Load Balancing (ELB)

A service that automatically distributes incoming application traffic across multiple targets, such as EC2 instances, in multiple Availability Zones, ensuring high availability and fault tolerance.

Encryption at rest

The practice of encrypting data that is stored on a persistent storage medium, such as S3 buckets, RDS databases, or EBS volumes.

Encryption in transit

The practice of encrypting data as it moves across a network, protecting it from eavesdropping during transmission.

End user computing (EUC)

A category of services that provides managed virtual desktops and streamed applications, allowing users to run full desktop software from almost any device.

Ethernet

A widely used networking technology for local area networks (LANs) that uses physical cables to connect devices and facilitate high-speed data transfers.

EventBridge

A serverless event bus service that routes events from AWS services, custom applications, and SaaS applications to various targets based on defined rules.

Fibre Channel

A high-speed networking protocol typically used to connect servers to shared storage systems, offering speeds up to 128 Gbps.

FINMA

The Swiss Financial Market Supervisory Authority, which governs financial institutions operating in Switzerland.

First in, first out (FIFO)

A type of Simple Queue Service (SQS) queue that guarantees message processing in a strict order and without duplication.

FSx

A fully managed file system service that supports various popular file systems, including FSx for Windows File Server and FSx for Lustre.

Generative adversarial networks (GANs)

A class of machine learning frameworks used in generative AI to create new data instances that resemble the training data.

Generative AI

A subset of deep learning that uses models like GANs and LLMs to create new, original content such as text, images, video, or code.

Governance

The framework of policies, roles, and processes that guides and controls how cloud operations are managed and aligned with business goals and risk tolerance.

Health Insurance Portability and Accountability Act (HIPAA)

A US law that mandates strict protections for handling protected health information (PHI) in the healthcare industry.

Hybrid cloud

A cloud deployment model that combines on-premises (private cloud) infrastructure with public cloud services, allowing data and applications to move between them.

Identity providers (IdPs)

Specialized services (like Okta or Azure Active Directory) that handle user registration, login, authentication, and session management, often integrating with AWS IAM.

Infrastructure as a service (IaaS)

A cloud service model that provides fundamental computing resources such as virtual machines, storage, and networks, giving users high control over their environment.

Infrastructure as code (IaC)

The practice of defining and managing IT infrastructure using configuration files or code, enabling automated, repeatable, and version-controlled deployments.

Injection attacks

Cyberattack techniques that involve inserting malicious code into data inputs (like web forms) to exploit vulnerabilities in a system's backend, often targeting databases.

Inspector

An automated security assessment service that scans EC2 instances and workloads for vulnerabilities and deviations from security best practices.

International Organization for Standardization (ISO)

An independent, nongovernmental, international standards development organization composed of representatives from the national standards organizations of member countries. It sets globally recognized standards for information security, risk management, and quality assurance.

Internet gateway (IGW)

A logical connection point that enables communication between an Amazon VPC environment and the internet.

Internet of Things (IoT)

A network of physical objects embedded with sensors, software, and other technologies that connect and exchange data with other devices and systems over the internet.

In-memory databases

Database systems that store their data primarily in a computer's RAM rather than on disk, enabling very high-speed data access and processing.

IPsec

A suite of protocols used to secure IP communications by authenticating and encrypting each IP packet in a data stream.

Jupyter

An open source web application that allows users to create and share documents containing live code, equations, visualizations, and narrative text, commonly used in data science and machine learning.

Kubernetes

An open source container orchestration platform that automates the deployment, scaling, and management of containerized applications.

Large language models (LLMs)

Advanced deep learning models trained on vast amounts of text data, capable of understanding, generating, and processing human language.

Least privilege

A security principle that dictates granting users or services only the minimum permissions necessary to perform their required tasks, and nothing more.

Local area networks (LANs)

Computer networks that connect devices within a small, localized area, such as an office building or a home.

Local Zones

Extensions of an AWS Region that place compute, storage, and database services closer to end users in major metropolitan areas, providing ultra-low-latency access.

Machine learning (ML)

A subset of artificial intelligence that enables systems to learn from data without being explicitly programmed, using statistical models and algorithms.

Man-in-the-middle (MitM) attacks

Cyberattacks where an attacker secretly intercepts and relays communications between two parties who believe they are directly communicating with each other.

Memory-optimized instances

EC2 instance types (R, X, and Z series) designed with large amounts of RAM, suitable for in-memory databases and data-intensive applications.

Microservices

An architectural approach that structures an application as a collection of loosely coupled, independently deployable services.

Migration strategies

Different approaches for moving applications and data from on-premises environments to the cloud, often categorized by the "6 Rs": rehost, replatform, refactor/re-architect, repurchase, retain, and retire.

MLOps pipelines

Automated workflows that streamline the process of building, deploying, and managing machine learning models in production environments.

Multifactor authentication (MFA)

A security measure that requires users to provide two or more different authentication factors to verify their identity, significantly enhancing account security.

MQTT

A lightweight messaging protocol commonly used in IoT devices for communication.

NAT gateway

A network address translation (NAT) service in a VPC that allows instances in private subnets to initiate outbound connections to the internet or other AWS services while preventing inbound unsolicited connections.

National Institute of Standards and Technology (NIST)

A US government agency that provides widely adopted frameworks for cybersecurity, including NIST 800-53 and the NIST Cybersecurity Framework (CSF).

Network access control lists (NACLs)

Stateless packet filtering rules that operate at the subnet level within a VPC, explicitly defining both inbound and outbound traffic allowances and denials.

Network Load Balancer (NLB)

A type of Elastic Load Balancer optimized for ultra-low-latency TCP and User Datagram Protocol (UDP) traffic, capable of handling millions of requests per second.

NoSQL database

A type of database that does not adhere to the traditional relational table-and-row model, offering flexible schemas for storing data as documents, key-value pairs, graphs, or wide-column tables.

Notebooks

Interactive development environments in Amazon SageMaker, built on Jupyter, that allow users to write and run code, visualize data, and document machine learning workflows.

Object Lock

An S3 feature that prevents objects from being deleted or overwritten for a fixed amount of time or indefinitely, supporting compliance requirements like write-once-read-many (WORM) storage.

On-Demand Capacity Reservation Pricing

An EC2 pricing model that allows users to reserve compute capacity within a specific Availability Zone for any duration, guaranteeing resource availability even during peak demand.

On-premises (private cloud)

A cloud deployment model where an organization hosts its IT infrastructure, applications, and data within its own data center, maintaining maximum control over hardware and security.

Operating expenditure (OpEx)

Ongoing operational costs that arise from the day-to-day usage of cloud services, such as compute, storage, and SaaS subscriptions, typically paid on a pay-as-you-go basis.

Passwordless authentication

A security method that verifies user identity without relying on traditional passwords, often using biometrics (fingerprints, facial recognition) or one-time passcodes sent to trusted devices.

Patch Manager

A feature within AWS Systems Manager that automates the process of applying operating system and software patches across EC2 instances and other managed nodes.

Pay-as-you-go pricing

A cloud computing pricing model where users only pay for the IT resources they actually consume, without large upfront investments or long-term commitments.

Payment Card Industry Data Security Standard (PCI DSS)

A set of security standards for organizations that handle branded credit cards from the major card schemes.

Peer-to-peer (P2P) networks

Network architectures where all connected computers have equal privileges and can directly share resources with each other without a central server.

Phishing

A type of cyberattack that uses deceptive messages (e.g., fake emails) to trick individuals into revealing sensitive information like login credentials or credit card numbers.

Platform as a service (PaaS)

A cloud service model that provides a complete development and deployment environment, including runtime, databases, and frameworks, allowing developers to focus on writing code without managing underlying infrastructure.

Portable Operating System Interface (POSIX)

A set of standards defined by the Institute of Electrical and Electronics Engineers (IEEE) to maintain compatibility between operating systems.

Primary key

A column or set of columns in a relational database table that uniquely identifies each row.

Principle of least privilege

A security best practice in identity and access management (IAM) that advocates for granting users or services only the minimum necessary permissions required to perform their specific tasks.

Provisioned input/output operations per second (IOPS) solid-state drive (SSD) (io1, io2, io2 Block Express)

EBS volume types designed for mission-critical applications that require consistent and high-performance input/output operations, such as large transactional databases.

Public key cryptography

A cryptographic system that uses a pair of mathematically linked keys (a public key and a private key) for encryption and decryption, where the public key can be shared widely while the private key remains secret.

Ransomware

A type of malware that encrypts a victim's files or systems and demands a ransom payment, typically in cryptocurrency, in exchange for decryption access.

Recovery point objective (RPO)

The maximum acceptable amount of data loss after an unplanned event, indicating how much data can be lost without causing significant harm to the business.

Recovery time objective (RTO)

The maximum acceptable downtime for an application or system after an unplanned event, defining how quickly a system must be restored to operation.

Refactor/re-architect

A cloud migration strategy that involves redesigning and rebuilding applications to fully leverage cloud native capabilities, such as microservices and serverless functions.

Region

A geographically distinct and isolated area within AWS that contains multiple Availability Zones, designed for high availability and fault tolerance.

Rehost

A cloud migration strategy, also known as *lift and shift*, that involves moving an application to the cloud with minimal or no changes to its code or architecture.

Relational database

A type of database that stores and organizes data in tables with predefined schemas, where data elements are related through common fields.

Relational Database Service (RDS)

Amazon RDS is a managed service for relational databases that supports multiple database engines, including MySQL, PostgreSQL, Oracle, and SQL Server. It automates administrative tasks such as software patching, backups, and database scaling, reducing the need for manual management.

Replatform

A cloud migration strategy that involves making minor cloud native optimizations to an application to make it work better in the cloud without a full redesign.

Repurchase

A cloud migration strategy that involves replacing an existing application with a new, cloud native SaaS product.

Reserved Instance pricing

An EC2 pricing model that offers significant discounts (up to 72%) in exchange for a one- or three-year commitment to a specific instance type and region.

Retain

A cloud migration strategy where certain applications are kept in their current on-premises environment due to specific constraints, dependencies, or recent investments.

Retire

A cloud migration strategy that involves decommissioning and removing applications that are no longer needed, freeing up resources and reducing complexity.

Retrieval-augmented generation (RAG)

A technique used in AI, particularly with large language models, to improve the quality of generated responses by retrieving relevant information from a knowledge base before generating a response.

Rightsizing

The process of optimizing cloud resources, especially EC2 and RDS instances, by adjusting their size and type to precisely match workload demands, eliminating overprovisioning and reducing costs.

Root user

The initial and most privileged user account created when an AWS account is set up, possessing full access to all AWS services and resources.

S3 Express One Zone

A high-performance S3 storage class designed for single-digit millisecond access times, storing data in a single Availability Zone at a lower cost, suitable for latency-sensitive workloads.

S3 Glacier Deep Archive

The lowest-cost S3 storage class, designed for long-term data archiving (12 to 48 hours retrieval time) that is rarely, if ever, accessed.

S3 Glacier Flexible Retrieval

An S3 archive storage class offering flexible retrieval speeds, from minutes to hours, for long-term data that is accessed occasionally.

S3 Glacier Instant Retrieval

An S3 archive storage class that provides millisecond-level access to archived data at lower storage costs compared to active storage classes.

S3 Intelligent-Tiering

An S3 storage class that automatically moves data between four access tiers (Frequent, Infrequent, Archive Instant, and Deep Archive) based on changing access patterns, optimizing costs without performance impact.

S3 on Outposts

An S3 storage solution that allows storing data locally on AWS Outposts hardware in an on-premises environment while using the familiar S3 API.

S3 One Zone-Infrequent Access (IA)

An S3 storage class designed for infrequently accessed data that stores data in a single Availability Zone, offering lower costs in exchange for reduced availability and no cross-AZ redundancy.

S3 Standard

The default S3 storage class, designed for frequently accessed data, offering high durability and availability by redundantly storing data across multiple Availability Zones.

SageMaker Savings Plan

A type of Savings Plan designed specifically for machine learning workloads in Amazon SageMaker, providing cost savings on usage.

Savings Plan pricing

A flexible pricing model that offers significant discounts (up to 72%) on compute usage (EC2, Fargate, Lambda) in exchange for a one- or three-year commitment to a consistent amount of compute usage per hour.

Security

The technical and procedural safeguards designed to protect data, systems, and workloads from threats, both external and internal.

Security Groups

Virtual firewalls that control inbound and outbound traffic for EC2 instances and other resources within a VPC, explicitly allowing only specified traffic.

Server Message Block (SMB)

A network file sharing protocol primarily used by Windows-based systems.

Serverless

A cloud computing model where the cloud provider fully manages the underlying infrastructure, allowing developers to run code and build applications without provisioning or managing servers.

Simple Storage Service (S3)

AWS's object storage service designed for high scalability, durability, and availability, used for storing and retrieving any amount of data from anywhere on the web.

Software as a service (SaaS)

A cloud service model that delivers fully managed applications directly to end users over the internet, accessible via a web browser, with the provider handling all infrastructure, maintenance, and updates.

Software-defined WANs (SD-WANs)

A virtual approach to wide area networks (WANs) that allows network configuration and management through software, offering greater flexibility and adaptability to changing traffic demands.

Spot Instance pricing

An EC2 pricing model that allows users to bid for unused EC2 capacity, offering discounts of up to 90% compared to On-Demand prices, but with the risk of instances being interrupted.

Standard Network File System (NFS) protocols

A distributed file system protocol that allows a user on a client computer to access files over a computer network much like local storage is accessed.

Storage-optimized instances
EC2 instance types (I, D, and H series) designed for workloads that require high sequential read and write access to very large datasets, featuring fast, local storage.

Subnet
A logical subdivision of an IP network within a VPC, allowing for organization and isolation of resources and enabling better security and efficient routing.

Sustainability
A pillar of the AWS Well-Architected Framework focused on minimizing the environmental impact of cloud workloads by optimizing resource usage and energy efficiency.

System and Organization Controls (SOC) reports
Audit reports (SOC 1, SOC 2) designed to assess how a service provider manages and protects data, focusing on financial reporting controls (SOC 1) or broader operational criteria like security and availability (SOC 2).

Tape Gateway
A type of AWS Storage Gateway that allows on-premises backup applications to use Amazon S3 and Glacier for virtual tape storage, replacing physical tape libraries.

Total cost of ownership (TCO)
A financial estimate that includes all direct and indirect costs associated with owning and operating IT infrastructure, encompassing hardware, software, maintenance, and personnel.

Transmission Control Protocol/Internet Protocol (TCP/IP)
A foundational suite of communication protocols used to connect network devices on the internet, managing reliable data packet delivery.

Transport Layer Security (TLS)
A cryptographic protocol used to establish secure communication channels over a computer network, commonly used for encrypting data in transit over HTTPS.

Trojan horse
A type of malware that masquerades as legitimate software to trick users into installing it, often leading to the infiltration of other malicious programs like ransomware.

Uninterruptible Power Supply (UPS)
Electrical apparatus that provides emergency power to a load when the input power source fails.

Volume Gateway
A type of AWS Storage Gateway that provides block storage to on-premises applications using the Internet Small Computer Systems Interface (iSCSI), with data either cached locally (cached mode) or stored entirely on-premises with backups to S3 (stored mode).

Wide area networks (WANs)
Computer networks that span large geographical areas, connecting multiple cities, regions, or even countries.

Workload
A collection of resources and code that delivers business value.

Zero-day exploits
Cyberattacks that target and exploit previously unknown software vulnerabilities for which developers have had "zero days" to create a patch or fix.

Index

rules engine, IoT core, 175

About the Author

Tom Taulli (@ttaulli) is a consultant to various companies, such as Aisera, SnapLogic, and Tad Health. He has written several books like *AI-Assisted Programming: Better Planning, Coding, Testing, and Deployment.* Tom has also taught IT courses for UCLA, PluralSight, and O'Reilly. For these, he has provided lessons in using Python to create deep learning and machine learning models. He has also taught on topics like natural language processing (NLP).

Colophon

The animal on the cover of *AWS Certified Cloud Practitioner (CLF-C02) Study Guide* is a golden palm civet (*Paradoxurus zeylonensis*). Endemic to Sri Lanka, these nocturnal mammals can be found in various habitats throughout the country, including lowland rainforests, tropical montane forests, shrubland, grasslands, and within the mountainous regions of the island.

Golden palm civets are quite small; their bodies are approximately 35 inches in length, and they can weigh anywhere between 3 and 7 pounds. Their coats, which are about 1 inch thick, can range from golden brown to dark brown, with their bellies usually taking a lighter shade of gold. Those from the montane forests are slightly darker, being more gray-toned wood-brown in color with a pale underside and a yellow-white tail tip.

Golden palm civets are solitary animals; they prefer arboreal environments and spend most of their lives in trees. Their diet consists mostly of fruits such as plantains, pineapples, mangoes, and guava, but they will also eat small reptiles, frogs, moths, and insects if resources are limited. Due to their solitary and elusive nature, little is known about the behavior patterns of these mammals, but they do rely on scent marking and olfactory cues to communicate with each other.

Currently, golden palm civets are listed as "Least Concern" on the IUCN Red List, but their habitats in Sri Lanka's hill regions have been slowly declining. Many of the animals on O'Reilly covers are endangered; all of them are important to the world.

The cover illustration is by José Marzan Jr. based on an antique line engraving from Cassell's *Natural History.* The series design is by Edie Freedman, Ellie Volckhausen, and Karen Montgomery. The cover fonts are Gilroy Semibold and Guardian Sans. The text font is Adobe Minion Pro; the heading font is Adobe Myriad Condensed; and the code font is Dalton Maag's Ubuntu Mono.

O'REILLY®

Learn from experts.
Become one yourself.

60,000+ titles | Live events with experts | Role-based courses
Interactive learning | Certification preparation

**Try the O'Reilly learning platform
free for 10 days.**

www.ingramcontent.com/pod-product-compliance
Lightning Source LLC
Chambersburg PA
CBHW061403210326
41598CB00035B/6076